INVERCLYDE

D0494785

CENTRAL LIBRARY		
1 2 JUL 2014	1 5 MAY 2015	
		1 2 AUG 2016
	2 0 OCT 2015	

INVERCLYDE LIBRARIES

This book is to be returned on or before
the last date above. It may be borrowed for
a further period if not in demand.

For enquiries and renewals Tel: (01475) 712323

Inverclyde Libraries

34106   003129835

AuthorHouse™ UK Ltd.
500 Avebury Boulevard
Central Milton Keynes, MK9 2BE
www.authorhouse.co.uk
Phone: 08001974150

*This book is a work of non-fiction. Unless otherwise noted, the author
and the publisher make no explicit guarantees as to the accuracy
of the information contained in this book and in some cases, names
of people and places have been altered to protect their privacy.*

© 2010 David M. Addison. All rights reserved.

*No part of this book may be reproduced, stored in
a retrieval system, or transmitted by any means
without the written permission of the author.*

First published by AuthorHouse 6/18/2010

ISBN: 978-1-4490-7816-4 (sc)
ISBN: 978-1-4490-7817-1 (hc)

This book is printed on acid-free paper.

By the same author

AN ITALIAN JOURNEY
A MEANDER IN MENORCA
SOMETIME IN SORRENTO
BANANAS ABOUT LA PALMA

Contents

Tuscany

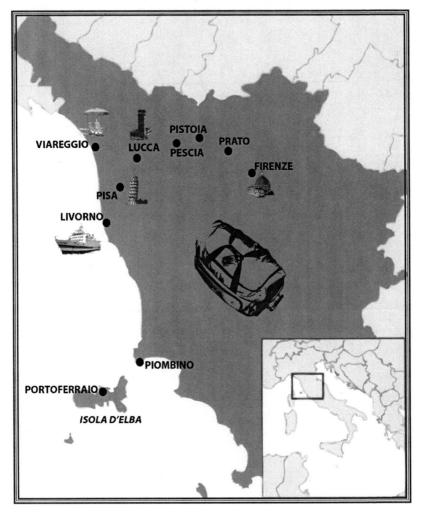

CHAPTER ONE:
THE CASE BEGINS

I'm tired. Apart from the lateness of the hour, and the travelling, and the cost of the taxi and the worry that we wouldn't get into the hotel, the stress of it all has taken it out of me. But now we are finally here and even if the taxi hadn't turned out to be that much cheaper after I had paid the extra tip and everything, it is a relief to find we have a room to ourselves and I have not had to make a fuss about being put in the dormitory smelling of pee.

Aaah! This bed feels rather comfy and it is wide too. A good chance we will not touch each other in the night and disturb each other. That's good too. I will, of course, have to consummate Lucca at some stage during our stay, for it is one of Iona's more curious foibles that we must engage in this ritual at every new place we lay our heads down to sleep. But it won't be tonight as she'll be too tired.

All my problems have melted away like insubstantial shadows. All's well that ends well. There's irony in that, for the next moment Iona's disembodied voice makes an announcement from the floor at the other side of the bed.

"The padlock seems to be missing from the case."

If in *Macbeth,* the knocking on the gate of Cawdor Castle just after Duncan has been murdered marks the first step towards the restoration of order, this, by contrast, was the knell that tolled the first of the insane events on this doom-laden holiday. Too tired to care about this apparently trivial matter, I dismissed it and luxuriated instead in the softness of the bed. But not for long.

"David, this is not our case!"

"What!" The bell is fairly clamouring now, going off like a burglar alarm in my head. In an instant, I have uncoiled like a spring and am beside Iona who is kneeling dumbfounded in front of the familiar green case that has been halfway round the world with us.

The contents are anything but familiar however. Some medicines I don't recognise and a new pair of jeans with the price label still on them. Never been worn evidently. No need to look any further. I close the lid, feeling sick to my stomach, cursing myself for the idiot I certainly am. Amazingly, in a supreme effort of self-control, Iona does not go off the deep end.

"For God's sake, you bloody, bloody fool! Did you not check you had picked up the right case? Did it not occur to you to stop and look at it? Even for a moment? Are you a complete and utter moron? What's wrong with you?"

I hang my head in shame. No point in explaining to her how it was all Dorothy's fault really. She would just say that I was trying to get out of it by laying the blame on someone else. But it really *was* Dorothy's fault.

"What are we going to do now, for God's sake? Have you thought of that?"

Good question. I haven't actually, not had time to. Evidently I have to get the case back to its owner of course and get mine back. But how? There is a label on the handle, just like ours, only black where ours is pink, with a little press stud that I have to undo first. I am little the wiser. The case appears to belong to a lady and I think her name might be Carla. I can't make out any familiar words in the address at all. It certainly doesn't seem to be Lucca anyway. That would have been too much to hope for, or Pisa or Firenze even. Probably some little village I have never heard of. It is a bit hard to tell, as although the writing is in block capitals, all the letters are squashed up together and it is nigh impossible to tell where one ends and another begins. The telephone number likewise. May as well give it a go though.

I put in the number I think it is, but all hear is silence. It's probably not the right number anyway so there is no use in persisting. Since I hadn't been able to get my phone to work in the taxi on the way here, maybe it doesn't work in Italy at all. Although it is very late to start proceedings such as this, I go out onto the landing and peer down to the reception area to see if the receptionist is there. It is a relief in a way to see that it is in darkness. I feel little in the mood for a confrontation with an irate Italian at this time in the morning, but I thought the owner might be relieved to know that some idiot was at least owning up to having the luggage, and we would worry about how to get it back to her tomorrow, well later today, as the chimes of midnight had already struck some time ago.

"I hate going to bed without doing my teeth," says Iona emerging from the toilet and speaking through them, clenched.

She should worry! What about me? At least she had packed her nightshirt in her hand luggage, whereas never mind dirty teeth, I have to go to bed in the pants I have been wearing all day and sweated into on seats of varying degrees of plasticity.

"And another thing! How am I going to get my hair done without a hair dryer, pray?" She is near to tears. This is a worse calamity than the absence of the toothbrush, evidently. The wisest course is to say nothing, not even "sorry" for that is likely to bring on another tirade about my idiocy. Anyway, she should be able to see from my hangdog expression that there is no-one sorrier than me.

Huh! I think bitterly. All the other worries I had had were little ones compared to this. Had it not been for this monumental act of stupidity, I could be lying in bed now thinking about the pleasures of exploring Lucca tomorrow and instead, here I am wondering and worrying about how on earth am I going to get out of this fine mess I have got us into. Some start to a holiday this is!

I didn't know then that this was just the beginning and it was going to get much, much worse. But the signs had been there, right from the start – if only I had been able to recognise them.

CHAPTER TWO: I HAVE FEARS

We had got such a bargain in the Ryanair sale that we just couldn't resist it, especially me. I was so carried away with the thought of a bargain that I didn't stop to think. I should, of course, have remembered after that time in Rome, when after dining out at a restaurant near the Spanish Steps, we had had to get a taxi back to the hotel because the buses had all stopped at nine o'clock. I could scarcely believe that in this, one of the top ten tourist city destinations in the world, and at the height of the summer season to boot, that they stopped so early. Who is public transport meant to benefit after all – the public or the drivers? I have a theory that in Italy at least, the bus drivers have second (and more remunerative) jobs as taxi drivers.

Anyway, it was only later, and too late, after having made the hotel reservation, that we discovered that by the time of our arrival at 11 pm, the buses and trains would have long since been tucked up in bed. I suppose, to be fair, they do have to get up early in the morning, but what is a poor pensioner, not even yet on a state pension, expected to do? I was horrified to discover that it was going to cost €60 or £55 for a taxi – for a matter of a mere 19 kilometres. Our return flights, for *both* of us, let me stress, from Edinburgh to Pisa, and at a rough calculation, a thousand times the distance, incredibly, didn't cost as much as that – or wouldn't have, had we not fatally decided to take an item of luggage with us that hiked the price up. No wonder therefore, I balked at that price for a journey which, at a pinch, I could do as a march if forced to do so, albeit with a suitcase, even if it did have little wheels that would be worn down to the hubs by the end of it.

Perhaps the fault lies with me, that I am out of kilter with the rest of society, that I see the world from the wrong end of the telescope, especially as far as prices are concerned. I am often accused by Iona of not living in the real world, since all my clothes (with the exception of my socks and underpants) once all belonged to dead men, and whose shoes, ever since their decease, I have been trying to fill. For this reason, amongst other canny purchases I make, I am accused of not knowing the real cost of things, and she might well be right.

Whatever the truth of that, it is certainly true that being fortunate enough to be a car owner, (despite being mugged by every Chancellor in practically every budget since the invention of the internal combustion engine) I have no idea what it costs to go anywhere by taxi, except a lot presumably, and perhaps those fares to Pisa are no more expensive than they would be at home. And perhaps my reaction has been skewed by what I paid for the airfares – the sort of prices that *do* belong in my world.

Even now, I can still scarcely believe it. It seemed too good to be true, but I have a piece of paper in my hand that feels real to me until I am told, like Neville Chamberlain, that the words written on it are not worth the paper it is written on. It certainly doesn't look like the sort of ticket that my mother-in-law for example would recognise, and I must admit though I have bought an e-ticket before, I still retain slight feelings of nervousness, vestiges of doubt that this flimsy piece of paper can actually guarantee my posterior a place on an aeroplane until I am actually admitted into the departure lounge.

I suppose my scepticism comes from being born in the wrong half of the 20th century. Technology has advanced so rapidly that I have been left far behind like an overweight old grandfather taking on six-year-olds in a sack race on sports day. Having said that, I have long since desisted from the practice of phoning people to ask if they have received my e-mail – which is at least a step ahead of my mother-in-law, who at 88, doesn't understand how you can receive mail unless it is delivered by the postman. The truth is, I just don't trust technology and with good reason too because it usually goes wrong with me.

And there was another thing that was worrying me – would we be able to get into our hotel? I had booked a double room in one we both liked the look of, through the Internet. It wasn't just the price that I liked, though that did have a slight bearing on my choice, as you might possibly have worked out. Part hotel, part backpacker's hostel, not only was it cheap, but close to the old walled city – but there was a downside. It would be closed by the time of our arrival. I knew that when I made the booking, was prepared for an extra charge but now, because of a delay in our departure, we were more than an hour late when we landed in Pisa. It would not be many minutes short of midnight, I reckoned, before we arrived, and I was worried about what we might expect when we got there.

Initially, I was delighted with my booking. It was only later I put the horse before the cart, so to speak, and read the ratings left by previous visitors. That was a mistake. The receptionists were described as ranging from very friendly and helpful, to downright rude and nasty and even more worrying for us – never being seen at all. Most worryingly of all, someone had written: "Don't let them put you in the dormitory in the basement – it smells of pee."

This contributor had booked a room, like me, yet that was where he had ended up. I got straight on the phone (at least as soon as it was free to call according to the terms of my phone contract) and talked to a young lady who, to my enormous relief, had very good English, and reminded her of our late arrival. Yes, that was all right, and we did have a double room, didn't we? Yes, we did. All the same, and call me paranoid if you like, so there would be no room for error, so to speak, I asked for confirmation of that by e-mail. If there were to be any trouble, there is nothing like a bit of paper to wave about, (like Neville Chamberlain) to prove what you had been promised. Yes, that would be all right too. I was all set to spell out my e-mail address but the receptionist preferred to give me the hotel's and said she would get my address from that. She gave it to me and I wrote it down and repeated it to her.

All seemed well, but I began to feel uneasy when no answering e-mail arrived and each time I phoned again I only got a ringing tone. That made me even more worried, as it seemed to confirm that the receptionists were hardly ever there and my initial contact with the English-speaking young lady had just been beginner's luck. My friend, Gardiner Dick, who speaks a bit of Italian, offered to phone on my behalf. After several attempts at getting through, he finally succeeded and gave me a mobile phone number with instructions to phone it as soon as I was on my way from the airport.

That was why I was just a little tad nervous as, having landed in Pisa, we approached the first taxi in the rank. My e-mail never had been answered, nor had it been returned as undeliverable. There was only one explanation I could think of – that it had been deliberately ignored. And why would they do that? Because they were intending to put us in the dormitory smelling of pee, that's why. Being without doubt the last to check in that day, and should they manage to let all the rooms, which they might well be able to do as there are only seven of them – I was afraid, very afraid, that that's where we would end up, in the basement with people snoring the roof off, not to mention other unsanitary habits they might have.

At the time I thought that was my biggest worry. Ignorance is not something you may die of, like the AIDS adverts in the Eighties, it is bliss sometimes – and this was one of those times. We had even managed to find a young couple with whom we could share a taxi, so that is why, as we headed for Pisa, I was blissfully unaware that we had the wrong case in the boot.

How did that happen? I'll tell you. And you will see that it really was all Dorothy's fault, just as I said.

CHAPTER THREE:
A CHANCE ENCOUNTER

In the beginning and back at Edinburgh airport, a chance encounter had seemed to signal a change in our fortunes, a happy encounter that could save us a fortune. But the gods, to adapt Sir Walter Scott's famous lines from *Marmion,* often weave a tangled web when they practise to deceive. I wouldn't mind betting that nine out of ten people are deceived into thinking that Shakespeare wrote these lines and which have always struck me as an appropriate motto for a lawyer's office. Which is ironic really, as that was what Sir Walter was by profession before he took to writing to get himself out of debt.

I was made aware once again of the truth of this aphorism when I happened to catch sight of someone I knew. I also knew that she had a villa in Lucca and I saw an opportunity to avoid that punitive taxi fare: perhaps we might be able to share one or cadge a lift from whoever is picking her up. She was walking away from me, towing a case big enough to have little wheels yet small enough to satisfy the restrictions they place on what qualifies as hand luggage nowadays.

I would have to admit to unseemly haste as I abandoned Iona and set off in pursuit of the other woman who was blissfully unaware of my interest in her. For how many yards I dogged her I couldn't say, willing her to turn round, reluctant to call out her name, hoping she would stop and turn round, catch sight of me and thus we could meet by accident, so to speak. If I have learned anything over the years it is, as far as the pursuit of women is concerned, it is better not to seem too keen.

"Dorothy…Dorothy…Dorothy…" How embarrassing is it to repeatedly utter someone's name to their retreating back only for them to be so totally unaware of the fact you have to say it louder and louder until it finally percolates the brain of the pursued (not to mention scores of others) that they are being addressed. It creates a sense of desperation – the very impression I was striving to avoid.

Finally, the lady did turn around and looked at me – without recognition. My heart sank. She must have been wondering who this person could possibly be who could recognise her from the rear, but whose face doesn't mean the slightest thing to her.

In a time briefer than it takes you to read this and certainly shorter than it takes me to write it, but what seemed to me to be an embarrassing silence stretching into infinity, the fog finally lifted from Dorothy's memory and the light of recognition switched on when she recognised me as the father of her son's wife's, brother's, wife. No wonder it took her so long to work out who I was. I can scarcely work it out myself. I suppose another way to put it would be I am her daughter-in-law's, brother's wife's father – though that scarcely seems much of a clarification. It does, however, make us remotely related by marriage and as far as I am aware, up till now at least, she considered me relatively harmless, so to speak.

"Oh, hello!"

She sounded surprised, as well she might.

"Are you going to Lucca?" Stupid question but I couldn't just breeze right in with what was really on my mind.

"Yes. I'm going with my sister and her husband for his sixtieth."

That was a blow but I tried not to show it as I carried blithely on, lest she got the idea that I was trying to pick her up.

"So are we. Iona's around somewhere. Shopping probably." The last sentence uttered in the sort of tone as if it were not of the slightest concern to me.

"We're sitting over there," Dorothy gestured vaguely off to the right and I automatically turned to look in that direction although since I had never met these people before, nor even, had I known them intimately, would I expect to pick them out amidst the multitude thronging the terminal building.

A pause ensued that felt more like a grinding halt. It still seemed too soon to leap right in with my modest proposal lest I appeared too anxious, but how to turn the conversation round to the matter of the moment? How to even begin a conversation with a person I had only met on two occasions previously? I couldn't think of anything in addition to what I had already said.

"You're welcome to come and join us if you want."

"Right thanks."

We fell into step as we headed in their direction. I had better take the plunge before we met them, and being immersed thus far in embarrassment already, I felt as if I might just as well go the whole hog.

"Er…how are you getting to Lucca from the airport?" I asked in as casual a tone as I could muster.

"I've got a friend coming to collect me."

I nodded. Then, while I was thinking of how next to approach the subject of our accompanying her, Dorothy added unexpectedly, "I'll be paying him the going rate – about €50 or €60."

Why did she tell me that? She must have thought I was trying to cadge a free ride. I felt myself blushing furiously although I was perfectly innocent of the charge. I was seeking damage limitation not annihilation. And whatever it said about the nature of their friendship, if she wanted to pay her friend and her friend wanted to accept payment, that was an arrangement made between consenting adults, but it nevertheless turned his vehicle into a taxi – did it not? All hope may not yet be abandoned. Confirmation of the price and desperation made me bold.

"Er…I don't suppose there would be any room for us would there?"

That stopped her in her tracks. She turned to face me. Oops! I wished I could have clawed the words back. It would have been better by far to have waited for her to have made the offer – if she ever did. Four in a car sounds plenty: six impossibly crowded, not counting the driver. Still, it might have been a people carrier and six into sixty is only ten and twice that is twenty, which was the most mental arithmetic I had done since I left school and which still sounded like a lot to me.

"Well you see…the fact is that we aren't actually in Lucca itself. We're up in the mountains."

"Ah, I see! No, no, no, no, no! Don't worry about it. It's no big deal. Really."

"We could possibly see about getting one back together," Dorothy proposed helpfully, as if to compensate for this blow, a blow which, to judge from its effect on me, she perceived must have hit me roughly in the region of my solar plexus. She was, apparently, not deceived for a moment by my numerous denials which I seem to have learned from the Lady Macbeth school of protestations.

"That's very kind of you but we'll be getting the bus back."

Who wouldn't at less than €3 a skull? Our return flight is well before bus bedtime. I was surprised she was not doing so herself, but then maybe her villa is not on a bus route or she wants to support her friend.

"I'll show you where you can get the taxis."

"That's very kind of you – thanks."

There seemed nothing else to say. It was mission unaccomplished, all hopes dashed apart from the one that

Dorothy had not come to the conclusion I was some sort of a cheapskate who was willing to go to any lengths, short of grovelling, to get a free ride into Lucca.

Dorothy said she had better join her relations and she'd see us there. I said I had better go and haul Iona out of the shops.

Although I spoke in jest, it turned to be nothing less than the truth. That was indeed where I found her. But it was nothing more serious than water for the journey, but at the sort of price that brought a tear to the eye and had we had the foresight to bring an empty bottle and applied it to our tear ducts, it would have gone some distance to making up for the taxi fare.

So that was how I happened to meet Dorothy. It wasn't her fault that we couldn't share her taxi or lift, whatever you want to call it. All the same, had we been able to, I probably would not have picked up the wrong case.

No, the real reason why it was her fault came later.

CHAPTER FOUR:
HOW THE CASE WAS LOST

We had barely time for the introductions to be made to Dorothy's relations, Leon and Tina, when the gate to our flight was announced and it turned out we were just about as far away as it was possible to be from the boarding gate.

Once announced, it provoked a mad scramble as if someone had shouted "Fire!" or let off a personally manufactured and pungent stink bomb as the place began to clear immediately. With no particular seats allocated, and should you wish to sit next to your spouse, as mine certainly does, (being so devoted – or more likely the devil you know being better than the one you don't, for Iona has had some unsanitary companions in the past) it is imperative to get as near to the front of the boarding queue as possible.

We sprang to our feet and hastily said farewell to our new friends who, on the other hand, started gathering up their belongings as if there was all the time in the world.

By the time we got to the departure lounge however, I was amazed and dismayed to find that we were practically at the end of the queue. It did not bode well for getting a seat together. Incredible to think that so many people could be travelling on this plane and it not even a Jumbo!

I left Iona who was concentrating on composing a text (probably to tell the children that we would be boarding soon) and took a stroll down towards the front. There was still no-one at the desk but a second, shorter queue had formed at right angles to the main one. When it came to passing through the narrow gap where they check your boarding pass, I could see that push would certainly come to shove, but even if we lost ground to many bodies, we would still get on the plane much sooner than by remaining where we were. The sooner we joined this queue the better, before others cottoned on too and got there ahead of us.

Filled with resolve, urgency and a new sense of mastery which I hadn't felt for the last twenty years, before I realised the truth, before I realised she only let me *think* I was the senior partner in this relationship, apart from age, I marched back to where Iona was still texting.

"Come on. Let's go!"

Without waiting for an answer, I picked up my hand luggage and turned to go, stepping over some annoying little bright yellow-and-red pieces of plastic furniture from a crèche which some careless child had left lying around. Designed to keep the little people happily occupied, it was at exactly the right height for short people like me to trip over and end up in occupational therapy.

"I've found a much shorter queue," I added over my shoulder, although as lord and master, there was no need for me to provide an explanation for my apparently eccentric behaviour.

I had a head start and therefore got to this new queue ahead of my dearest partner in greatness, only I didn't feel so great seconds later when I realised my appalling mistake. I just had time to register it before she joined me, the notice that even the most myopic could not fail to see, (had they gone close enough): PRIORITY BOOKING Q HERE. Too late, I remembered that this no-frills airline permits passengers, at an extra cost, to board the aircraft before cheapskates like me.

"That's the priority queue, you moron!" Iona pointed out redundantly. "Now we'll have lost our place in the queue! Thank you very much!"

She stomped off and all I could do was to follow her sheepishly. I was only trying to help.

If the walk back from the wicket to the dressing room for a batsman out first ball is the longest walk on the planet, short of that of a prisoner on death row to the execution chamber, this walk back to whence we have come was no shorter. It wouldn't even matter so much, if no-one in the queue knew us, but of course there are some who do now. And another thing: my hat makes me conspicuous.

It is a very fine hat indeed but not the sort of hat you would wear if you didn't want to draw attention to yourself such as if you were robbing a bank or going into an Ann Summers shop. No doubt scores of people had probably witnessed this incident, doubtlessly hardly containing their glee as they followed the queue jumper's progress (or lack of it) and his shameful return to the very back of the queue.

But the real shame was meeting up again with Dorothy and her relations. They were the very last in the queue but for another couple, and now us, which made conversation not only possible but out of politeness, unavoidable.

"Do you know what this idiot has just gone and done now?"

Iona was really addressing Dorothy and Leon and Tina, but it was impossible for the couple between us not to hear, nor those in front of her too, at the very least. They almost certainly did know what I had done as they had witnessed it with their very own eyes, but Iona was certainly going to tell them anyway.

"And serve him right too!" she added bitterly when she had finished, referring to our new position on the starting grid.

"There will be plenty of seats for everyone," Dorothy remarked calmly, possibly in an attempt to reassure Iona that she would be able to be seated next to the most dearly beloved.

I wanted to tell her, yes of course, I knew that, that I know standing is not allowed on planes, and I only did what I did because Iona wants to be sure of sitting next to me, not some malodorous stranger who bores her from here to Pisa with an account of his latest operation.

However, I decided that that subject was best left alone and instead turned the subject to Lucca and asked Dorothy if she knew where our hotel was. Lucca is not such a big place after all and being just without the city walls, I thought she might just have heard of it. She hadn't. But someone else had – or at least had heard something that interested him.

"Did I hear you say you are going to Lucca?"

The speaker, standing just in front of Dorothy, was a young man in his early twenties wearing a university scarf and a three-quarter coat. He was with a young lady whose long brown hair was cascading from beneath a knitted woollen beanie. They looked as if they might be engaged and sure enough, when I got a chance to get a closer look, she was sporting a diamond solitaire on the finger normally reserved for that purpose.

"Yes."

"So are we!"

This was providence indeed! How the gods lead you on, sport with you, snatch you up from the depths of despondency and lift you up to the heights of exultation all in a moment!

"Would you like to share a taxi?" I asked.

Even before I heard the answer, I knew what it would be. Why else would an impecunious young couple speak to an impecunious retired couple like us, unless to share a taxi? And to think how this nearly did not happen! If I had not left the queue, we would not be standing where we are now. And if we hadn't talked to Dorothy we might have stood next to each other, totally unaware of our shared destination. And just in the nick of time too, for the queue had started moving at last, the people standing in groups broke up and we began to string out in order to file through the boarding gate.

There was time only to establish that they were not staying at the same hotel as us – that would have been just too much of a coincidence and I wanted to say something like "let's try to get seats together on the plane" as having found them, I didn't want to lose sight of them again. But by the time we got through the gate, not more than a minute behind them, they were nowhere to be seen. They must have legged it for the plane.

That was the last we saw of them although I had been keeping my eyes peeled for them. Not on the plane, not on the short bus ride to the terminal building, nor in the immigration hall. By this time I was getting increasingly anxious. At immigration, I joined one queue while Iona went in the other. I was first through, for once having chosen the quicker moving of the two.

In baggage reclaim, the first carousel was the one for the Edinburgh flight and the first bag I saw was our bag, not just on the carousel, but precisely programmed so that it reached the curve just as I did and all I had to do, in the neatest bit of baggage retrieval it has ever been my good fortune to experience, was to put my hand down, pick it up by the droopy handles, set it down, pull out the extending rigid plastic handle, put it into an upright position and I was ready to go. Looking back now, I should have known no-one is that lucky, especially me.

But I was distracted, already swivelling my neck like a ventriloquist's dummy, searching for the young couple, but in a further coincidence, it just so happened that Dorothy and her entourage arrived at precisely that minute. Even a few seconds later would have been enough, enough for me to have looked at the case more closely, and had I done so, I would, without a shadow of doubt, have noticed the fatal error that was to have so many repercussions and which was to colour the entire holiday.

I would have looked for the red-and-white ribbon attached to the handle, not because I am an Aberdeen supporter and it is their colours, but because when we were travelling around Peru, our guide had attached a ribbon of the national colours to the luggage of everyone in the party, so while we did nothing, he went and retrieved our luggage, all part of the service.

Iona and I had thought it a good method of distinguishing our baggage from the common herd and had kept it there ever since, with the addition of a further distinguishing factor – and this was Iona's idea – a pink luggage label to replace the black one that came with the case. Pink is not a colour I am partial to, but it does seem to be very popular with little girls – and one of my nephews, when he was very young.

Nevertheless, I permitted the pink luggage label to stay (as if I had any say in the matter) despite its clash with the red-and-white ribbon because I could see the sense in having such a distinguishing mark. It was a bit like having an "A" branded upon our case, not for "Adulteress" as in Nathaniel Hawthorne's *The Scarlet Letter* but "A" for "Addison." A case sporting such a feature would be far and few between, I reckoned.

But I did not check, nor notice the absence of these features. Instead I fell into conversation with Dorothy, exchanging phone numbers while we waited for Iona to arrive.

That was how we ended up with the wrong case. Although I was partly to blame, it never would have happened but for Dorothy, as you can see.

What I did not foresee, apart from the impostor case, there was going to be another slight problem before we arrived in Lucca, before the real problems began.

CHAPTER FIVE:
EN ROUTE TO LUCCA

As soon as Iona joined us, we headed for the exit although it was against my instinct. I felt I ought to hang around the baggage hall, for surely the young ones must stop here, unless of course, they had not checked in any luggage, as evidently neither had Dorothy & Co. Even so, you would have thought that they might have waited there as the spot where they would be most likely to meet us. But I was powerless to check our relentless progress to the exit. Like most people, when you arrive at an airport, the first thing you want to do is get out of the place as quickly as possible and get to your final destination, and Dorothy and her group were no different.

Just inside the exit doors, Dorothy was hugged and kissed like a long-lost relative and which she reciprocated in kind – which all took a bit of time. You know how the Italians are. I presumed this was her driver and friend. They certainly looked friendly enough. But where was our young couple?

I needn't have worried. They must have been lying in wait for us, just inside the exit too, though it was the young man who recognised me first. Thanks to the hat no doubt.

"Want to share a taxi?" he asked, like we had never met before, like a tout.

Perhaps during the flight, they may have wondered if we had changed our minds, perhaps worried about it for the entire flight. They needn't have worried about that. But they had only just met me of course.

"The taxis are over there," Dorothy said with a casual wave of the same arm that had pointed out her relatives earlier. The difference this time was that I could see what she was pointing at. Straight ahead, as I would have seen anyway, as anyone without a white stick could not have failed to notice, was a long white line of taxis, lying in wait for customers like great white sharks.

"I'll call you," said Dorothy. "Maybe you can come up to the villa for lunch one day."

"That sounds great. Thanks very much," I called back as we headed towards the taxi rank.

Being the most senior male by a mile, I took charge of operations.

"How much is it to Lucca?" I asked the driver in the first car.

"Fifty or sixty euros."

Just what I was expecting and yet I hesitated. Perhaps it was negotiable. And perhaps the taxi driver was a mind reader, for he added, "Meter," nodding at a contraption in the facia of the dashboard.

"Can you take all of us?" I asked, indicating my companions.

"Yes."

"All right then."

He sprang out, opened the boot, the case belonging to someone else was stowed away with the hand luggage, the others piled into the back and I was left to sit beside the driver.

Minutes later we were on the motorway and with us safely on our way, I fished out my mobile phone. It was a bit dark to see the number on my piece of paper, but each time I typed in the numbers, I ended up with the same result – a dead sound. The battery was fully charged, the signal strong and I knew it was full of money. Furthermore, I was sure I had copied down the number from Gardiner correctly, aware of how vital it was to get that correct. But just then I was struck with an idea that filled me with horror – what if *he* had heard it wrongly in the first place?

But I dismissed this idea almost instantaneously. No, I am sure he would have taken just as much care as I had done. Perhaps it was something else, like I was meant to put in the code for Italy first, (whatever that is) or leave out a zero or something as I have done in the past when I have sent texts from abroad.

"Do you speak English?" I asked the driver.

"Poco. A leetle," he replied, taking his right hand off the wheel and indicating a small gap between forefinger and thumb. I understood. Perhaps if I talked slowly he would understand me too.

"I can't get my phone to work. Do I need to put in something before the number?"

By way of an answer, he reached above his head and I repeated my question hoping that the light that was now flooding the car might also shed some light on my problem. How much he understood, I couldn't say, but by way of an answer, he picked up his phone from the tray on the dashboard and indicated that I should pass him the piece of paper on which I had written the number. With one eye on the road and the other on the keypad (I was glad he had two) he keyed in the numbers, listened a moment, then passed the instrument over to me. It was certainly ringing all right.

"Hello," I said when someone answered. It might even have been the very person I talked to before. "This is David Addison here. We have booked a double room with you (no harm in reminding them) and this is just to let you know that we are on the motorway now and we will be with you very soon."

"That's fine. I am expecting you."

"Thank you. Goodbye."

"Goodbye."

"Thanks."

With a great sense of relief I handed the phone back to the driver and let him switch it off, which he did, followed by the light. This was going to mean a bigger tip than usual. Still, what did that matter? It was such a relief to be on our way with the taxi fare halved and secure in the knowledge that we would, at least, be able to get in to the hotel and not stand about freezing, waiting for someone to come and let us in.

There was still the slight concern of the dormitory smelling of pee, but there was nothing I could do about that at the moment and if turned out to be a problem, I'd just have to cross that bridge when I came to it.

CHAPTER SIX:
AN ALARMING DISCOVERY

A light so bright that it sears the eyeballs, even at this early time in the morning, is poring in through the open, outer door of the toilet. Someone, I suppose, must have left a light on during the night. But it is extinguished as soon as Iona gets up, first as usual, and closes the door to perform her ablutions.

In a curious sort of arrangement, they have built some sort of porch on to what I call the "pabby." Pabby is my childhood word for "toilet" sometimes shortened, when I am feeling lazy, to "pab" which is not unusual (as Tom Jones might sing). I think my greatest legacy would be to get that word, or its abbreviation, into the Oxford English Dictionary. Not in my lifetime, of course. But for some reason, Iona hates the word and is just as determined to stamp it out.

I can see no practical reason why they should have done this, for it does diminish the size of the room somewhat, though I imagine, this double door arrangement is an effective soundproofing system. I never saw the point of people having *en suite* bathrooms in their own houses when they don't have to queue, unless they have teenagers in the house, who, when they are not sulking or skulking in their bedrooms, are usually to be found in the bathroom trying to improve on nature. It seems to me, (not exactly known for taking the harder route when an easier way presents itself) the height of laziness not to walk a short distance to get to the pabby. I would have thought the further you got away from all those embarrassing plops and tinkles the better, particularly in times of illness.

I was right about the double doors. Not a sound can be heard. She takes a much shorter time than usual, naturally, with no hair to wash.

"Come on, get up!" she says in a tone that brooks no argument, like when she says, after making yet another of her exotic meals, "Perhaps you would like to clear up in the kitchen."

I hear no question mark and have transposed it as spoken and as heard by me. Hercules, I am sure, had an easier labour of it when he cleaned out the Aegean stables, (are all those pots and pans and utensils strictly necessary?) but if that is the price you have to pay for delicious meals, so be it. This is precisely the same tone she is using now when she says, "You've got a case to get back to its rightful owner."

Don't I know it! Have I not been thinking about it all night? Are my ankles not black and blue with where I have been kicking myself all night? If not, they should be. Ever reluctant to get up in the morning, I am especially so this morning.

They say that people who are near death but who have not died, or who have, but have been resuscitated, report being drawn to a bright light and also report with what extreme reluctance they left that light behind. Feeling like death itself, I hobble off to the bright light coming from the pabby and it would be so easy to slip into *easeful death* in Keats's phrase, like someone intent on suicide and head towards that light and just keep going, leave all my troubles and cares behind for Iona to sort out.

Selfish swine, I think as I realise that the light is not artificial, but the sun streaming in the one and only narrow window. I tweak back the net curtain and squint at the sky. Cloudless blue. The sun is in the heavens and all would be right with the world if only I had stopped for a second, two seconds at the most, to check I had picked up the right case. Now, instead of wandering around Lucca in this heart-warming sunshine, I am going to have to spend an endless amount of time getting rid of this case – and getting ours back. If only it were grey and gloomy, that would have been better, more in keeping with my mood, like Ruskin's pathetic fallacy, but I tell myself not to be so pathetic, though I defy this sky-splitting sun to lift my spirits with its brilliance.

Just as well my mother-in-law is not with us, I reflect, as I squeeze in between the space created when the two halves of the shower cabinet are drawn apart. This must certainly be the smallest shower in Lucca. I can hardly fit in myself, but at least the water is warm and there is a little bar of soap and shampoo in little sachets that you can only open with your teeth, being careful to make sure all the shampoo is at the bottom otherwise you end up with a mouthful of shampoo.

I never brush or comb my hair, unless with my fingers, and after washing it, all I do is give it a brisk rub with the towel and that is me ready to go, so the absence of a hair dryer doesn't bother me a jot. And it's also quite nice not to have to shave for once, but on the other hand, it is with some repugnance that I have to put on those underpants again, over my lovely clean bottom. Well, clean bottom anyway.

I hope Gisele is going to be there, I am thinking, as I undo the luggage label that I hope she will be able to decipher. Seated behind the wooden chest-high desk, it had come as rather a surprise to me, though it wouldn't have in London, or Edinburgh even, to find that the receptionist was a black woman. Probably she was the very one whom I had talked to on the phone from Scotland. The badge on her blouse told me that her name was Gisele.

From our brief meeting last night when she had taken our passport details and then shown us to our room, she had appeared to be friendly enough. She had even tried to carry Carla's bag upstairs for us but I gave her Iona's bag instead, since she was so insistent on carrying something. That was another reason why I hadn't spotted the impostor: both bags felt equally as heavy. If they are charging you for 15 kilos, you jolly well make sure that 15 kilos is what you take.

The first thing I had noticed about the room after its dimensions, not large, but not that poky either, was the big, solid, red headboard with the muslin cloth behind it, which gave it a rather medieval look, appropriately enough for this medieval city. There was a wardrobe to the left of it, a table and a chair to the right, and a wooden cupboard contraption that Gisele had opened.

"Kitchen," she had explained, with what I interpreted as a tone of pride and after which I somehow got the feeling that this could be the best room in the hotel. And to think I was worried about ending up in the basement in the dormitory smelling of pee!

There was an aluminium sink and a couple of hot plates. There didn't appear to be any pots or pans however, nor any dishes, though there was a jam jar out of which some sad-looking eating utensils were peeking forlornly over the top.

"Kitchen!" I had repeated. "Wow!"

Gisele had appeared so pleased with this response, it hardly seemed worth pointing out these rather vital deficiencies when we had absolutely no intention of doing any cooking.

Now, as we head downstairs, I've no idea what I'm going to do if Gisele is not there, or if there is no receptionist at all, or if it turns out to be one of the unfriendly ones.

But she is, thank God! As I slide the luggage label over the desk I explain what has happened. Being a woman, she can multi-task, listen to me, even if it is in a foreign language and read the label, or at least attempt to. From the way her brow is puckered, I can see this latter task is a bit of a challenge, even to one with her abilities. Her hand strays towards a mobile phone on the counter beside her, then pauses. Instead she says something that I can't quite make out, but it sounds as if it begins with an "I."

"Is that where she comes from?"

Gisele repeats the same strange-sounding name. It does not get me a great deal further forward other that it does indeed seem to begin with "I" and seems to end with an "ah" but as for the rest, it remains as obscure as ever. Iona, however, seems to have cottoned on. Being musical I suppose, she has a better ear for such things. But more than that, it seems to have a profound effect on her for she is gasping like a landed fish. For the life of me, I can't see why on earth it should knock the stuffing out of her like this.

"Isola d'*Elba*?" she croaks.

Elba! Is that what Gisele was saying? If she had said "Elba" I would naturally have got it straight away. After all, I don't normally go about saying the "Island of Iona" or the "Island of Mull," though people do tend to talk about the "Isle of Skye" for some reason. That "I" of "Isola" had really thrown me. I presumed it was the name of some obscure village. Now I see the reason for Iona, the wife's, reaction. I am leaning on the desk with my elbows to support my legs which seem to have gone a bit wobbly. I have no clear idea where Elba is exactly, but the very fact of it being an island must mean it will be more difficult to return the case. After all, at one time, the British had thought it remote enough to banish Napoleon, although they had been wrong about that, so maybe I am also wrong about how hard it may be to get to.

"Isola d'Elba," Gisele repeats. She appears to be a lady of very few words but they have the power to strike fear into me.

With a great deal of foresight, (which would never have occurred to me) Iona has brought the guide book with her and which has a map of Tuscany spread over the inside covers. No doubt she was prepared for the owner living in some obscure place which neither of us had heard of before. Now it is useful to see where Elba is exactly.

How stupid was that, to put Napoleon so close to the mainland? And yet it looks a long, long way from Lucca. Why couldn't Carla have lived somewhere on the mainland? It would have been nice if she had lived in Lucca, but Elba looks

as if it is as far away as you can possibly get and still call Pisa
your local airport. In Scottish terms it looks the equivalent of
getting from Edinburgh to Arran – not the easiest of journeys.
But at least in Scotland, we can speak the language.

That which had seemed bad, had just got a lot worse.

CHAPTER SEVEN: ANOTHER SHOCK

Iona and I are still in shock as Gisele reaches for the phone and frowning with concentration, her thumb moves over the digits as she types them in, pausing between each one as she deciphers it. Breathlessly we wait. Is it the right number? Eventually she speaks, in Italian of course, but I do recognise some words such as Lucca and the name of our hotel. Gisele writes something down. It looks like a telephone number. The conversation ends.

"That was signora Cremona," she says. "She can't talk at the moment, but she has given me her husband's number."

Well done, Gisele, you are a star! What a relief! In far away Elba, I imagine Carla must be feeling the same thing. Without saying anything more, Gisele's thumb moves again and at last she speaks as someone apparently answers. This time I catch the name *signor Cremona* and *sì, sì, sì,* as she writes down something being dictated to her. It looks like an address. Great! Now we have a phone number and an address we can read! I had hardly dared for so much progress so soon.

Gisele pushes the phone away from her, seems to be staring at the scrap of paper as if there was something not quite right about it or as if committing the address to memory and says nothing for what seems an eternity. Meanwhile, she has us in the palm of her hand. It wouldn't surprise me if she were a drama student: watch for her on ITV someday, (that's Italian TV by the way) for she is a mistress of suspense.

At last she passes the slip of paper across the desk. "That is signora Cremona's telephone number, and that is her address."

Portoferraio. We pore over the map but it is too small to show any details. Elba just looks like a little green goldfish swimming away from the mainland.

"Your luggage is at Pisa airport," Gisele continues. "When they are getting their luggage, they will phone to the airport and you can get yours."

I had no doubt that that was where my luggage would be. It would have been too much of a coincidence, too inconceivable that Carla was as stupid as me and had not noticed she had the wrong bag until she got home. No, I can picture the scene as a bag like hers, but not hers, went past her. Perhaps she had stooped to pick it up, noticed the red-and-white ribbon, or the pink label, or both, and had checked her move. Then she would have become increasingly anxious as fewer and fewer bags were left on the carousel, then the crowd thinned out until all that was left was the bag that looked like hers, endlessly going round and round – which is when the dread suspicion that was beginning to form in her mind turned into the awful concrete certainty.

Now, instead of speeding merrily on her way, she would have had to report the loss, filling in endless forms in the lost luggage office. And what if she were in a race against time to catch the last ferry of the day? Another dread thought clutches at my heart. Will I have to pay for her to stay in a hotel overnight, if she had missed her ferry because of this?

I had also hoped, in a vague sort of way (more than I dared to give voice to, lest the gods snatched it away) that if I appeared at the airport with Carla's luggage, the airport might have taken care of it, would send it on to her and would give us ours back. Now it sounds more like a hostage threat, or like negotiations prior to the exchange of spies during the Cold War. I want to know if that is airport policy or whether that is signor Cremona's ultimatum, but Gisele doesn't know.

So what do we do now? Nothing at the moment as Gisele takes a key from a young man, who, indicating a blackboard advertising a continental breakfast for €8, asks where he has to go. She tells him it is not available but there is a café round the corner to the left. That is useful information for us too, but I wonder why, if the breakfast is not on, why the blackboard had not been taken down? It seems to be getting-up time as young people start drifting downstairs and hang about the lobby. Backpackers. Students. We are the oldest by far. Cheapskates.

"Do you know of a company that will send the bag to Elba? You know, a carrier, that will maybe send it express?"

Gisele looks doubtful. "Maybe you should post it?" she suggests.

Maybe I should have let her carry the bag upstairs after all, then perhaps she would not have made such a ridiculous suggestion. Has she got no conception of how heavy it is? That to post a bag of that weight and size would cost a fortune? Just because I am a mature adult and not a backpacker or a student doesn't mean that euros just drop out my bottom every time I go to the toilet. Having retired very early, I don't look as old as a person on a pension, which I am, but it is only an occupational one and I have to be as economical as any student. But I don't want to confess that to Gisele. I shake my head vigorously.

"No! No! Very heavy. Far too big and heavy to post! A carrier would be better."

Wordlessly, Gisele reaches for a phone book and leafs through it until she finds the equivalent of Yellow Pages. At last her finger pounces on an advert and she rings the number. This is going to cost a fortune in phone calls I think, but there is nothing else for it.

Nothing seems to be happening. I presume it is ringing, but no-one seems to be answering and at last Gisele hangs up, studies the phone book again and tries another number. Meanwhile, Iona slopes off. Where is she going? Back to the room apparently, but why? What if there are important decisions to be made? It seems an act of folly on her part, to leave that to me. She looks so tired and depressed I hope she is not off to hang herself. But with what? It won't be with the hair dryer cord anyway.

Ah! After a few moments in which I listen in suspense, it begins to sound a bit more hopeful. Gisele speaks for a few moments then hangs up.

"This firm will deliver your bag by tomorrow. Do you want that I call a taxi for you?" She seems poised to act as if it were a rhetorical question. As simple and easy as that. Problem solved.

That sounds like good news and easy. But let's not be too hasty. Apart from yet another taxi fare, perhaps costing a fortune in itself, no price has been mentioned and Gisele had hung up before I had had a chance to ask her to find out, as I would certainly have done had I been able to follow the conversation. She apparently takes me for someone for whom money is no object, but had she stopped to think for a minute, she should have realised that if that were the case I wouldn't be staying in a hotel-cum-backpackers' hostel like this. Maybe she is a spendthrift. She can't be earning that much, yet I know people like her who have hardly two pennies to rub together, yet do not hunt about for the best bargain, but just spend willy-nilly as if they had all the money in the world. That's why they'll never be as rich as me.

Besides, that was just one company. Maybe I could get a better deal from another one. I won't know until I try but I don't want to try Gisele's patience; she probably has plenty to be getting on with and I can't ask her to spend the morning phoning company after company only to end up with possibly only saving a euro or two. And it would be too embarrassing for words if she said no anyway.

"Er. Thanks. You've been very helpful, but I'll maybe try the Tourist Information Office first…"

Sometimes I get an idea, one that I think up all by myself, and this sounds like one of my best, at least to me. Of course, it may not be any use. For all I know, the services provided by the Tourist Information Office extend no further than doing things such as booking hotel rooms and providing guided tours, and has absolutely nothing to do with poor benighted travellers, especially if their problems are of their own making. Perhaps that is a job for the police. In which case, I will ask them.

It is only the slightest of shrugs, but Gisele pushes the phone away and nods. Just then Iona comes down the stairs, dressed in her outdoor clothes. So that was it! Just as Gisele is economical with words, there was no need for Iona to speak on this occasion. I haven't known her all this time and not learned that she is not best pleased with me and furthermore, she is hungry and wants her breakfast as soon as possible. It doesn't do her much good as I have to go upstairs to get my hat and jacket, which I set about doing immediately, only pausing to thank Gisele again for her help which she acknowledges with a slight bow of the head, as before.

By the time I come back down, although it is only a moment later, Gisele has disappeared, as have all the backpackers who were hanging around. For all we know, the entire hotel could be deserted. We close the heavy wooden door behind us, the kind of door you might expect to see in a manor house or stately mansion as this probably was once upon a time. We turn to the left, but before we have gone very far, I don't know what made me think of it, but suddenly I remember I have left my pouch in the room. My pouch, which has all my money, my cards, my passport and, not least, the little bit of paper that shows I am the rightful owner of the luggage at present residing in Pisa airport somewhere. Not that it matters really, as long as Iona has enough money to pay for the breakfast and the hotel is as empty as it appears to be – as I also point out to her at the same time as admitting my omission.

"Oh, you'd better go back for it, I suppose!" she responds testily.

It is but the matter of a few minutes to fetch it, but must seem longer by far for the tired and hungry one, who, she informs me, has not slept well and now has to hang around in the frosty air, for although it is deceptively sunny, the air has not yet had time to warm up. I suppose you could say that that reflects her attitude towards me at the moment too.

The café is not far. To the end of the street, turn left and it is on the corner, at the end of the street opposite the church of Santa Anna. It's called the Scilla. Scylla would seem more appropriate as far as I am concerned, caught between the Scylla of Iona's anger and the Charybdis of Carla's bag hanging like an albatross around my neck.

Three little wrought iron tables with matching chairs are on the pavement outside although no-one is using them. Breakfast, Italian style, consists of crowding into the little café not much larger than the shower in our hotel where you stand, not naked, but snappily dressed, not with a bar of soap in your in your hand, but a pastry or a croissant wrapped in a paper napkin, while your espresso, no more than two swallows at the most, rests on a little shelf at elbow height along one wall while, in a corner, a machine hisses and spits like an expectorating cat.

Although I too, normally have breakfast on the hoof, we sit outside on the iron seats, where, though I can't speak for Iona, the cold permeates my nether regions. The coffee is scarcely any warmer. I have a latte; Iona, who is to coffee as I am to whisky, (though I have yet to succumb to my drug at such an early time in the day) has an americano, which is hot. With this infusion of her drug (with perhaps the paltry help of the pastry) she seems somewhat revived, unlike our conversation, which is desultory.

We set off towards the town. No problem about in which direction to head. Straight on from the Scilla to the traffic lights, the same lights where we had had to stop last night and I had had my first glimpse of the famous walls, and, I have to admit, I had been more than just a bit disappointed. Short and squat, they are crowned not with crenellated battlements, but trees. There hadn't been time for the usual research before leaving, so I had no idea of what to expect as far as the walls were concerned but I had hoped for something like Carcassonne, towering walls and turrets half as high again – and these just don't measure up. They are too like me, too short and too fat. Nothing noble, nothing impressive, nothing majestic; just ordinary, like me, and as far as I can tell, from this preliminary impression, too thick by half.

They are still a bit of a disappointment, at least from this range. Only as we get closer, do I begin to appreciate them more and it is only when you stand directly beneath them that you realise they are in fact pretty high, not rising straight up, but sloping upwards at a slight angle off the perpendicular. And it is only when you get right up to them that you see that they are composed of thousands of tiny little bricks, thin and rectangular, like Roman bricks. How many bricks must it have taken to build this wall? And when you think how they go right round the city, and not just in a circle either, but have enormous spade-shaped bastions too – it is truly mind-boggling. But, impressive though all that is, it is not those that impress so much but their thickness.

We are standing outside the Porta Santa Anna which is pierced by a road for vehicles and at either side, a path for pedestrians and cyclists. In the distance, we can hear the *Nee-naw* of an ambulance rushing off to some invisible emergency, the third time we have heard it today and it hardly begun. And bicycles abound too. Never have I seen a bigger infestation of bicycles since Amsterdam. As a motorist, I detest them, especially when they come in pairs so you can't get past them and you have to slow down to 10 mph. Even solitary cyclists are a pain in the butt, (them too, let's hope, sitting on those razor-sharp seats, a form of torture, inspired, I am sure, by Hieronymus Bosch) as you never can be sure that they won't suddenly swerve into your path and you have to give them at least as wide a berth as a car.

Here, as a pedestrian, they are no less pestilential. They come up behind you on well-oiled wheels and silent, pneumatic tyres and the first thing you know anything about it is when they pass you so close to your skin that you practically jump out of it. It would take only the slightest deviation from your path and the merest wobble on their part to bring about a collision, and unlike the ambulances, there is no warning bell, no Ting! Ting! to warn you of their approach, like I had on my bike when I was a boy. Unlike the collision between a cyclist and a motorist however, there is not the slightest doubt who would come off better, every time, in this merger of metal with flesh.

Passing through those oh, so thick walls, the first thing we see, cannot fail to notice, is a memorial plaque to a WWII war hero. Someone has been here recently for a bouquet of withering flowers in cellophane is hanging next to the plaque. But after this eye-catching piece of vegetation, the eye is drawn to the living, to the numerous trees that adorn the piazza which we now find ourselves in, the Piazzale Verdi.

In a piazza of such a size, if not munificence exactly, surely the Tourist Information Office must be nearby, for, with a bit of luck, we seem to have entered the city through one of the principal gates. A line of yellow buses is straight in front of us, and over to the right, a lot more, only blue. The bus station, apparently. How convenient for our future trips – once we get rid of the Albatross.

What we are looking for *must* be somewhere here about. I need a sign. And there it is, pointing apparently to the left-hand side of the piazza, where an impressive, two-storey building with a covered balcony and a wide arched entrance with glass doors gazes out at the bus station directly opposite.

Inside, it is roomy with a desk in an island in the centre and racks of bicycles for the hire of. If you can't beat them, join them.

I don't have to wait. A young lady named Roberta, so her badge says, is ready to help.

"I bet you've never had a problem like this before," I begin.

"Don't worry," she says, smiling. But she hasn't heard my problem yet.

I launch into my explanation and she listens, rapt, then to make sure she has understood me properly, sums up the problem.

"So, you picked up someone's luggage by mistake at the airport and you want to know the best way to return it?"

"Yes. Here is the owner's phone number and address." As she reads, I explain about my own bag being held hostage. "Do you know if that is the airport's rule or is it signor Cremona's idea?"

Roberta shakes her head. I was right about her never having a problem like this before and before I can stop her, she is phoning the number on the slip of paper. I was going to suggest could she phone the airport to find out, but it is too late now.

"Sì. Sì." Roberta rings off. "That is the airport policy," she tells us. So now I know. And now signor Cremona knows that retrieving my bag, not returning his, is my priority.

"Er...I was wondering if you could phone a carrier company and find out how much it would cost to send it to Elba?"

Roberta riffles through the phone book, phones a number. No answer. Tries another. No answer. This is getting worrying. But it is a case of third time lucky – for someone answers at last and presently Roberta asks me, "How heavy is the bag? How big is it?"

"Fifteen kilos. About three feet by one foot?" I look at Iona for confirmation, who nods. "Er...that is...I mean about one metre long," and then pulling my hands apart, "by so much high."

That's about the best I can do. I had left school long before the enforced conversion to metrification and had never bothered trying to learn it, remaining true to the old faith and only picking up what little I knew by unavoidable contact with it such as 75cl in a bottle of wine and 70cl in a bottle of malt. And never having had any cause to measure anything since then, centimetres and millimetres, as well as the rest of that metre family remained strangers to me, apart from kilometres I suppose, which I must admit I do approve of, rather than miles, as they disappear beneath your wheels with much more satisfying rapidity.

Roberta relays the information. We all wait. Presumably the invisible man (or woman) is punching numbers into a calculator.

"Sì. Sì." Grazie." Roberta's face is impassive as she breaks the connection. "The company will come to your hotel and pick the luggage up and drop it off at signora Cremona's house. Based on that weight and size, the charge will be – " she breaks off to write a figure down on a scrap of paper, then goes over it again so it stands out, big and black and bold, before turning it round so I can see it. She needn't have bothered. I could read it perfectly well upside down and thought I must be dreaming. Maybe Roberta couldn't believe it either, which is why she went over it again, or was she just delaying the moment before she had to break the bad news?

"€243!" It's not a dream but a nightmare. Had it been a reasonable sort of price, that would have been the beginning of the end of our problems. Bye, bye Albatross, I might have felt like singing. It is so utterly preposterous, risible, that I can't help making a snort of derision. Why, the flights and the hotel together scarcely came to that, I explain to Roberta.

But of course I didn't really need to tell her that. She already knew it was a non-starter, otherwise she would not

39

have hung up without asking me first if I wanted to go ahead. There seems little point in asking her to try another company or ring those numbers again if that is the target price.

"What about the Post Office?" I ask. That which had seemed so preposterous might not be so preposterous after all. Surely it couldn't be any worse.

Roberta is brilliant. Without demur, she picks up the phone again. All in a day's work. But there is no reply from the Post Office, at least nothing that is any use to me.

"It is only an answering machine," Roberta informs me. "You will have to go there yourself."

My heart sinks. That sounds as if it may present some problems. A plague on this "progress" which prevents you from speaking to real people. If only Roberta had been able to speak to someone we might have had some sort of idea if it was worth our while going there or not.

"This is how to get there," Roberta says, drawing a street map of the city towards her and marking the Post Office on the map. It looks a long way, right across the city in fact.

"Thanks. Thanks a lot. You've been a great help," I tell Roberta, taking the map and, for some reason, the scrap of paper with the €243 written on it. Maybe I still can't believe it yet.

"Another possibility," Roberta adds, as if a sudden thought had just occurred to her. "There is a travel agent here, on the Piazza San Michele," and taking the map from me again, she marks with a circle, the said square. "It may be that you will have to go to Elba yourself."

"Thank you, thank you. I am very grateful for everything you have done."

It is nothing less than the truth, but the truth is that my heart is very heavy indeed as we head in the direction of the Post Office. Go to Elba! Meet Carla face to face! Anything but that!

CHAPTER EIGHT: AT THE POST OFFICE AND OTHER PROBLEMS

I give the map to Iona. She is the navigator. She is, after all, an ex-geography teacher and loves maps, even if she does not love me very much at the moment.

First step of many is to go up the Via San Paolino, not the main street of Lucca actually, but a main artery, or should that be vein, for it is not all that wide. But that is the joy and the attraction of a medieval town – they were never built for vehicular traffic, though that does not deter them entirely, and certainly does not deter the bikes. Lucca lies on the Lucchese Plain, as flat as a pancake, or Holland, if you prefer, which explains why there are so many of the two-wheeled nuisances.

But before we set off, we are distracted by a freestanding poster of Puccini at the corner of the street. He looks rather dapper, effete even. Not my idea of a composer at all, especially a composer of operas, though to be honest, I don't know what such a person should look like, but if I had had to guess from this larger than life-size photograph what this bloke did for a living, I would have said a gentleman, or a gambler or a gigolo. It's partly because of the cigarette languidly held between his fingers, apparently forgotten, and his natty suit with waistcoat – but mainly because of his hat, a sort of light-coloured bowler. It is not nearly as stylish as mine (but then what could be?) but on the other hand, it does go with his suit. He looks quite the man about town, a big spender who would be happy to spend some time with any lady beautiful enough.

But what do I know? I know next to nothing about him, not being an opera fan, mainly because of those screeching sopranos who set my nerves on end, just as the sound of nails

41

scraping on a blackboard does, or the sound of a wet finger run round the rim of a glass. But he does have some very good tunes to his credit, I must admit, especially if they are sung by a tenor such as Pavarotti, as anyone who watched the BBC TV coverage of the World Cup hosted by Italy in 1990 knows – *Nessun Dorma* having been chosen as its signature tune. It is, as the poster informs us, the 150th anniversary of the great man's birth, here in Lucca. Puccini I mean, not Pavarotti, who has unfortunately, recently left us, and who knows, the two Ps might be up there together now, the latter regaling the former with his greatest hits?

A group has gathered round this handy meeting point and a guide is holding forth on something. But not for us, any of the attractions of Lucca, not until we get rid of the Albatross. First things first, but off to the right, set back from the Via Paolino, Iona spies a row of little shops, amongst which is one which looks as if it might sell toiletries. Indeed it does, so now we have toothpaste and toothbrushes, but not unfortunately any mascara, which is apparently, almost as vital as the former. Cheered a little at least by these purchases, we set off again.

I lag behind as I try to phone Dorothy. I don't know how exactly, but she may be able to help. After all, she got me into this mess in the first place. Roberta had told me she thought that I needed to put 0039 in front of the number. No use. Neither is 039 or plain 39. Since I am phoning a UK number, I try 44. This time something different happens. It is in Italian first of all, then English. I can't even understand the English the first time round and it takes a second attempt. Apparently I am barred from making any calls. Well, I don't know what I did to deserve that, but at least now I know.

Calls, no. But what about texts? I fall further behind as I try sending one: *We've got a bit of a problem here. Could you phone me please?* And because, in all likelihood, Dorothy wouldn't recognise the number, I add *David* just so she would know whom the message was from. To my surprise, it goes.

Who can tell what results my text may have? Things can only get better.

Not immediately they don't. To be fair to Iona, the map is not that clear and we are in a medieval city after all, with narrow, winding streets. But the Post Office is behind the Duomo and that shouldn't be that hard to find, should it? But it is. We are lost.

But it is a small city and if you wander about enough, you are bound to find what you are looking for eventually, especially if it is as large as a cathedral and one of the city's major attractions. Initially, we come to a church, the San Giovanni with another of those freestanding Puccini posters standing outside it. It tells us that this is the church where Puccini's father's funeral service was held. Even if I had wanted to, I couldn't have got in since it is firmly shut up.

Then suddenly, we find ourselves in the Piazza San Martino, with the church forming one side of it and the Duomo straight ahead. There is nothing to tell us that we are nearing our goal until we are nearly out of the piazza and I catch sight of *Poste E Telecomunicazioni* written on the side of the building ahead of us. Going up the steps, we find ourselves in a vestibule and passing through that, we enter the Post Office proper.

It's unlikely that we would ever have come here but for the Albatross, not having any intention of sending any postcards, but if we had, we would probably have got the stamps from the *tabacchi* where we had bought them, so this is a chance to see a snippet of ordinary Italian life.

On the left, the whole side is given up to desks, but they are not all the same apparently. Just inside the entrance is a machine that dispenses tickets, like at the delicatessen counter of some supermarkets. But it is not a case of taking any old ticket. Fortunately we have enough Italian between us to work out that the desks on the left are for banking customers, while those on the right are for people like us who want to post something.

Only it isn't a queue, it's much more civilised than that. There are plenty of seats, enough for all, though some prefer to stand until they hear the announcement, or in our case, until the red dots above the desk come up with the letter and number on our ticket – PO 49. On previous trips to Italy, I had not been unduly impressed with Italian logic, but this seems to me an eminently sensible idea and far better than the system back home where you stand in a snaking queue for sometimes twenty minutes. You may not be served any quicker under this system, but at least you get a seat. PO 44 is being served at the moment.

At last it is our turn. Here we go. Deep breaths.

"Do you speak English?" I ask the clerk. Seeing the blank look on his face, I resort to the little Italian I think I know. "Parlare Inglese?" No doubt it is not the sort of Italian ever spoken by a native unless with learning difficulties, but it should be good enough to convey my meaning. But even before I attempted my translation, I knew the answer.

He shakes his head in what might be construed as in a sad way, but that might just have been me pathetically hoping he was empathising with me. I was afraid this might happen and now it has. How do we overcome this slight communication difficulty?

"Do any of your colleagues speak English?" I ask hopefully. "Te amigos, parlare Inglese?" I try and, for added measure, make a gesture to include his fellow workers to left and right.

He shakes his head again. What does that mean? Does that mean they don't, or they aren't his friends, or does he still not understand me? Surely he must know a bit of Spanish even if he doesn't know any English. We're all in the big happy European family now and what's the point of that if we can't borrow a bit from each other's language?

"I want to send a bag," I tell him, making a pantomime of carrying a bag and then pushing it away from me.

Whether he would have understood that or not, I don't know, because meanwhile, on the small piece of paper with the big price, Iona has drawn the bag with its dimensions and 15 kgs next to it and then an arrow from it pointing to ELBA. The clerk looks at it and all is instantly clear. Words! Who needs them?

"Sì, sì," he says, nodding enthusiastically and then following that up with a string of Italian. Now it is our turn to look bewildered. Making a sign to follow him to the end of the row of desks, he shows us a big box in brown paper with masses of sticky tape wound round it like a mummy. I nod to let him understand that I realise I must put the case in a box and wrap it up so securely that not even Houdini himself would be able to get out of it.

"Quanto costa?"

I've no idea if it is proper Italian or not, but anyway it provokes a response, though not one I can understand. I hand him back the piece of paper, indicating that he should write it down. He scrawls some figures in a big loose hand and hands it back. No! It can't be true! €15.90! Especially when you compare it with the price on the other side of the paper. It is far too good to be true. There must be some mistake. He can't have understood me. A euro a kilo to send it all that way to Elba! But I don't know how to ask him if he's sure, that he hasn't made some mistake.

Instead I ask him in the best Italian I have, "Quanto giorno arrivare?"

I think he has understood my meaning and I am reassured by the single finger he is holding up, and it not even the middle finger either. Again, I can hardly believe what I am hearing – and seeing. The next day and at such a reasonable price too! Everything I could possibly have wished for, never would have dreamt of in my wildest dreams. What a wonderful institution the Italian Post Office is! And to think that I had nearly had a fit when Gisele had first suggested it! And thank God that I hadn't let her order me a taxi to the carrier's! But why, therefore do I have such an overwhelming feeling, not of gladness but of foreboding? It can't just be the slight matter of where on earth, never mind Lucca, am I going to find a box to put the case in, not to mention the brown paper and sticky tape?

"Grazie, grazie."

Iona is similarly despondent as we make our way down the Via Santa Croce towards the Piazza San Michele. Like me, she thinks there is far too big a difference between the carrier's price and the Post Office price and the latter cannot possibly be right.

"Do you know what I think?"

Although she is going to tell me anyway, I say, "No. What?"

"I think we should take it to Elba ourselves. I think we should make it part of the holiday. Make it an excursion, see Elba at the same time."

And I would see Carla, or her husband at least. I don't think that's a very good idea for a start, never mind what it would cost for another. In my opinion, two very good reasons *not* to go anywhere near Elba

"Hmm. I'm not so sure. Let's find out what it would cost first." (Please, God let it be a fortune!)

The travel agent Roberta mentioned is directly across from the church of San Michele. It is very small with two of a staff and no customers. It's funny how the girl asks me in English, before I even have time to open my mouth, how she can help me. Perhaps it's my hat. Maybe she thinks I'm an Australian. Some people do. I can forgive her that; it is such a relief to find she speaks English.

"How would I be able to get to Elba from here?"

You would think that she was asked this question every day in life, for the answer comes pat.

"You would have to take the train to Pisa, then get a bus to (and here I couldn't make out what she said) then you would have to change buses and get a bus to (and again I couldn't make it out but it sounded as if it began with a P) and then you would have to get the ferry."

Good grief! I look at Iona in despair and she looks suitably shell-shocked too. I don't like the sound of all those changes and, of course, we would have to get a taxi to Carla's house and then repeat the whole process again in reverse. I'll worry about the details later if I have to, but first of all, I need to know how much would it cost.

"For two people? €75."

"And what are the times?"

I try vainly to write them down; not very easy when I can't make out the places she is talking about, apart from Pisa. And a balance has to be struck between starting at an ungodly hour and a time that would give us time to get there and back at a reasonable time of day. One thing seems certain: it is going to take so long to get there, (even if we don't miss a bus) and bearing in mind that it gets dark early, it won't give us much time to see anything of Elba – unless we spend the night. Our hotel was so cheap one night wouldn't matter – as long as we could get one at a similarly bargain basement price – and as long as the basement did not turn out to be unsanitary.

"Can you book us a hotel?"

"Not for one night, no."

At this time of year it should be easy enough to find a room ourselves – but how would I be able to find out the best bargain?

"You would like me to book the tickets? It is only one ticket for the whole journey."

Well, that does make a difference I suppose, if we didn't have to go about buying a ticket for each stage and it might not be so difficult as it sounds, all those changes – as long as I had it all written down for me, and if we could find the bus station and the right bus and do it all in between one bus arriving and the next one leaving, though having to hang around for ages for the connection would be just as bad in my view, as having to rush to catch one. It sounds far too much hassle for me – and at the end of it, a meeting with Carla, who would naturally be delighted to be reunited with her luggage but of whom the same could not be said of me.

"No, not just now, thanks. We'll think about it. Grazie."

If it has anything to do with me, she should read that as a no. Whether she does or not, I couldn't say, but as far as Iona is concerned, it is a maybe. Outside, in the Piazza, Iona drops her bombshell.

"I still think we ought to go to Elba."

"What? Are you mad?"

This is definitely what I do *not* want to hear. When she gets a bee in her bonnet, it can be extremely difficult to dislodge. I am beginning to feel a bit like The White Queen in *Alice in Wonderland* who could believe in six impossible things before breakfast. I suppose it all depends on how late she began it and even although it is getting close to our lunchtime, that's the third, if not "impossible" exactly, but certainly *incredible* thing I've heard in the past few minutes: the carrier's price, the Post Office's price and now this. At this rate, with a bit more time, I could easily make it six before lunch.

"You heard how complicated it was – and how expensive it would be, especially if we have to stay the night. And that doesn't even include the taxi. And how would we get around Elba anyway? By taxi?"

"Well, where do you think you are going to get a box big enough to put that bag in?"

That is a very good question indeed, because I haven't a clue.

It turns out that that *was* the last incredible thing I heard before lunch for, as we head towards the Tourist Information Office, out of courtesy to let Roberta know of our progress, we stop off to buy a sandwich from a little café on the Via San

Paolino which the Santa Croce renames itself after it leaves the Piazza San Michele.

"Do you really think it can be that cheap?" I ask Roberta after relating what had happened at the Post Office.

"Yes. Why not, if that is what they told you?" she suggests with a shrug.

Ah, but did they understand exactly what I wanted? And yet, what was there not to understand about Iona's drawing? Although Roberta's reply hardly seems a ringing endorsement, I am almost inclined to half-believe it may be true after all.

"There's just one problem," I tell her. "I have to put it in a box and wrap it up with brown paper and sticky tape."

"The Post Office will sell you a box."

It could not be more music to my ears than if she'd told me I'd won the lottery. "And brown paper and sticky tape too?"

"Yes, why not?"

Why not indeed? I resist an impulse to jump over the desk and hug Roberta to death, which would be quite easy to do as I am practically floating already. The Albatross, while it is still there of course, nevertheless feels as if someone is supporting it from below and an enormous weight has been lifted from my shoulders, not completely, but considerably.

And here's another thing. As we emerge from the Tourist Office, the sky, which had gradually become overcast, culminating in a faint smir of drizzle, has now brightened up and in fact, before we reach the hotel, the sun has become so warm that Iona must divest herself of her fleece. Could my mood possibly be influencing the weather, rather than the other way about?

At the hotel, Gisele is at her desk and has to be told of the latest developments. I resent the time spent and it is a bit churlish of me, after all her kindness, but I am impatient to get that bag on its way and let the holiday begin. Its little wheels are fairly spinning as they clatter noisily up the Via San Paolino, through the Piazza San Michele, onto the Via

Santa Croce. So far straightforward (as the far as these streets are straight) and without recourse to any maps either, with us beginning to get the hang of the place – or so we thought.

We know we need to go off to the right somewhere, but should it be this one? Doesn't look familiar. Well, maybe the next will. It doesn't, but we seem to have proceeded too far in a westerly direction as PC Plod may have put it, and instinct tells us it is right to turn right. Hmm! Don't recognise this little lane either. Lost again, but this time with the inconvenience of towing Carla's lost luggage behind me, trying to ignore the curious stares of the good burghers of Lucca who cannot help but notice the curious spectacle of a funny-looking man in a funny hat taking his case out for a walk, like a pet dog.

Finally, after wandering through a maze of side streets, by happenchance, we come across the Duomo and from there we do know where we are. In a few minutes, hopefully, that which Carla has lost, will be on its way to her.

Because it is now lunchtime, there is only a skeleton staff and it takes a great deal longer than last time. Eventually, presenting ourselves before the clerk, but not the same one, unfortunately, though I can see him at a desk further along, I point to the Albatross on the floor.

"Parlare Inglese?"

No, of course she doesn't, hadn't her friend or colleague already told me that? Oh for Roberta now or Dorothy and why, for that matter, has it taken so long for her to get back to me?

"Box?" I make the sign of rectangle over the Albatross as if putting it in a coffin, then mime furiously wrapping it up with tape. "Box?" I repeat. "Buy?" rubbing my thumb and the tips of my fingers together.

She shakes her head sadly. Definitely sadly this time, but it is not as I first thought, with non-comprehension, for she gets up and returns in a short while with a box. It is flat at the moment, but I can see, we all can, that there is no way that Carla's case will fit in there. It is not even worth trying to make it up. My hopes are dashed again, but whether on the rocks of Scylla or Charybdis, I couldn't say. But perhaps, if two boxes were put together…Well three would be better, but I am not so sure of what "three" is in Italian.

"Due?" I make a sign of joining them and taping them together.

"No possible."

That was in Italian, and I understood it completely. I also understand that there is no possibility of even trying it out to see, though I am still fumbling for the words to ask precisely that. My mouth must be opening and shutting like a goldfish. If I had been able to say something, I would be stammering. Iona, however, has had enough.

"Let's go!" she says and without waiting for a response from me, starts heading towards the exit.

My heart is as low as where the Albatross lies, as not too gently, I seize it by the neck and follow her outside where it has started drizzling again.

CHAPTER NINE: A PAPER CHASE

Back to square one. Looking for a box. A box for me would do, if I can't find a box for the Albatross. And if finding a box for it is not already difficult enough, it has just got a great deal harder – for by now the shops, or the greater part of them, are closed for the afternoon siesta. That means they will be closed for approximately the next two hours, it having begun an hour ago and if the sleepyheads can drag themselves out of bed to open them again that is. I am not adverse to forty winks in the middle of the day myself, but three hours is a bit much, and rather inconvenient, especially for us in our present predicament, I have to say.

I am going to have to find a box – and fast, or else the spectre of plan B, going to Elba, is going to rear its ugly head again. The search is on, in earnest this time. Logically, a supermarket would be a good place to find one, and, what's more, it may even be open at the moment. There's just one snag – we haven't seen any sign of one, nor would I expect to, as they would all certainly be in the "new" town somewhere. If I am to get a box, then it is going to have to be from one of the shops here – except most of them are shut.

It is funny, when you start looking, you begin to notice things you would normally not pay any attention to. Most tourists for example, would not show the slightest interest in flattened cardboard boxes outside the shops, probably would scarcely even notice them. But there am I, not just noticing them, not just looking at them, but raking through them, while Iona looks the other way. She is not with me. No good. Just small boxes, big enough to post a dead parrot in, but definitely nothing large enough to dispatch an Albatross.

And so the search goes on down the Santa Croce, I feeling increasingly despondent as each shop that has put cardboard out for collection, probably about one in ten, fails to produce any results. Furthermore, I am beginning to hear time's winged chariot drawing near and the spectre of Elba looming ever closer. Desperate situations call for desperate measures.

"Scusi. Excuse me. Do you speak English?"

I have gone into a clothes shop, the sort of shop I would never, ever enter in normal circumstances. For a start it has more zeros on the price tag that I would ever contemplate and secondly, it is like walking into Henry Ford's world, where you can choose any size and style of garment you like as long as it is black. It never ceases to amaze me that the young should be so addicted to that gloomy non colour – unless of course it is an expression of their pessimism at all the pressures they are under personally and the state of the planet, generally. I don't blame them for that. I would hate to be young nowadays. I would probably dress in black too.

But the third and the main reason why I would never ordinarily darken the door of such an establishment is I am convinced that if they got a customer aged on the wrong side of thirty, once he (or she) left, without buying anything naturally, the sales assistants would snigger and say: "Did you check that wrinkly who was in here just now?" So what on earth they said about me, after I had left, about the geriatric who came in to buy not clothes but a cardboard box, I prefer not to think about.

Ah, ah! This might be more hopeful – a United Colors of Benetton shop, even if it is closed at the moment. It just so happens that Carla's case (and ours) was made by Benetton. Surely they must have some boxes and made to measure too! They have not put out any boxes at all for collection, but when they open, it might be worth my while going in to ask.

"Don't be ridiculous!" La Belle Dame Sans Merci snorts. "You don't imagine that each case comes individually packed do you?"

"Well, they might," I retort. Drowning men clutch at anything, but it seems reasonable to me that Benetton would wish to protect their precious goods from the slightest scratch, for some shoppers can be notoriously picky, preferring clothes that no-one else has worn before or goods which no-one else has used before, just to give two examples.

Nothing I can do about it at the moment anyway, so the search goes on. At the end of an arcade I can see a shop which is open, and not just open, but wide open because it does not have any doors at all, only shutters which have been cranked fully up so I can see right into the shop and even from this distance, I can see a pile of cardboard boxes on the floor which look as if they might be about to be thrown out.

Leaving Iona to wait in the street, I set off down the spick-and-span arcade, the click-clack of the wheels on the marble tiles rumbling and echoing in the confined space. Alerted by this noise, the young lady assistant, who is standing alone in the shop, never mind the whole arcade, stops doing whatever she was doing and watches me coming. It strikes me it is like a scene from a Western, (especially with me wearing my hat from Missoula, Montana) where all have fled, leaving the stage empty except for two protagonists and which is going to have fatal consequences for one of them at least, usually the bad guy. There is no doubt as to which of us that is, the rumbling of the wheels an ominous accompaniment to what the assistant must see as the approach of this sinister-looking stranger in this deserted arcade while she, her scalp prickling with the beginnings of fear, is powerless to flee or take cover or call for help.

As I get closer, I can see that I am heading towards a clothes shop, and as I get even nearer, that it is a women's clothes shop, and as I get nearer still, to my horror, one of those that seems to specialise in underwear of the more lacy and diaphanous kind rather than the purely functional. Now it is my turn to feel alarmed as I realise that the girl must be

54

wondering what a weirdo like me is doing in a place like this, wondering why I am towing a bag behind me – unless it is to put her body parts in – after.

I slow down, but that only has the effect of making the click-clack of the wheels sound even more sinister as if to presage the moment that whatever my intentions are, the climax is just about to be reached. Perhaps she is clutching at straws herself, that it may not be as bad as it seems: perhaps I am some rich American who has come to buy a whole caseload of undies for his trophy wife; or perhaps she is wondering if I am a cheapskate who has merely come to browse; or just a pervert who likes ladies' underwear. What she *isn't* thinking, as I can tell from the stricken look on her face, is that I am a harmless husband who has strolled in, in search of a sexy piece of lingerie for his wife, even if it is for himself really (only not to wear). She is still rooted to the spot – can only wait to serve, as Milton did not quite put it.

"Do you –" I croak, and have to stop to clear my throat, " speak English?"

She nods.

"Er…I wondered if you had any more boxes. Bigger boxes." This said with a gesture at those discarded on the floor and then spreading my hands apart in a gesture meant to dispel any doubts that large boxes, not busts, is the reason for my visit and there is no cause for alarm.

But even as I said that, I can see that the boxes that I had seen from afar are far, far too small for my purpose and that the original contents must have contained nothing more than a handful of 34C bras (which scarcely contain a handful themselves): in other words, these boxes are about big enough to bury a blackbird and a very far cry indeed from an albatross.

She shakes her head with wide-eyed wonderment. The power of speech seems to have deserted her.

"Grazie," and spinning on my heel, I make those little wheels on the case spin as they have never spun before (and that is saying something) and without looking back, make for the exit – and some fresh air. I can only speculate as to how big the look and how deep the sigh of relief the young lady gave to see me go, but I don't need to speculate on whether to try any more shops for boxes or not. I am certainly not going through all that again. I'd rather swim through shark-infested seas to Elba and fling myself on Carla's mercy.

"No use," I tell Iona, though there really was no need to say anything, unless it was to cover up my embarrassment.

The gods truly love to sport with you – for just a moment later, with despondency at its lowest ebb, what should present itself but a possible source of salvation! The most unlikely sort of salvation, admittedly, a sort of straw, not blowing in the wind, but floating on the water, the sort of straw that a drowning man swimming to Elba with 15 kilos of baggage on his back may clutch at.

Angels, it is said, present themselves in the most unlikely of forms, in which case this may turn out to be one now. Rather like the pestilential bicycles, it is silent, for it is powered by electricity, but a great deal larger. However, having said that, it is tiny compared to those that we have back home, rather like one of those Matchbox toys I used to collect as a boy. This has been specially scaled down, adapted to fit the narrow streets of Lucca.

And just what is this potential angel on wheels you may be wondering, dear reader? The answer, is what we in Scotland call a scaffie cart or lorry and which, if you live south of the Border, especially the further south you go, you might know as "a refuse disposal vehicle" which, in my opinion, sounds rather posh for what it is, like calling the people whose job it is to collect and dispose of household waste, "garbologists" – rather a far cry from when I was a boy, and in order to encourage me to do my homework, my mother warned that if I didn't, I would end up as a "dustman" as we called them then.

It was only after it had passed me and turned up a street to my right that I noticed that it was piled high with flattened cardboard boxes and some of them looked as if they might be the sort of size I was looking for. Surely amongst that lot there must be a box big enough to suit my purpose! Some may hesitate, nay would never contemplate liberating something from a scaffie lorry, but after my shame in the shop, I have none left. Besides no-one knows me here. Furthermore, if t'were to be done, *t'were well it were done quickly*, for if this vehicle and others are going around picking up all the cardboard boxes in Lucca there is not going to be one left for me is there? The stakes have just been raised again, for I realise now I am in competition and in a race against time.

The citizens of Lucca then, those fortunate enough to be in the right place at the right time and not already having retired to bed, are treated to the rare and never to be repeated unedifying spectacle of someone (thank God they don't know who) chasing after the aforesaid vehicle, gesticulating wildly at it in the hope that the driver would catch sight of me in the mirror and stop. Though on reflection, I now realise, unless curiosity got the better of him, this might have had the opposite effect and the driver would have put his foot down harder on the accelerator. I am able to do all this wild windmill waving because, although I originally set off in pursuit accompanied by the Albatross, it soon became apparent that I was being outstripped and the only solution was to abandon it if I had any hope of catching up with the scaffie cart.

With another gesture to Iona that she should look after the abandoned one and thus unburdened, I sprint after the lorry with its precious cargo, and drawing level, make signs to the driver that I wish her to stop, for it turns out that the driver is indeed a lady. Well, female anyway. Maybe my signing is not very good. In fact, I know it is not, for after our son, George, who is deaf, married a deaf girl whose parents are all deaf, I went to signing classes and it was the hardest thing I have done since trigonometry and I was rubbish at that. Still, having said that, you might have thought that, bad though it may be, my signing would have been sufficient to make the driver understand that I wanted her to stop – but it isn't.

There is nothing else for it. In two or three strides of my magic boots, I have nipped ahead and stepping into its path, I hold up both hands as I image King Canute did in the days of old, and commanded the little lorry to stop. It does when it comes into contact with my stomach. It doesn't hurt very much, well not at all actually, as I am wearing a padded jacket. I never thought it was a potentially life-threatening situation but I never intended it to be as close as it was – after all, that was how Houdini died after being hit in the stomach when he wasn't prepared for it. And although I was prepared for the cart to stop, the driver was obviously not prepared for a lunatic throwing himself in front of her vehicle.

I am not entirely stupid however, as in a time shorter than it took her to bring her vehicle to an emergency stop, I realise that she is not likely to best pleased with me and asking a favour of her, even if I could make her understand what I wanted, this might not be the best time in the world to choose.

"Scusi. Scusi." If only we were in Germany I would know exactly what to say to apologise for my precipitate behaviour as I had studied it in school, but we are not, and I am aware of how inadequate this sounds: more like a feeble apology for accidentally brushing my big fat belly against the bonnet of her vehicle, rather than what she must perceive as an apparent suicide attempt, but the sort only a lunatic would make as the most likely result would only be a few bruises – if that.

Defence is best form of attack, so they say, so I plough straight on in English and in sign language, to explain the object of my desires. Not her, if that is what she is thinking, an admirer driven mad by desperation to fling himself in front of her to draw attention to himself. I can't make her understand what I really want, just as I can't understand what she is telling me, which is maybe just as well. She lets me have a volley of Italian with both barrels before letting out her clutch and moving out of my life, forever I hope. Hopefully, if she should meet me again she will not recognise me, but a distinctive hat can be a dangerous thing.

I am a lucky person, in a manner of speaking though. Iona has just arrived in time to observe what I hope she understands is a piece of normal social intercourse between an Italian scaffie cart driver and me and too late to observe the unconventional method by which I had brought about this encounter. In fact, she misconstrues the situation so badly that she thought the sign the lady had made, describing circles with her forefinger in the region of her temple meant she was going to turn round and then presumably, I would be allowed to rake through her cart to my heart's content.

Which just goes to show you Iona is not always right because she doesn't turn round and she doesn't come back.

CHAPTER TEN:
INSPIRATION STRIKES

We are no further forward. In fact, you could say, the options are diminishing by the minute, but since the scaffie lorry had taken us up this street, well so be it, let us try it. Let the exploration of Lucca start here, even if it is with the troublesome suitcase.

The street turns out to be the Via Fillungo, the main artery that bisects Lucca from north to south, and the main shopping street. They must be very rich, the lucky Lucchese, for even more than those on the Santa Croce and the Via Paolino, the shops look very expensive indeed: designer wear designed to diminish the bank balances of those with more money than dress sense, or just about any sense you would care to mention in fact, but especially taste, for the only sense of taste they must have to buy something from shops such as these, must be in their mouths.

Here is something a bit different though, something that I have never seen before. It is a jeweller's shop with its name, "CARLI" written in gold block capitals over the door, but what makes this different is the frontage which has burnished wooden panels and shelves below the plate glass windows. It has a distinctly medieval look and I like it a lot, which, coming from someone who would normally avoid a jeweller's like the plague, is saying a great deal.

And talking of jewels, a brown sign tells us we are heading for the Piazza Anfiteatro, one of the jewels of Lucca, the site of the ancient Roman amphitheatre and retaining its original oval shape as the medieval shops which were built outside it, followed its contours. But before we reach there, at a street corner, stacked against a shop window, my eye catches a pile of flattened cardboard boxes, and not only that, but they look as if they might be the very size I am looking for.

With a hopeful heart and fingers trembling with excitement, I pick up the first box in the pile and make it into a box again. It certainly looks as if it may be the right size. With mounting excitement, I lower the Albatross into it – and it does fit, more or less, a little bit bulgy at the sides perhaps, but it is a soft case and with a bit of judicious pressure, I am sure, could be persuaded to fit better. But I don't want this box. I'm a bit picky now. And if anyone who happened to passing should assume that I am looking for the best one to make a bed for the night, I couldn't care less. Even Iona is caught up in the excitement of the moment and is helping me look for the driest and sturdiest. This one is a bit wet; perhaps one of these at the back will be a bit drier. This one feels the best, still a bit damp, but it will do.

We must make an odd-looking couple, Iona with this three-foot-long flattened box under her oxter and me towing an Albatross behind me, though to other people, it would just look like an ordinary case. Just then, whom should we meet, coming from the amphitheatre, but our taxi companions of last night.

"I'm Dinah," Dinah had said, "and this is Rod."

It seems they were destined to be a pair, but it's not too surprising that we should bump into each other in the old part of town, especially near the jewel in the crown.

It's their lucky day because they are treated to an explanation of this strange spectacle and they do look suitably impressed. It might have been a tale of woe, but now with that life-saving box, our troubles would seem to be nearly over, for surely, finding some brown paper and sticky tape should not be nearly so difficult. So while it certainly is a tale told by an idiot, as Macbeth would have put it, unlike his story, mine is about to have a happy ending, for finding the box has been a major breakthrough and my heart, which had once been heavy, is now light and carefree.

If only the shops were open, I would be case-free all the sooner. Although we do not have high expectations of getting what we need from a little shop like a *tabacchi,* it is worth a try and we can see one across the amphitheatre. But in spite of my impatience to see the end of the case, we don't make a beeline for it, but instead, cannot help but stop to admire our surroundings.

If the amphitheatre's immediate appeal stems from its pleasing oval shape, much of its charm depends on its irregularity, for there is not one roof that is the same height as its neighbour, not one building that is not higher or lower, not one house that is not wider or narrower than the one next to it. What they do have in common however, are windows with green shutters, some open, some shut, some with window boxes and some without, most without flowers or plants but some with, adding just a touch more colour to the pleasing shades of yellow ochre, terracotta and white in which the buildings have been tastefully painted. Below them are the cafés and restaurants with their canopies and gay tablecloths providing another splash of colour. One half of the piazza is bathed in bright sunshine, the other in shadow. Naturally we are standing in the sun and this winter sun is surprisingly warm, as hot as any summer's day in Scotland.

Reluctantly, we step out of this warm winter bath and step into the shade, a sort of acclimatization for the dinginess of the *tabacchi.* It is one of those old-fashioned shops that looks as if has been stuck in a time warp since before the War, with little wooden boxes in tiers behind the counter. There is only one customer, a man buying cigarettes and this gives us a chance to have a look around while he makes his choice. There is no apparent sign of any wrapping paper, but amongst all the smoking paraphernalia, the pipes and pouches of tobacco, the cigarette lighters and cigars, there are non-smoking items too:

newspapers and postcards and a thousand and one different types of knick-knacks, and there are also some long drawers on our side of the counter that might well contain what we are looking for.

Just as the smoker is paying for his purchases a little old lady wanders in. I sign for her to go ahead as I think it may take some time for me to get my message across. She has come in to buy lotto scratch cards. So many choices of cards and so many decisions to be made, but instead of being irritated by the inordinate length of time she is taking, I begin to become more interested in her. She might have been handsome once, an object of desire, with scores of lovers.

For the second time that day, I think of my mother-in-law, who, in her prime, bore an incredible resemblance to Ingrid Bergman, though you would never think so now. This old lady is definitely not one of the rich Lucchese, more like a poor old widow investing her pension in a dream. She certainly does not buy her clothes out of those fancy shops on the Via Fillungo: for a start she is far too old and for another thing, I suspect those shops are not so much for the well-heeled natives, but traps for tourists. To my surprise and dismay, she spends an amazing €23 on tickets, as she probably does every week, and returns to the privacy of her modest flat which she probably shares with at least two cats, to have a jolly good scratch at the cards and then has to scratch a living for the rest of the week when they all turn out to be blanks as she has just spent the best part of her pension on them.

I have been too distracted by her to have given much thought to preparing what I am going to say but I do know that it would be a waste of time to ask this old timer if he speaks English, for he looks as if he has been here at least as long as when the shop was fitted out and has probably never been further than the city walls in all his life. Yet I have no alternative but to speak to him in English, but very slowly, and with a heavy dependency on sign.

"Paper? Brown? Wrap that up?" and I point to the Albatross. At which point, as if we had rehearsed it all our lives, Iona, like a conjuror's assistant, remakes the box with a couple of shakes, and almost as quickly, and with a flourish makes it clear *that* is meant to go in *that*. Which is my cue to make signs of wrapping it up, or so I hope to convey, like poor Jack's broken crown in the nursery rhyme, though, on this occasion, we could dispense with the vinegar. After all, we are not going to eat the Albatross – just send it. Which reminds me of the story about the unsanitary child, smelling like the basement of our hotel allegedly is said to do, whose teacher, as tactfully as she could, sent the child home with a note drawing the parents' attention to this problem – only to be rebuked with the following immortal response: "Oor Delores is sent tae school tae be lernt, nae smelt. She's no an effin' geranium."

And who can say whether we got our message through or not? While the gist of what we want to say seems as clear as crystal to me, it might be as opaque as mud to the shopkeeper – or perhaps he does understand and really does not stock any brown paper at all, even in those long drawers behind us that look as if one of them, at least, might contain reams of them, while one of those smaller boxes behind him, I am perfectly sure, contains bottles of vinegar and sticky tape. At any rate, whether he understands us or not, or takes us for itinerant and inferior showmen, not worth donating a euro to, we understand his response perfectly: the universally recognised shake of the head (apart from in Bulgaria and Albania) and which means we go away empty-handed.

There is nothing more we can do at the moment, so we may as well stroll about until the shops open. Going down the Fillungo and then taking a meandering lane that takes us past the prison, we finally end up in the Piazza Santa Maria and one of the six city gates – the Porta Santa Maria, funnily enough. The piazza is crammed with parked cars and bicycles. The bicycles are for hire and although the cars are not, there happens to be, next to the bike hire place, a car rental office. It is closed and unfortunately there are no adverts or posters to give us a hint as how much it might cost, but driving to Elba or at least to the ferry terminal might be another possibility, certainly would appear to be a lot less complicated than the public transport and might give us a chance to explore some of the area around Lucca too.

But sending the case by post is still the frontrunner. There is a *tabacchi* stall in the square and more in hope than expectation, I reckon I may as well try asking again for brown paper. It does, after all, seem to be more of a newsagent's stall than a tobacconist's and where else would you expect to get brown paper from, but a newsagent's, though bearing in mind that this is Italy, the most logical idea is not necessarily the correct one. Predictably, there is no brown paper, or else I had failed to make myself understood again. What I really need, I suspect, is a supermarket where I can just serve myself.

At the Porta Santa Maria, as well as going through the tunnel beneath the walls, you can climb onto the ramparts. From this elevated position, I reckon, we may be able to spot a supermarket in the new town. Climbing the sloping path to the top of the ramparts lets you see just how high they actually are and which means they do give us a commanding position over the new town. Unfortunately from our point of view, in their wisdom, the planners began building at such a distance from the walls that it is too far for either of us to make out if there is a supermarket or not. There is something that might be one, but it is too far away to tell with any degree of certainty.

Since we are on the ramparts anyway, we may as well continue. The top is very broad – so broad there is a road, wide enough to be classed as an A road, and bordered on either side by a path and an avenue of trees. That is how thick the walls are, the widest I have ever seen. The occasional car comes crawling along, but it is basically a pedestrian and bicycle precinct, but it is so wide there are bags of space for all.

It all makes for a very pleasant walk, with the autumnal leaves gently gyrating as they tumble to the ground to form a multicoloured, crunchy carpet, with, on our left and further below our feet, the old town with its higgledy-piggledy arrangement of houses with their burnt-orange roof tiles, not one orange but composed of several variegated shades according to age and the effect of the sunlight. And soaring above them, the skyline is punctured with a handful of slender bell towers, like fingers pointing to heaven. And if we look over them and into the distance, we can make out a range of mountains far, far away. It would all be quite perfect – if only there were not a third article in this relationship that stalks our every step.

We only go one stop, so to speak, to the next path leading down from the ramparts and as we have been walking for hours, the legs are beginning to weary. Besides, Iona is having caffeine withdrawal symptoms and suggests we should stop for a rest. That's a good idea as it means I can have a beer. There will be plenty of time to come back and walk the walls later and without the encumbrance of a bag, so any way you look at it, it seems a good idea. But before we do, we linger to admire the rear of the Palazzo Pfanner, a tasteful edifice in green and white with elegant balconies and staircases and a formally laid-out garden graced with statues and a pool.

As we descend the path, we approach the Chiesa San Frediano from the rear, not its best side as soon becomes apparent as we come into the piazza of the same name, for high on the façade is a magnificent mosaic of Christ and the Apostles in gold and blues. It is a pity that the sun is in the wrong direction, putting the mosaic in shadow, for what is already impressive must be truly magnificent when the sun brings out the iridescence of the colours. Or, should it never shine again during our visit, it may not matter, for I can see that it must be floodlit at night, which may be nearly as good.

The cafés are aligned on the right side of the piazza as we come into it. The first appears to be closed because there are no tablecloths laid out, however there are at the one next door. As it is only a beer and coffee we are after, not anything to eat, one is as good as another and we need search no further. We plonk our bums on the same hard, wrought iron chairs they have at the Scilla and study the menu. Not much studying required for Iona, who knows what she wants - an espresso, a transfusion of caffeine straight into the veins. As for me, the choice is a lot more difficult. Bottled beer or *spina,* 50cl or a litre, and then which brand, and which offers the best value for money? It is just as well that the waitress takes her time before coming to take our order.

And so we sit, eventually, with our drinks, for it takes almost as long to serve them as it took to order them, but that is fine – it gives us longer to rest, restore our energy. It is rather a boring experience for Iona, for *the rest is silence* as Shakespeare once wrote, as I am writing and I can't write *and* talk, as I am a mere man and can't multi-task. I am writing up my notes, for, having less and less of a retentive memory these days, I must write down every last detail in case I should ever write a book about this visit. There is quite a lot to write about and her coffee being a great deal smaller than mine, 25cl I should imagine compared to my litre, and it being hot, she needs to drink it before it gets cold, whereas I can afford to spend time over mine. In short, her drink is long since gone, while mine is still long and cold, as I can't drink *and* write at the same time either, let alone think.

"How much longer are you going to be?" she says at last, the elastic of her patience having obviously just snapped.

But for that interruption to my writing and my train of thought, who knows if my moment of inspiration would have ever come? Probably not and even now I still do not know what made me think of it, unless it was to avoid the basilisk stare of La Belle Dame Sans Merci that made me keep my eyes downcast. I couldn't help but notice the tablecloth with the name of the restaurant and its address printed upon it, with its bright red logo, but now I see it in a completely new light, have been about as slow on the uptake as the service, as I realise that the very tablecloth upon which I am writing, not literally, though I could have done so had I wanted – is made of brown paper! A couple of these, at least, should be sufficient to cover the case with ease.

"You can't!" says Iona, but it is already too late for I have beckoned the waitress over and before I have time to change my mind or let La Belle Dame Sans Merci talk me out of it, by pointing to the box and the case, I have explained to her the novel purpose I have in mind for the tablecloth.

"Momento!"

How much of that she has understood, if any, I can't say, but a moment later, just as she said, a young man appears. He seems to be the boss although he looks scarcely any older than her, but he does speak English.

"I wonder if I could buy one of your tablecloths," I begin. Although I will need two, better to begin modestly some instinct tells me, and if that is all right, I can always ask for another one.

"I will give it to you," he tells me after I have explained.

Exactly what I had hoped he might say, but "buy" sounded better than "have" and of course it means a bigger than normal tip so it amounts to the same thing in the end anyway.

"Er...do you think I could have two please?" and I show him how big the box is when it is made up.

He nods and goes away. I sit down, pick up my beer and take a celebratory pull. I can hardly contain my elation and it's all I can do to remain seated and not do a jig in the street. But when my saviour does not reappear with the tablecloths, but instead joins in the carefree laughter and banter with a group at the next table who appear to be friends as well as patrons, I begin to wonder if he has completely forgotten our conversation and doubt and fear begin to make me feel down in the dumps again. I can't bear the suspense. I *have* to know. I down my beer much more quickly than I normally would and stand up to put on my jacket and scarf to draw attention to the fact I am about to leave, hoping that this will bring about the desired response.

But the only response is from the waitress to whom I am able to sign that I would like the bill and I sit down again. When it comes, I include a 10% tip and in the pocket of my jacket, have ready to hand what I consider would be a reasonable tip for the tablecloths, considering their importance to me is far and beyond their monetary value.

I stand up again and put on my hat. Perhaps that was what I should have done the last time, for it being the only one of its kind in the whole of Italy, (I would have thought) it is obvious no-one would leave that behind, except by accident. In any case, it has the desired effect, and to my relief, without me having to say anything, the boss goes inside and returns with a couple of tablecloths. Instead of merely giving them to me however, he places them on an empty table and peels off a plastic backing that I hadn't realised they possessed. It would have been better if they had been left on, more robust and less likely to tear but I don't like to point this out in case it sounds as if I am being too fussy.

Instead I thank him profusely and in exchange for his two large pieces of brown paper, I give him one small blue piece in the currency of the realm, and a great deal of other realms beside. He looks at the note in astonishment, and it crosses my mind he may not have expected a tip at all. Or maybe he thought €5 was far too much for a pair of tablecloths.

His services to us are not quite over however,

"What is the Italian for strong sticky tape?" Iona asks him.

He tells us.

"Could you write it down, please?" she asks.

He could and he does, on a scrap of paper with little squares on it which the continentals seem to find indispensable but for which I can't come up with even one reason as to why you should want such a thing unless it is to make what is written on it harder to read. We have no problem working out what he has written however as he prints in big black letters with a broad felt-tip pen: *Nastro Adesivo Grande.*

"And do you know where we could buy it?"

"Up to the top of the square, turn left and the shop is on the right."

"Grazie! Grazie! Grazie!"

Could the nightmare be about to end at last? Hopes are high as we set out with the case for what we hope will be the last time.

CHAPTER ELEVEN:
THE MAD HATTER

We find the sticky tape shop easily. But our problems are not going to end that easily. It is shut. In fact it doesn't look if it would be a likely place to stock such a thing and if we hadn't been told it did, we probably wouldn't have tried in there at all. Italian logic, I mutter to myself bitterly.

But I was wrong. Presently we come to a much more likely looking suspect – a big artists' materials shop. This must have been the one the waiter had meant all along. Would we have stumbled upon it on our own I wonder? Probably – but only after we had trailed all the way to some supermarket or other only to find they didn't stock it.

"Nastro adesivo grande, per favore," says Iona like a native and the assistant takes a massive roll of it from a shelf behind her, just as easy as that – and what's more, it only costs €1.50! That has to be the best bargain in Italy! (I wonder how much a couple of sheets of brown paper would be? I am sure they must stock it). I feel my troubles beginning to melt away as we make for the Post Office. The Albatross does not feel nearly such a burden now – though I am very glad of the little wheels all the same.

Rumble! Rumble! Rumble! The noise is deafening as we trundle the bag over the flags, to the astonishment of a group of tourists. I had noticed them earlier being given a talk in front of San Frediano. They turn round, surprised to hear what must sound to them like a tank coming up behind them and stop and step aside to let us past. It's best to do that when tanks are steaming up behind you. Not for the first time, but hopefully for the last, we have the power to make heads turn. They may know something about the amazing mosaics of San Frediano, but they'll never know the meaning of this amazing sight.

We have been walking for ages. Surely we should have come across the Post Office by now? I have a feeling that we have come too far north and possibly too far east too. We are in a part of town we have never been before and there are no familiar landmarks and very few people about. It doesn't matter which way Iona turns the map round – she can't make head or tail of it. Naturally I am impatient at this hold up. Leaving her metaphorically scratching her head, I cross the street to a man who is standing outside a shop, probably waiting for his wife who is trying on a new hat.

"Scusi, dov'è Post Office?"

Years ago I once watched a Teach-Yourself-Italian programme on TV and even bought the book that accompanied the series, but was too lazy to do any homework. I was really watching it for the scenery and the bits of Italian culture, though the lady presenters made it worth watching for that reason alone, as I vaguely recall.

Even if I can't remember what "Post Office" is, although I had seen it emblazoned on the side of the building not so long ago, my meaning should be perfectly clear, should it not? Not to this man it is, who looks at me with the sort of blank, wide-eyed bewilderment as if he had just been addressed by a lunatic.

"Telegraphico? Dove?" I try again, hopefully.

It's not any better. The first word might not even be a real word in Italian, and the second makes me acutely conscious of speaking pidgin Italian although I know enough to make the second word have two syllables, the last of which the inhabitants of the most violent prison in Scotland, at a place near me, love to tack on to the end of practically every sentence, just to make sure that their meaning is clear.

"Grazie," I tell him, more as a way of bringing our brief acquaintanceship to an end than in gratitude for all the help he has been.

"It's down this way," I tell Iona, who presuming that I have been given instructions from the man, follows in my wake. And wake is the appropriate word, for I am off at a rate of knots with the air of someone who has the courage of his convictions, but in reality only has an instinctive feeling that this is the direction in which we should be heading.

When I look over my shoulder, Iona has stopped and is looking at the map again. Obviously *her* instinct tells her this is not the right way. She signs me to come back to heel and without waiting to see if I am following, sets off down a side street. Grumbling, I rumble after her. The rumbling stops but the grumbling grows when Iona comes to a halt not much later to study again, with increasing frustration, the worthless piece of paper in her hand – which does my temper no good at all. In the heat of the moment, of course, I have totally forgotten that but for my stupidity, we would not be in this position at all.

I don't have a great deal of time for maps of cities, preferring just to stroll around, go to whatever attracts my interest. I dare say I may miss some sights but I might make some serendipitous discoveries along the way, hopefully. And neither does Iona on this occasion, who declares this the stupidest map she has ever seen in her life and she has spent a quite a few years studying maps, let me tell you. I haven't tried looking at it myself, but merely by looking around me I can see that we are on the fringes of the city, near the wall. We *have* come too far north and too far east, just as I had thought. I may only have a pigeon brain but I have a pretty good sense of direction. If only we had continued along the trail I had been blazing...

So now we head in the direction that my brain dictates, parallel with the walls, heading south and sooner or later, we must come to either the Post Office or something we recognise – like the Duomo. But we don't. We are still as lost as ever.

I stop a passer-by with the same words as I had addressed the man earlier. He seems a bit taken aback at first, but then starts speaking, in Italian of course. He does point us in a certain direction however, and gives us a great deal of other directions besides, which I pretend to understand. We can always ask again if need be. It seems the wrong direction to me, but when someone is kind enough to give you advice, it is best to follow it, especially as he is so insistent that we should go down that street there, the way he has just come. Not to do so would be very rude indeed. Besides, he may be watching.

So completely against my instincts, we do as he says. Truth to tell, of all the possible people I might have asked, I am regretting asking *him*. I only did because he happened to be passing at the precise moment I was feeling most exasperated and I spoke without stopping to think if he looked like the sort of person who might give me a sensible answer, or indeed be able to understand what I was trying to say in the first place. So, it was only when he started giving his lengthy directions that I began to notice his appearance.

There was a famous poster once, released by President Nixon's political opponents featuring a close-up of his physiognomy with its heavy jowls with their seven o'clock shadow and at the bottom a caption which read: "Would you buy a used car from this man?" The question of course, was rhetorical, but if anyone had asked me: "Would you ask directions from this man?" I would have said "No" most certainly and most definitely, "No."

And who would ask directions of a man wearing a hat, the type that makes me think of Peruvian shepherds or Nepalese Sherpas, the worst of all hats in the world, a knitted garment like a balaclava with the front missing, with long floppy ears like a spaniel's and with thick pleated cords with tassels at the end like Gretel's pigtails. It is impossible to take anything that a person wearing a thing like that says seriously, for it is the most ridiculous and unbecoming hat in the world – the sort of hat no self-respecting person would wear unless they were completely mad.

As soon as we can, (and with a glance over my shoulder) we take the first street on our right, then right again – which should take us back to where we started, more or less, then if we go left again...But wait a moment. What's this? My heart sinks as there is no mistaking this person coming towards us and there is no chance of him not recognising us either. How embarrassing!

"Come here!" Gretel is signing with a great deal of energy. He is waiting for us at the corner of the street where I would have turned up to the left.

No words are necessary. On the wall of the nearest building, he draws an air map of the way we should go. Ah, I see it now! That makes it a lot clearer – I don't think. On the contrary, it looks extremely complicated and means the Post Office must be miles away. He is taking his task extremely seriously, studying my face to make sure I am following every twist and turn. Unfortunately, I can't understand a word he is saying, but I nod and nod and nod as if everything is perfectly clear and not following a survival guide to the Hampton Court maze. Actually, I think there is one word out of the many that I do understand. It sounded like *bicicletta* but that couldn't have been right because what that could have to do with anything I couldn't imagine, unless we were so far away we'd be best to hire a couple of them to get there.

At last he stops speaking and looks at me as if to say: "Did you get that?" I couldn't bear to hear it all again, but avoid the lie by saying nothing but by nodding emphatically and then thank him profusely for the degree of dedication he has shown in his efforts to be helpful. Pointing up the street, he jabs his finger at it. This at least, I do understand and thanking him one more time, we set off.

It is not a very long street, probably the shortest street in all of Lucca unfortunately and not only that but straight and when, after a few moments, I check to see if my helper is still there, and he is, sure enough, standing where we had left him. The pigtails swing gaily as he nods vigorously in encouragement, to which I respond with a cheery wave. He seems determined to help, damn him!

Funnily enough it is the bicycles I notice first, masses of them parked outside. The second thing I see are the steps and then I recognise it is none other than the entrance of the Post Office. We have approached it from the rear (as my instincts told us we would) which is why we hadn't recognised it.

It seems to my pigeon brain that if I hadn't asked Gretel for directions, had trusted to my own instincts, we would have stumbled upon the Post Office by a lot less convoluted means and a lot sooner too. And another thing – what on earth were all those directions on that air map he had shown me, with all those instructions to turn left and right and go straight on, when all I had to do was to go straight on for a hundred yards? And another thing – now that I come to think about it, he did have a sort of mad glint in his eye, like the Ancient Mariner's, who liked nothing better than to stop a wedding guest out three and bore them to death with his traveller's tales.

Admittedly, I was the one who had stopped *him*, and I was the one with the Albatross, not he, and I was not going to a wedding – in fact, ever since I had arrived in Lucca I had felt a divorce was more likely. But these converse matters of detail aside, there is one thing we might possibly have in common. There is more than a hint of the supernatural in Coleridge's poem, and it occurs to me that perhaps the gods had judged that I had not yet quite atoned for my sins, and Gretel had been sent to try me, just to turn the rack one further notch at the very moment when I thought that the end of the Albatross was in sight.

But before we enter the Post Office, or as I regard it, the hallowed precincts of Heaven, where I will finally get rid of the Albatross for good, I turn round to wave a final farewell to Gretel. According to his air map, we should now turn left or right, I can't remember which, but I would have thought, since we were still within eye contact, he could have semaphored what to do next, for whatever his air map showed, it was certainly not that we had arrived at our destination.

But he has gone. As an agent of the gods, had he done his best to send us on a wild goose chase and realising his game was up, has scarpered? Or is there a more rational explanation? Have we been in the company of the equivalent of the village idiot all along – Lucca's own lunatic, the Mad Hatter?

CHAPTER TWELVE:
THE CAVALRY ARRIVES

In the vestibule of the Post Office, we set about making the box postage-proof. Every seam is treated to a strip of the tape, both the inside and the outside. It is murder on the teeth and my mother-in-law would not approve of the way her daughter is gnawing into it like a rat at a cable as she was always taught to use that little dispenser thing on the Sellotape with the serrated edge and never, ever to use her teeth, as it was very bad for them. But what else are we expected to do?

Once the coffin is secure, the body of the Albatross is laid irreverently to rest, but not before I enclose one of my cards on which I write: "Very sorry for all the trouble I have put you through." Huh! If she only knew all the trouble it had caused *me*. But then again, I deserved it and she didn't. One day, maybe, she will be able to laugh about all the stress and hassle I had caused and the card may be a nice souvenir which she could show her friends and say: "This is the idiot who took my bag" and maybe, just maybe, one of them will be curious enough to buy one of my books, even if it is in a foreign language.

Now for the tablecloths, with the printed side down of course. I smile to think of Carla's reaction when she tears the paper off and reads the name of the restaurant on it and no doubt she'll wonder how I came by it – why I just didn't buy a couple of sheets of brown paper, like anyone else. But no doubt, she'll just shrug her shoulders and conclude anyone who is daft enough to pick up the wrong bag would be perfectly capable of a little eccentricity like this.

Round and round the tape goes, lengthways and breadthways and along the edges again. I am glad we have yards of it and we may as well use it to ensure, as much as we can, that the box stays in one piece. We make a good team, Iona and I. One lifting the box, one taping, passing the tape underneath and passing it back. I am beginning to sweat with the effort of it all when suddenly I feel something vibrating in my jacket pocket, followed by the sound of frogs croaking. It takes me by surprise, but only because it hardly ever happens. It is not a plague of frogs being sent to try me further: only my phone ringing and I am so used to people texting rather than phoning me, that I am not quite sure how to answer it.

Fumbling, I press a button. "Hello? Hello?" I can't be sure if I have pressed the right one.

"Hello?"

"Hello?" (This could on forever.)

"Dorothy here."

Of course! Who else would be phoning me when hardly anyone ever does and in Italy to boot? It was so long since I had sent the text, I had more or less completely forgotten about it, and during the wrapping up of the parcel, (to which Iona is now manfully managing to attach the final strip of tape) I had been far too busy to have given it a thought.

"Oh, hello!"

"You mentioned you had some problem?"

At last I am able to say something a bit more constructive than "hello" but just as I am getting into my stride, Dorothy cuts in.

"Who am I talking to?"

"David. David Addison."

Why is she asking this? She knows I have a problem of some sort, so she must have received my text and that is why she is phoning. What's *her* problem? Good grief, surely she couldn't have forgotten me already! We're practically related, for God's sake!

I hear a sharp intake of breath, then, "Oh!" Then there is a pause followed by the resounding tinkle of a penny dropping. "Where are you?"

"At the Post Office."

"The main Post Office?"

"Yes."

"We're just round the corner at a café in the piazza near the Duomo."

"Really?" It's unbelievable. After all this time, without hearing from her, it's incredible that she should be so near. I know precisely where she is, just a stone's throw away.

"I'll be with you in a minute."

"That would be great. Thanks. See you."

She is as good as her word and arrives just as the last strip of tape has been rasped around the sarcophagus of the late and unlamented Albatross. Hardly in the nick of time, but better late than never, and Dorothy's expertise in Italian may be needed yet before the Albatross is finally despatched to the care of the Post Office. I am still not entirely convinced that it can be as simple as presenting the mummified box to the clerk who will not even raise an eyebrow and merely go about sending it on its way as if it were an every day occurrence for people to send suitcases like this by post. What if it's too heavy or there is some other objection - about the way it is wrapped for example? Or what if they want to see what's in a parcel of this size, to make sure it does not contain body parts? It would break my heart to have to open it up and start all over again - especially to have to find more brown paper. I daren't go back to the café and ask again.

There is plenty of time as we take our ticket and wait to be served, to give Dorothy all the gory details. "It wouldn't have made any difference anyway," she says. "I wouldn't have known where to get a box – or brown paper either, for that matter."

Well actually, she could have helped, because I still can't believe that I have understood the clerks properly, particularly with regard to the cost. It can't *possibly* be that cheap. What if it turns out to be as expensive as the carrier – or more? Anyway, we are just about to find out, for it is now our turn and my last chance to make heads turn, for the bag in its box is far too heavy and unwieldy to pick up, and the other customers are treated to the sight of me pushing an outsize parcel along the entire length of the polished marble floor to the front of the desk. You can see them thinking: "What the... could he have in there? If it's what I think it is, that must be his mistress. So who is the other dame?"

Dorothy takes over and the clerk, yet another one, cranes her neck to look over the desk to see what is to be despatched. Perhaps people do send parcels that size every day and perhaps in Italy, they do regularly send body parts through the post too, for she does not turn a hair, but merely gives me a form to fill in with my name and address and Carla's. I know how to do it in the Italian way with the surname first, then I am told to take the box over to the scales at the end of the row of desks.

Naughty Carla! Whatever her body type may be, she is overweight. The bag weighs more than 16 kilos, more than a kilo overweight. Of course there is the box to take into account, not to mention the tablecloths and masses of tape, but that shouldn't amount to much, certainly not enough to take it that much over the limit. The extra weight must be due to all the troubles she had packed.

The flimsy top copy of the form I had filled in is attached to the case, while I am handed the illegible duplicate carbon copy. Illegible, not because I can't read my own writing, but because it is so faint. I put it in my pouch along with my money as I realise what an important document this is – my proof of posting, should the case get lost between here and Elba. I am relieved to see the clerk writes Carla's address on the box for good measure and then she tells me to go back to her desk. That is the last I see of the Albatross and strange to say I did not weep – not even tears of joy.

Mind you, I felt like it, especially when the price of committal is confirmed as €15.95. I would have willingly paid twice that. There's just one other thing though. I ask Dorothy to find out when it will arrive.

"Friday. It's too late to catch the post today."

That's a pity, but at least I was right about it taking only one day to get there. The Italian Post Office must surely be the winner of the Most Wonderful Post Office in the World Competition.

"Would you care to join us for a drink?" Dorothy asks, now it is all over.

Music to my ears! Of course I would! Have I not got something to celebrate? I have just saved myself something in the region of €225.

Leon and Tina are sitting outside at a table at the front of the café with a glass of red and white wine respectively. In front of the café is a fountain and beyond that the Duomo. While it may be an attractive enough setting at present, it will be much improved when all the litter is removed.

Lucca had been host last week to a festival of computer games (of all things) and there are marquees everywhere. I am glad that it is over, for not being a fan of computer games in the first place, I would have been more than a little disgruntled had I been here last week because you can't see any of the buildings in the piazza without enough canvas to equip an armada getting in the way. What's more, to judge from the number of marquees, the place would have been crawling with geeks getting in my way too. Thankfully the geeks seem to be all gone and the marquees are in the process of being demolished which is why we can see so much paper and plastic strewn about.

"What would you like?" Dorothy asks without sitting down.

We'll have the same as Leon and Tina.

A waiter arrives in due course with the wine and little pieces of toasted garlic bread (a treat for me) while Tina and Leon (and Dorothy again) are treated to the details of the case of the wrong case, told by the idiot himself. Dorothy has her own tale to tell however and reveals why she had sounded so surprised to find herself speaking to me on the phone. She explains that she hadn't replied earlier because she had thought it was from David at work and the last thing she wanted to do was a bit of long distance problem solving. For one thing, she was meant to be on holiday and for another, God knows what it would cost her to call Scotland on her mobile because there was no telling how long it would take to sort out the problem. She must have been relieved that I was a much smaller problem than she had anticipated. In fact, it was all but resolved before she turned up.

"When I called you just now, although we were only yards away it would have cost a fortune as it would have had to go through to my service provider in Scotland then back here."

"Oh? Would it?" I had no idea. I feel as if I should offer to pay for it, except she might feel insulted.

"Yes. You would have been able to get me if you had tried putting 44 in front of the number. You can try it, now," she adds, picking up her phone as if she were expecting it to ring in a few moments.

No point in telling her I don't really want to, especially if, as she says, it costs a fortune. I'm prepared to take her word for it, prefer to speak to her in the old-fashioned way, face to face. But I must save my own face in case she thinks I am a skinflint. Feeling rather guilty at the expense I had put her to, I feel the least I can do is phone her and apologise, and hope she does not keep me talking. Thankfully it doesn't work. As the anonymous voice had already told me, I am barred.

Presently, as the light begins to fade and the moon peers over the roof of the Duomo and lights begin to come on in the administrative building next door, giving it an inviting, cosy glow, I begin to feel a cosy interior glow myself. My troubles are over. It may be true that we do not have any luggage to call our own, but what does that matter? Would anyone like another drink?

We all would, even Dorothy who needs a bit of persuading, as she is driving. After a while, as there is no sign of the waiter coming, I go in to order them, and having taken the order, instead of telling me how much it comes to, he puts the drinks on a tray and takes them outside. If he is surprised to see me still hanging about inside when he comes back, he doesn't show it. Perhaps he had thought I had been at the toilet all this time. It wasn't wasted time though. I had read the labels on the wine bottles (to see what we were drinking) and helped myself to crisps and nuts from bowls on the counter.

"How much is that?"

"Altogether?"

"Yes."

You would think I had never been abroad before, let alone to Italy, not to know that you pay at the end, not as you go along. It is too embarrassing to say no and too late now to tell him I had changed my mind, for that would make it even worse. He picks up a fistful of receipts and starts ringing them up on the till. Good grief! Will he never stop?

"€37," he announces. It could have been worse, a lot worse – they might have had a full-blown lunch but obviously have only had a snack with the wine. Anyway it is Leon's special birthday and Iona and I had partaken of some of the wine had we not, not to mention the matter of the phone call too, so as well as salving my conscience somewhat, the voice of reason in my head tells me it is a small price to pay for all that.

It is only when Tina says she had better go in to pay, that I reckon I had better admit to what I had done in case she is charged again as had been my unfortunate experience once before.

"That's very generous of you," Dorothy says. In the fading light it, I can't see if she looks shocked, but was that a hint of surprise in her voice?

I look as modest as I can and raise my glass, with the remains of its contents, to the birthday boy, "Happy birthday, Leon."

We Scots have a saying – *mony a mickle maks a muckle,* which is to say that all these unconsidered trifles are beginning to add up and transform the bargain winter break that I had snapped up into a tale of a different hue. And Dorothy is determined to compound the felony. Whatever she thought of my taxi shenanigans earlier and despite the gathering gloom, she sees me now in a different light – as someone who doesn't think twice about splashing out on the afternoon's carousing of people he scarcely knows. Knowing that I am without my medication, the antihistamines which prevent my urticaria, she is insistent that she will press her Italian skills into service again in a chemist's to help me buy what I get for free back home.

"No! No! It's all right really," I protest in alarm. Goodness knows how much that would cost and after all, I should get my case back on Friday and I can last till then.

Not only that, but she is going to take us to Upim, a cheap department store where Iona can get some mascara and face cream and I can get some cheap underwear and socks. Funny that. Her needs are more to do with the most seen, mine more to do with the unseen, more or less. I suppose that means her mind is on higher things, while mine tends to the less salubrious.

I'm not too resistant to spending some euros on some new clothes as, regrettably, I am forced into buying that sort of thing from proper shops as I have already explained and it's not as if I couldn't do with some new underpants anyway. In fact, it's just as well my companions do not possess x-ray vision or it is doubtful they would have sat anywhere near me. In fact, it's only the willing suspension of my own disbelief that allows me to sit down on them myself.

When it comes to letting go of an idea, Dorothy is a bit like Iona, a bit like a dog with a bone, or to put it another way, a bit like my grip on a £5 note when it comes to spending money on clothes.

"Are you sure you wouldn't like to go in here?" Dorothy asks, stopping outside the wide-open, welcoming door of the brightly-lit *farmacia*.

"Yes, really."

"Are you sure? You'd be best to get them while I'm here to help you."

My resistance crumbles. Maybe she has a point. My urticaria occurs when I am under stress so there is every chance that after today I could end up looking like the Elephant Man and God forbid, there may be some problem and we don't get our case back on Friday after all. Besides, they may not stock them and I might be spared, as I was with the phone call to Dorothy, just at the other side of the table.

"Well, I suppose it can't do any harm to go in and look."

But this *farmacia* has shelves and shelves and drawers and drawers of medicines and the white-coated assistant knows exactly what Dorothy is asking for and knows exactly where to lay her hands on my drugs in this cornucopia of drugs. The funny thing is they sound exactly the same in English and I bet if I had gone in and just uttered their names with a rising intonation, I would have ended up with the same drugs and been nearly €20 the poorer. When I add that to the bar bill, I reckon I could have a pretty good meal out for that but all have I ended up with is a handful of pills and a couple of glasses of wine.

But Dorothy means well. Her fist impressions, she must admit, were completely erroneous: her distant relation is not averse to spending money like water.

At the entrance to the cheap department store we say our farewells and thank her for everything she has done for us. She promises to phone me so we can arrange a time to go to her villa in the village somewhere in the mountains where there is the best pizza place on the planet. And, what's more, she will come and collect us.

That sounds good to me. You never know, we might find ourselves at a loose end and that would be a very pleasant way of spending an afternoon.

CHAPTER THIRTEEN: AN INTERESTING CONVERSATION

If my luck had been out when I picked up the wrong bag, it was back when we went to Upim because they were having a sale. I am wearing my new boxers, a pair of new socks and have even splashed out €10 on a new shirt. That got rid of another €30 that was burning a hole in my pocket.

I have had a shower and the clothes I had been wearing are hanging on the heated towel rail to dry. They would dry more quickly if I could get it to work, but I can't, no matter which way I twist the valves at the bottom. Nevertheless, with a bit of luck, they will have dripped dry by the morning and I can rotate my clothes, with the exception of the socks, which I won't need to wash because I had bought a bargain pack of five. I am, apart from my face, quite presentable. I might even keep the beard. It covers up my red face. Besides, think of all the time I'll save – time I'll spend lying in bed a bit longer in the mornings. It never crosses my mind to think of the money I'll save on razor blades.

Iona, however, is not so fortunate. Her hair is looking flat but that is preferable to the birds' nest it would resemble if she washed it, and to add to her misery, when we emptied our purchases on the bed, there was no sign of the mascara, although according to the receipt, we had paid for it. I remember seeing it rolling about on the desk and the assistant catching it before it fell on the floor, but I don't remember seeing it again after that. I don't see how it could have fallen out of the bag but it is certainly not here now.

On Dorothy's advice, we are going to the Baralla for our evening meal. It should be easy to find because it is behind the amphitheatre and if there is one thing we do know for certain about Lucca, it is how to get to the amphitheatre. Her guiding spirit is with us as we make our way there along the Via San Paolino but somewhere along the way our attention is drawn, like moths, to a restaurant with a candle burning in a lantern outside.

It is called the Rusticanella Due, and looks pleasingly rustic with commensurately basic prices to match and whose menu includes such regional specialties as wild boar and domestic rabbit. Well I presume it wasn't wild, as it doesn't say so, though it would be safe to say it would not have been too chuffed to find itself in the pot. We would almost certainly have patronised this place had it not been for Dorothy's advice. Because it is so near it would have saved our legs, having walked for miles today already, and it is quite a step to the amphitheatre. And what's more, I wouldn't mind betting that the Baralla is not the cheapest restaurant in town, that Dorothy's recommendation will be based on the quality of the food rather than price, as she can now see that such a trifling matter wouldn't bother me in the slightest. There is no telling when the phone call will come summoning us to the villa and she is sure to ask what we thought of the Baralla and it would be best to have an answer ready.

Somewhere on the Fillungo, we bump into Dinah and Rod again and bring them up to date with the latest instalment of the case saga. They are heading for a restaurant they had seen earlier, off to the right somewhere. It was on the point of my tongue to ask if they would mind if we joined them, as being married now for more years than not, and having had more hot dinners alone with Iona than stars in the Milky Way, their company would enliven the evening, forgetting of course, that as young lovebirds, the stars are all in their eyes. They would much rather have a romantic meal *à deux* than share it with a couple of old wrinklies like us.

But mercifully, some angel or other whispered in my ear it wasn't a good idea so, happily, I didn't make the proposal and thus saved them the embarrassment of a downright refusal or an acceptance they would have been too polite to show. Instead, I merely wished then *buon appetito* and said we'd probably bump into them again tomorrow.

All Dorothy had said was the restaurant was behind the amphitheatre, but how can you tell where the back of a circle is? I do happen to know how you can tell the back of a tree though. Well, no-one hides *in front* of a tree, do they? And everyone does the toilet *behind* a tree. Since the Baralla is not in sight, it must be hiding round the other side. There is nothing else for it but to walk round the outside of the amphitheatre until we come to it. But which way? Somehow it seems natural to turn to the right which means going in an anticlockwise direction or widdershins, the preferred method for witches when they danced round churches in order to conjure up the Devil.

It becomes dimmer and dimmer the further we go round and it seems less and less likely that a restaurant will be conjured up out of the mirk. But it seems as tedious to go back as to go on, as Macbeth, who knew a bit about witchcraft, or at least thought he did, concluded. Our persistence is rewarded however with the first glimmers of light emanating from around the corner like the first fingers of dawn creeping over the horizon. Then not just one, but two restaurants come into view. The Baralla is the second one. If we had turned left rather than right, we would have been there all the sooner, a decision which might have crucial consequences, for this place is hoaching and there are two couples ahead of us, although as far as I can see, there is only one table for two left.

While they are being attended to, it gives me a chance to take the place in. It appears, at first glance, to be a vast cavernous area with a brick barrel-vaulted ceiling supported on pillars of the same material and which gives you the impression that you are beneath the amphitheatre, back in Roman times, or at least in a medieval banqueting hall. It is not as vast as it appears however, as the far wall largely consists of huge mirrors.

At last it is our turn. The table is still vacant.

"Have you a reservation?"

This appears to be the boss, a grey-haired, prosperous-looking man with a blue-and-white striped shirt with the cuffs undone. Maybe he hadn't had time to finish dressing before the rush, or perhaps it is a form of ventilation, as he looks rather hot and harassed. The waitresses too, seem rushed off their feet – the whole place seems to buzz with activity. I get the impression that the mass of patrons had arrived not long before us.

"No, I'm afraid not."

His chin juts out as he scans the room for an empty table, and then, instead of directing us to the unoccupied table that he can not have failed to notice, he dismisses us with, "Five minutes," before rushing off, leaving me with my jaw hanging open and the words "Why can't we have that one?" unspoken on my lips.

In actual fact, it is less than five minutes when we are ushered to a table near the back. This is a much better table, although there is a risk of catching ourselves in the mirror if we are not careful. Behind me is a dresser built into the brick containing phalanxes of neatly regimented glasses and, to my right, a fireplace on whose mantelpiece are untidy piles of paperbacks, many of which are in English. My seat commands a view of the restaurant as I am the writer and need to observe people, while Iona faces the wall which has no writing upon it, unfortunately, as she could have spent the time reading it.

It is not too difficult to make a decision as what to eat, although the choice is wide. When in Lucca, naturally, you have the regional specialities. But first there is the wine to choose, the house wine naturally, a litre of course, and red as we are already pretty much decided as to what we are going to have and although Iona tends to prefer white, red would be better suited to what we are going to eat. The boar for me, the rabbit for Iona, but of course in this democratic marriage arrangement we have, (where we have a joint bank account but she also has her own) we will taste each other's. In addition, Iona suggests we have a side order of olives and white beans because the olives and olive oil from Lucca are reckoned to be the best in all of Italy. We also have a litre of *aqua frizzante* to spin the wine out.

The wine comes with the *coperto*, and that's what I love about the continent – it doesn't cost the shirt off your back to get a litre of pretty decent wine for half the price you would pay for just an average bottle back home. In fact, it costs a euro less than the shirt I am wearing at the moment and you can relax and enjoy the anticipation of the culinary delights to come – but you must beware of eating all that delicious bread and filling yourself so full you don't have room for the main course.

Now that the order has been given to the waitress (with whom I have instantly fallen in love) it is time to write up the notes which are seriously behind and if I don't get them made up soon, I might forget vital details in the same way that when you waken up from a nightmare you know something horrible has happened, but your brain has mercifully blanked out the worst parts as to recall them might drive you over the edge into madness. But for me, these are the precise details I want to remember. Maybe that is a sign of madness in itself, or perhaps it explains why I was irresistibly drawn to walk widdershins round the amphitheatre. Or it could be, as my mother said, I am just plain perverse.

Just as well I hadn't invited Dinah and Rod to join us after all, or I would never have been able to get on with the notes. As for Iona, it can't be much fun for her, what with only those glasses to look at or the blank wall and only the occasional grunt from me by way of conversation. But then she should never have suggested that I should take up writing as a hobby, so she has only herself to blame. I suppose she could help herself to one of the books on the mantelpiece if the boredom gets too bad and what's more, there is every possibility she might be able to finish it.

Ah, here comes the food, and the waitress brings a bottle of olive oil to add to the beans, just in case we should not have enough and it is gratifying to see that according to the label, it does comes from Lucca as I had hoped it might. May as well have some, although it doesn't really need it but it is supposed to be good for you and when in Lucca...

For once, I am glad I am having my boar not Iona's bunny. I tend to find that after having made my choice and after the dishes finally arrive, I like the look of what other people have chosen better. This could easily be prevented if only more restaurateurs would provide pictures alongside the description of the food. It's not that the rabbit is not delicious, it's just a bit fussy to eat with all those little bones – as if she didn't have enough to pick with me already. Or maybe choosing the boar just came naturally to me somehow.

Whatever truth there may or may not be in that, it is very tender with a delicious sauce or gravy and instead of potatoes, it comes with polenta, which makes an interesting change for me. It is fine as long as it is hot, but as it gets colder, it congeals into a solid mass like porridge with jaundice.

Iona has a sweet, naturally, while I being sweet enough already, don't have one which means I can get on with the notes and finishing off the wine while she has something to occupy herself with. But there is a problem. It's all I can do to keep writing and having writ move on, for to stop would let them see that I had overheard, that I was eavesdropping on their riveting conversation and they would not only stop, but be morally outraged at this invasion of their privacy and call the owner. It takes a massive effort of will to pretend that I am completely unaware of their presence and to keep my head down, to resist the urge to stare open-mouthed at the speakers at the next table. Next table it may be, but the occupants may as well be at ours for all the distance between us. If Dinah and Rod had accepted my invitation to dine with us, this pair could scarcely have been any closer. With all respect, however, Dinah and Rod could scarcely hope to match them for interesting conversation.

They are a couple of American women, each sharing the most intimate family secrets. It's almost as if they were nursery school children, unable yet to distinguish fact from fiction, unaware of how specious their tales are, vying to out-trump each other with stories of their horrendous relatives. Perhaps because Iona and I have spoken so little, they don't realise we can understand every word they say, but if they had been less caught up in their own conversation and paid more attention to the way I had given the order to the waitress (apart from adoringly) they might have noticed I spoke a form of American. Or perhaps to wash their dirty laundry in public, in front of two perfect strangers whom they'll never see again doesn't bother them in the slightest.

With my eyes, I tell Iona to tune in, though she hardly could not for they are making no effort to keep their voices down or speak in a conspiratorial whisper, which I would have thought more appropriate, considering their subject matter. Wordlessly, Iona sends the message back that she already is receiving the *Voice of America*.

"*My* brother-in-law," the one facing me is saying, "was arrested for indecent assault. *For two women at the same time!*" Drawing breath for dramatic effect, she continues: "He just came up to the first one and told her how beautiful she was and that he was in love with her. She told him to get lost, but he tried to kiss her and when she resisted, he pushed her – you know where, *with both hands!*" Pause, during which the other makes suitable comments of shock and horror, after which the speaker goes on: "But he wasn't finished. He came back and pinched her friend in the butt, then put his arm round her from behind and grabbed her – you know what." More appropriate remarks from the listener while the speaker contemptuously dismisses him with: "I never liked him. I always thought there was something creepy about him. And he is an *alcoholic*," she concludes in a lower register as if that put the lid on it.

This is followed by a discussion on the speaker's sister's reaction to the attack and how they have kept it quiet from the rest of the family.

Now it is the turn of the one sitting beside me. "*My* brother-in-law's father is *in prison*," she responds, conjuring up an ace from the bottom of the pack or where she may have been keeping it hidden below the table. "They only caught up with him thirty years after it happened." A dramatic pause during which the silence gets heavier and I hardly dare to breathe in case I miss the next bit, yet force my fingers to write something, lest they detect my ears are out on stalks. "He sexually assaulted two little girls for years. He began when they were only three and six." A further pause to permit an appropriate response. "There were allegations that there were others, but they couldn't be proved. My sister never took to him. He was always making sexual innuendoes to her, well any woman, as a matter of fact. And he was always "forgetting" to do up his flies," she adds finally and conclusively.

This is followed by a general discussion on black sheep in the family and the perils of marriage. It is of particular interest to me as I am a black sheep myself. Surreptitiously, I look to see if the one across from me is still wearing a wedding ring. She is. Unfortunately I can't see whether the one sitting next to me is or not.

"You just have no control over your in-laws do you?"

"Just like your children, when they grow up and start going around with people who you can see are clearly unsuitable. I mean, you can instil them with all the values you like, then they meet someone and they go flying out the window."

"That's so true," agrees the other.

"You know my oldest daughter, Jackie…? Someone touched her where they shouldn't and her boyfriend went looking for him with a *knife*. Fortunately he didn't succeed in stabbing him, but he was cut a bit." Sounds of shock and sympathy in response. "Actually, I don't see what she sees in him. But what can you do? If you say anything, that just makes them more determined to go against you."

The listener affirms the veracity of this universal truth and they expand on the difficulties of being a mother these days, especially to teenage girls, and the terrible state of the nation generally, from which I gather they are not exactly regretting the imminent retirement of George W. Bush. As a matter of fact, we had left on the night of the Presidential election, a bit of bad planning on my part as there is little to beat as a little bedtime activity, lying in bed till the early hours of the morning listening to the election results coming in. I only found out that Obama had won when we were at the café with Dorothy and the others - a result we all toasted heartily.

The lady beside me leaves to go to the toilet presumably and also leaves an awkward silence behind her. With no-one to talk to, and with neither Iona or I talking to each other because what we are desperate to say cannot be said in her presence, I am the one more relaxed now, getting on with my notes, while Iona has finished her pudding and has nothing to do. In fact, I am beginning to sweat in case Iona *does* say something, for that would reveal to our neighbour that I was an English speaker and it terrifies me that she might leap to the conclusion that I was some sort of crypto-rapist making notes on them as potential victims and accuse me right there and then in front of everybody, for seen from her perspective and that of her friend, rapists are roaming the earth.

There being no question of any eavesdropping at the moment and my recollections having ground to a halt for the moment, I feel it is safe to look up and appear to gaze into the middle distance, but in reality, to take a close look at her. You probably could have correctly guessed her nationality without her having to open her mouth. She's blonde, though not naturally so, and a bit on the tubby side as many Americans tend to be, but far from obese. It is noticeable she is wearing make-up but in a reasonably subtle way, so there is nothing particularly showy or flamboyant about her, or her dress, to make her stand out unless it is her jewellery of which there is a great deal, especially on her fingers, but even that is on the more tasteful side of vulgar. She looks like any other middle-class mom from Middle America and you would never guess to look at her that she had so many skeletons in the family cupboard.

I can't help but ponder how it came to pass that these two, both so far from home, should happen to be in Lucca at the same time and what had prompted them to divulge these family secrets that even some of their own family weren't aware of. Furthermore, no names, apart from the daughter, Jackie, had been mentioned which leads me to conclude that they don't really know each other all that well. And where are the husbands I wonder? Have they been left behind while the wives get to know each other better as they tour Italy or Europe?

Never once does she meet my eye, not even a flicker to check that I am not staring at her rather than the distant horizon, not even a glimpse at my notebook, out of curiosity, to see if she could possibly make out a word, even if it were upside down, that might give her a clue as to what I could possibly be finding to write about all this time. Not the slightest interest either in so much as throwing me a glance to see what a weirdo who spends all his time scribbling in between courses looks like. It's just incredible how uncurious some people can be. Instead she begins to rummage in her handbag and although she must be as familiar with the contents of that as the back of her hand, it takes some time for her to produce her credit card.

When her friend comes back, I get my first chance to get a proper look at her. About the same age, dark, and also unmistakeably American, though I was unable to make out if she was wearing a ring or not. She picks up her glass and drains it off.

"I hate to leave it behind, but I can't possibly drink any more."

"Nor can I," says the blonde.

It is just not their conversation that is incredible. They are referring to their half-litre carafe of red wine that has at least a glass left in it, if not more. They had been well embarked on their main course (and conversation) before we arrived and had had a sweet, but with so much to talk about, while we had nothing much to say, we have caught them up. Now they are ready to go, but I want to linger, for I have a plan. Our wine is not quite finished and Iona doesn't want any more either which is not surprising as it just doesn't go after a sweet – another reason why I never have one.

I watch our dining companions get up and go, still without a glance in our direction from either of them, then I check the floor in case they have dropped something they might need to return for, keep my eyes open for them to pass the big arched windows outside and when I am sure I saw them do just precisely that and that they have passed out of my life for ever, I reach swiftly for their carafe and tip the contents into ours. Speed was of the essence, firstly in case the waitress whisked it away before I could act, and secondly, and this is the greater danger – before La Belle Dame Sans Merci could stop me.

What's so wrong with that? They would just throw it out anyway, unless we are expected to believe that behind the scenes, there is one huge cauldron into which the waitresses pour all the leftovers from punters stupid enough not to drain their carafes down to the last drop and which is subsequently recycled into new carafes. Frankly, I don't see anything wrong with that either as I am a passionate believer in not wasting anything and that is exactly what I am doing – preventing waste, because you can bet that in a classy restaurant like this, that's just what they do – pour all this perfectly good wine down the sink. It's just not right.

Like Little Jack Horner, although not quite in the corner, I feel as if I have pulled off quite a coup and I am rather pleased with myself. La Belle Dame Sans Merci, however, is outraged, especially when she looks hurriedly around to see if anyone has noticed.

They have. The family at the table in the corner, next to the fireplace certainly did, if no-one else, for they are leaning over the table in a confidential manner, looking in my direction and hurriedly looking away again when they see me looking at them. But for the moment I have got off with it as she does not want to create more of a scene than I have created already by reprimanding me in public.

"Just wait till I get you out of here!" Scow Ling mutters darkly.

It has to be admitted that does cast rather a pall over my triumph. However, with regard to our neighbours on the other side, I have, in fact, been watching *them* out of the corner of my eye for some time, for the man, husband, father, call him what you will, even Will if you like, is another of God's duplicates and his name is Graham. That's because he is the spitting image of my good friend Graham Duncan. "Good" as he is doing lots of good works in South Africa where he is a missionary and why it can't possibly be him with someone else's wife and daughter. Still, just in case he is leading a double life, I can't help but keep stealing a glance at him from time to time because the resemblance is so strong. He, however, shows no sign of recognising me. But then again, maybe he is terrified I come up and greet him with: "Hey, Graham, does Sandra know you are here, you old rascal!"

There is another reason why my attention should be drawn to this family however, as the daughter, who must be about fifteen, is the strangest-looking child I have ever seen. She obviously gets her looks from her mother poor dear, who is no oil painting herself. She has the sort of profile that you see of witches in children's books or Hallowe'en stories, like a crescent moon, with a prominent jutting jaw and a concave face with a pointed nose that exceeds the chin for prominence.

What a contrast to our waitress whom I now call over so I can get the bill. She is the dark and sultry type, which is my type, with a hint of Asian blood about her if I am not much mistaken. Naturally I do not express to Iona this admiration for what appears to be this Indian-Italian combination, but it does seem to me to be one of God's better ideas and leaves me reflecting on the unfairness of life, that some can be born beautiful and others not, and like choosing your in-laws, there's nothing much you can do about it.

And I also reflect on the unfairness of my own situation when, by preventing that wine from being thrown out, I thought I was doing something good, but instead find myself in trouble, just as Jack probably got a whack from his mum for using his thumb instead of a spoon, and which the nursery rhyme neglects to go on and inform us.

Such beauty in a waitress deserves a larger than normal tip of course, while €43 does not seem too extortionate for the meal considering it had been very good indeed and had included a litre (and a bit) of wine, of which I had the lion's share, though you would never have guessed I was a lion unless it was the one from *The Wizard of Oz* if you could have seen into the state of my heart which is as tremulous as a mouse's knowing that a different sort of reckoning is about to be faced for my misdeed.

Already, in my head, I can hear the band begin to strike up a sombre tune as I prepare to face the music. But before that, I need to put my foot up on the chair recently vacated by the American lady on my left in order to tie my shoelaces.

"Have you had your shoes off all this time?" La Belle Dame Sans Merci cries, aghast.

"Yes, of course. Why not? We weren't about to go anywhere were we? And my feet were loupin' with all the walking we had done today." And by way of mitigation, I add, "You should have felt the heat coming off them!"

"No wonder those people were looking at us and sniggering all the time!"

"Who? The family with the father who looks like Graham Duncan?"

"Who does it matter who he looks like? They were looking at us and laughing at us! How dare you make a fool out of me like this! Just wait until I get you outside!"

There are some days when you just can't do anything right.

CHAPTER FOURTEEN: THE STRESS GOES ON

It is my idea to eschew the Pasticceria Scilla on the corner and have our breakfast somewhere in the more interesting surroundings of the old town, which doesn't meet entirely with Iona's approval. I have no particular place in mind, but one of the piazzas with the architecture as a backdrop has to be more interesting for people-watching, while she on the other hand, is more interested in coffee than anything else and would rather have it sooner rather than later. Furthermore, if we are going into the old town, she wants to go directly for breakfast without stopping to look at anything that takes our interest. I shake my head sadly. She really should do something about her drug dependency.

But first, I would like to go into the Tourist Office. It won't take a moment. Now that we have sent the bag off, it may be worth contacting Carla to let her know it is on its way and should arrive tomorrow. In addition, I want to give Carla my phone number so she can phone me as soon as it arrives, for if there is one thing that Iona desperately wants, it is to wash her hair and if there is something she needs even more than that, it is her cross-stitching. And if there is something I desperately need it is for her idle hands to have something to do, otherwise I might just find them round my throat.

It is disappointing to see that Roberta is not on duty today. A German couple are being attended to by someone else who is fluent in their native language which is a pity as otherwise it might have been over a lot sooner. The tourists seem extraordinarily inquisitive while the assistant is determined to be helpful and answers each question in a great deal of detail, while I hover in the background, like the Invisible

Man feeling increasingly embarrassed at eavesdropping on this conversation, even if I don't understand a word, but too afraid to drop out of earshot, because that is precisely the moment another tourist would choose to come along and take my place. Besides, if I stay there, it might dawn on the assistant that I want some attention too.

If I am feeling uncomfortable, then Iona the Caffeine-deprived is feeling more irritated by the minute. This was meant to have been just a brief stop, but how could I have anticipated this? A couple of times, the German couple seem to be on the point of departure, gathering leaflets and other bits of paper together, which they do, I am sure, because they know it gives me hope, but then one of them thinks of a supplementary question and then we are off again on what could be the history of Lucca since Roman times by the length of time it takes to answer. They have a word for it, the equivalent of which does not exist in our language: *Schadenfreude.*

But, at last, finally, there is nothing more to be said and they part, lifelong friends by now I should have thought and, as I step up to the desk, I can see why the lady was so good at German because the name on her badge tells me she is German too – Beate.

"I hope your English is as good as your German," I begin in a light-hearted tone of voice, as if I hadn't minded in the slightest being kept all this time, nor was in mortal fear of my wife.

"Yes, I hope so."

This doesn't sound too promising. I should have known not to try the jocular approach with a German: there isn't time for humour in the serious business of getting through life – they are all about business-like efficiency – which is why she had done such a good job in sending her native language speakers on their way.

It is necessary to explain the background from the beginning before I proceed with my request. Finally, I get to the point and push the proof of postage with my notebook with Carla's address and phone number in it across the desk.

"Could you please phone this number and let them know that the case is on its way and ask them to let us know when it arrives?"

Beate studies the documents I have placed before her, especially the phone number – all the way to Elba. Was it my imagination, or did I see her eyebrows shoot above the rims of her glasses? Pisa may be the local airport for Elba but it doesn't look as if it is a local phone call from Lucca.

"I can't make this phone call."

That sounds decisive and final. All the old feelings I had experienced yesterday, of despair and depression, come flooding back. I am sure I can feel the clunk as my heart hits my boots.

"But Roberta phoned for me yesterday," I manage to get out. "You know Roberta?"

"My colleague, yes?"

"Well, she phoned this number for me yesterday."

As I say it, I hope I have not dropped Roberta in it. What if she was not supposed to have done that? After all she had done for us, the last thing I want is for her is to be hauled over the coals on my account, but I couldn't think of anything else to say at that moment that might persuade Beate to make that phone call. I know I couldn't cope with it on my own. Besides, it would mean having to speak to Carla personally and I'm too frightened of her, assuming she could speak English in the first place of course.

"Tell me again," Beate says, patiently.

Phew! At least I have got a reprieve, another chance to explain my situation. If only Roberta had been here, there would have been no need for all this, but just as patiently as Beate had asked, I explain and having explained, I feel my heart soar into its rightful place again because I think I may have made a breakthrough.

"Ah, at last, I see your situation. Now you have explained it to me, I understand. Yes, of course I can make that phone call for you. Now, what is it you would like me to say?"

She is already picking up the phone. She is determined to be as helpful as she was to the German couple, though they were probably asking boring things about hotels and restaurants and transport to Pisa and Florence, like normal tourists. This unusual request might make her day and it might make mine too if we get the right answers to our questions. And now that Beate is prepared to be so helpful, I feel I can make a supplementary request: since she has seen the proof of postage, would they consider releasing my luggage?

But it's no use. Carla's husband is happy to know that his wife will soon be reunited with her case, but still won't relent from his right to retain ours until hers arrives. And within my heart of hearts, I didn't really expect to hear anything different. I probably would have done the same thing had the situation been reversed. What if it had all turned out wrong and all of Carla's possessions were there, apart from her underwear? He'd be in really big trouble – but nothing half so bad as I would have been, if I had had as much as a peek to see what she had in her case once we realised it was not ours.

But it is progress at least in the sense that the Cremonas know they should soon be reunited with their bag and signor Cremona has promised to phone the airport as soon as it arrives in shipshape condition.

"Er...Would you mind phoning the airport and giving them my mobile phone number so they can phone me when they get the all clear from the Cremonas?"

Beate doesn't mind, and just for good measure, I slide the hotel's business card, which I had picked up on impulse, across the desk as well.

"Or they could try to reach me at this number, if they prefer," I say, being as helpful as I can in my own way.

We thank Beate profusely for all her help. She came up trumps after all.

And now to breakfast. However, in the Piazza Cittadella, by chance, I happen to meet a very interesting person indeed: none other than Giacomo Puccini himself, wearing a three-piece suit, bow tie and a rather haughty expression. He is sitting, very relaxed, in a chair, his left leg thrown carelessly over the other so the ankle is resting on the right knee and with the inevitable cigarette (or is it a cigar?) barely held by a couple of fingers as if it was almost too much effort to hold. It is a very recent bronze statue and dominates this little piazza.

Iona, meanwhile, has been investigating the two cafés facing each other, trying to weigh up which would be better for breakfast and having made up her mind, takes a seat outside one of them, but in not nearly such a relaxed manner as Giacomo and the only thing remotely to do with smoke is that which is coming out of her ears (or is it steam?) at the inordinate length of time I am spending with Puccini, and which builds up to a full head when I tell her I don't want to go to either of them.

This is a piazza so small and enclosed I suspect no winter sun ever penetrates and I want to sit in the sun, for it is another spring-like morning with a refulgent sun set in an azure sky. Instead, I modestly propose that we go to the Piazza San Michele, the former Roman forum which is so large there is bound to be a café in the sun. Besides, there is not much to do in the way of people-watching here, the most interesting being Giacomo and he's not going to be doing anything very interesting. He even, very rudely, has his back to us.

She is now my Chinese wife, Scow Ling, as she stomps off up a narrow canyon which fortunately is not very long and which leads us into the vast Piazza San Michele which is bathed in sunshine and where a café, the Turandot, with a gay yellow awning, is in full sun and full of patrons wearing dark glasses. This is more like it and off we set across the piazza, hoping that there will be a table at the front in the sunshine and we will not be forced to sit under the awning in the shade.

One table is in part sun but what is really annoying is that right in front of us is an unoccupied table with a man's jacket draped over the back and the longer we sit there without being served, the more annoying it becomes when its owner does not reappear. Probably a German, I mutter to myself uncharitably, wishing I had the courage to change places with the jacket. But at last it dawns that there is no waiter service and that you have to go inside to order what you want and if you want to be sure of a seat when you come out, then it is not unreasonable, if you are on your own, to sling your jacket over the back of any seat available. That is probably where the owner of the jacket is now and he may not even be German.

Iona goes in to see what she would like to eat with her americano and having chosen, re-emerges to guard the table with instructions that I am to make the order and wait. But after fighting my way through the heaving group of humanity inside, I take one look at the choice of croissants and pastries on offer and decide this is not for me. The only way I could make an order would be to point at what I wanted and this is no orderly queue: it is every man for himself and whoever can shout his order louder than his neighbour or attract the assistant's attention in some way is going to prevail – which means it is going to take ages for me to be served, time when I could be outside sitting in the sun. Iona, who doesn't care as much for the sun as me should be in here, while I should be out there. She's got it all wrong. Besides, if someone does queue-jump her, she is better equipped to deal with the situation.

I am surprised by the violence of her reaction. It seemed a reasonable suggestion to me but apparently I have made a very great error of judgement indeed. I am left speechless as she gets up, snatches her bag and snaps that she is going to the café at the other side of the piazza and that is the last and final time she is moving and if it is not in the sun, well that is just my tough luck, for she is going there and not moving a further step until she has had something to eat. She doesn't fool me though. I know what she really wants and why she is so short tempered. Drug withdrawal symptoms.

So that is how we come to be in the much less frenetic Bar San Michele, and apart from being served right away, we have a table in the sun on which a notice in three languages urges us, for reasons of hygiene, not to feed the pigeons – as if we would, and what's more, it affords a much better view of the proceedings in the piazza.

Not so far away, for example, a man is playing a saw to the accompaniment of a tape from a ghetto blaster. I love the sound of a saw: it seems to me to have an ethereal, transcendental quality and what could be a more appropriate background sound as we sit with our croissants and coffees looking at the façade of San Michele?

Meanwhile, across the piazza, I can see that that table in the sun is still unoccupied, apart from the jacket still draped over the chair. If I had been sitting behind it in the partial sun, the steam would have been coming out of *my* ears by now.

Yes, we are far better off over here and the view of the church is better too. A good decision of Iona's to move. But for these benefits there is a price to pay. The €3.70 at the Scilla has escalated to an incredible €8.20 here. It is just as well that it is in euros and not the sort of money I understand or I would certainly have fainted on the spot. You live and learn.

It will be the Scilla from now on.

CHAPTER FIFTEEN:
AN IMPERFECT SAINT

The façade of San Michele is notable for three reasons. At the very top, at the pinnacle of the façade, like an enormous eagle in its eyrie, stands the statue of the saint and even with the naked eye I can see how crude it is, but through the binoculars it becomes even more evident just how unsubtle it is. Even if you can ignore the tin hat he appears to be wearing, like a WWI veteran, (his halo I presume) there is nothing remarkable or exquisite about the saintly features: the face is big and round and as devoid of expression as a Christmas pudding or like the orb he is holding in his left hand. That resembles a water balloon which, with most unsaintly behaviour, Michael, like a prankster schoolboy, looks poised to drop on the unsuspecting public below - not to mention the spear which he holds carelessly in his right, the tip pointing earthwards and which, if he were to loosen his grip, would result in much more serious consequences than his water bomb.

The whole thing is monstrously too big - there is no sense of proportion here: no thought seems to have been given as to how its size should be commensurate with the scale of the church; no thought seems to have been given to the point of view of the beholder below. It may be at the pinnacle of the eponymous church, but I'm afraid the statue of St Michael is its worst feature and its only use may be to serve as a contrast to the splendours below. I feel rather like Blake, who marvelled at how He who made the lamb, could also be responsible for the "tyger." How could the same hand possibly have made the exquisite carvings of the rest of the façade?

The short answer is – they couldn't possibly. It took three centuries to build this cathedral-like church. Begun in 1070, most of what we see dates from the 12th century and this monstrosity *must* belong to a different era, from a time after all the master craftsmen had gone on to take master classes in the sky and left such a dearth on earth that this is the best they could come up with.

It is hardly a crowning glory to the marvels that undoubtedly belong to the rest of the façade but this St Michael does have a unique and hidden attribute - his huge metal wings actually move! It's true: if you look behind the façade which sticks up like a sore thumb above the roof, you can see the stairs which little men equipped with large poles mount on festival days to make the wings move. On windy days they are redundant and the wings are moved by the breath of heaven alone, which must be a pretty impressive sight because they are at least as long as an albatross's but a great deal more bulky. To see them flapping about on their own must be an unforgettable sight.

So much for point one. The second most remarkable thing about the façade is the way you cannot fail to notice the incongruous way so much of it sticks out so far above the roof. It reminds one of the façade of just about any saloon or any hotel in any Western you have ever seen. You would imagine the roof would meet the tapering top tiers of the façade, but the roof is much, much lower. This design was not intended to be inspirational or innovative. Sad to say, it was a case of the eye being bigger than the stomach, of the Lucchese having bitten off more than they could chew. The money ran out and they had to lower their expectations - and the roof.

The third, the best and most remarkable feature about the façade is the infinite variety of decoration on the columns, not two being alike. Ruskin apparently spent an age drawing them. It is endlessly fascinating to look at them collectively, then study them individually through the binoculars to observe the details more closely. You name it, they've got it here, like a column emporium, where if you see one you like, you could order that style for your portico: chevrons, diamond lozenges, crosses, barley sugar twists; stripes like an American tie, running from right to left, some running in the opposite direction; some carved in high relief, some in bas; while still more look as if they had been painted, looking for all the world like a roll of carpet and one jazzy one with black vertical zigzags on the white marble that would be perfectly at home in the psychedelic Sixties.

But just a minute, what's this? Surely this one and that in the same row are the same? These are the plainest columns of all decorated only by four rings and a double pair at the top and bottom. Back and forth my binoculars swing until my arms ache and it seems the crick in my neck will leave a permanent crease, but I can't detect any difference apart from the natural variegation of the marble. And that's another thing – the marble is a different colour, not white, but brown. With the naked eye I look again and surely there is another the very same on the tier above, and another. In fact the more I look, the more I see. Unless I am much mistaken, these must be replacements for the originals that have weathered away.

If they are the plainest, then most ornate of all are the columns with figures carved on them. And that's not all, because, remarkable though all these idiosyncratic styles may be, at the top of each column is a gallery of carved heads, not gargoyles either but distinct individuals whom you would recognise if you passed them in the street – as you might well have done if you had been alive 600 years ago when this church, church mind you, not cathedral, was completed in the 14th century, for that is exactly what they are - real portraits of real people - the celebrities of their day. You knew you had made it in medieval Lucca when your mug was on the façade of San Michele, the equivalent of having your name up in lights.

And that's not all either because above this portrait gallery of the great and the good, runs a black-and-white inlaid marble frieze of animals which is arguably the most charming feature of the entire façade. It is rather hard to make out what they are (especially at this distance) because they are rather stylised, but amidst the menagerie I can definitely make out bears and birds that an ornithologist might be able to identify for certain, but to me look like flamingos and ostriches and what either of these could possibly have to do with Lucca, you would have to ask Saint Michael himself because I haven't a clue.

And I haven't even begun to tell you about the blind arches and the detail on them and you may be relieved to know that I don't intend to. It is hardly surprising it took four centuries to complete this monument to God (apart from the slight problem of raising the cash) with all this attention to detail. But this is the sort of detail that you need the eyes of a hawk to see from the ground and which I can, only thanks to the power of my binoculars.

These fascinating columns topped with the realistic busts obviously must be older than that articulated saint on high with his almighty wings, but without their supporting role, he would never have had a place to perch. But despite being lower in a physical sense, they are far higher in artistic terms, as anybody with half an eye can see, (let alone anyone with binoculars). If much of the detail on the columns could be compared to icing, Saint Michael, archangel though he may be, articulated wings though he may have, – he is definitely not the cherry on the top.

CHAPTER SIXTEEN:
ON SAINTS AND A SINNER

The inside does not match the splendour of the outside, and that in my experience, is typical of Italian churches or cathedrals, as I have written elsewhere. You can have inner or outer beauty, but not both, or so it seems, and so I comfort myself with that thought each day as I shave, though not for the two past days as it happens. Having said that though, the interior of St Michael's is very pleasing in its plainness and simplicity, not like some baroque or rococo examples I could mention.

Down the vastness of the interior, the eye is drawn to an enormous 13th century Byzantine wooden Crucifixion which stands in the apse. It is the work of Berlinghiero Berlinghieri who, whatever else you can say about him, which is probably not very much unless you are an art historian, nevertheless has a very fine ring to his name. Christ, incongruously, is sporting a very fine pair of gold lamé breeches with black buttons all down the front. His poor outstretched, crucified arms, if they were hanging naturally by His sides, (oh, if only!) would reach to His ankles and are as skinny as frankfurters. Typical of Byzantine art however, He doesn't seem too distressed by the situation and looks as if He could hang about there all day.

The cross is noticeable because of its prominent position and enormous size, but the second thing that the eye is naturally drawn to, glowing like ruby, is a little gem of a painting in the first altar to the right of the Crucifixion and like it, it was executed by an artist with another very fine name indeed - Fra Filippino Lippi, a name he inherited from his more famous father, Fra Filippo Lippi. The lad was a chip off the old block evidently, although in actual fact, he was a pupil of Botticelli, otherwise known as "The Little Barrel" - a soubriquet I imagine he was not particularly proud of. This painting has recently been restored which is why it glows with such a quiet luminosity in the dim interior of the church which is almost monochrome, apart from this and Christ's gold lamé breeches.

The subject matter is the four saints, from left to right – Roch, Sebastian, Jerome, and Helena. The painting is remarkable for the absence of the Holy Family but apart from that and the vibrant colours, I like it for the scenario it depicts. St Helena is the one I know best, the mother of Constantine, the first Christian Roman emperor. I once was very close to her in the Vatican museum, only feet away from her tomb, a massive sarcophagus made of porphyry.

She looks rather wistful, as well she might. We all have our crosses to bear, but she literally has the True Cross to carry. She stumbled across it on a visit to the Holy Land and this is her lugging the great big bit of timber back home. It looks a hell of a burden for a slip of a woman like her to carry.

You might have thought that one of the other saints would have offered to give her a hand, at least taken one end of it, even if they didn't carry the whole thing for her. But no, Jerome who is standing right next to her, has his head in a book and it is such a Good Book, he can't put it down, not even for a moment. It's as if the others are not there at all as far as he is concerned. He is lost in his own little world.

As for the other two, well there is no point in asking them either – they are far too wrapped up in each other, particularly in showing each other their legs. Sebastian, whom you recognise because of the arrow, though he is holding it, rather than scores of them protruding from his person like a pincushion, is wearing a pair of bright red knee-highs that clash violently with his bright orange robe. (His mother should have told him.) Perhaps he borrowed them from Jerome as they are precisely the same shade as his robe. Whatever their provenance, he seems very proud of them as he has hitched up his robe to show them to St Roch and thus exposing a glimpse of knee which I find rather shocking.

St Roch, on the other hand, not to be outdone, and who is wearing a fine pair of black leather boots, unlike poor Sebastian who is only in his stocking soles, has hitched his robe up even further and more daringly, to show an expanse of thigh. I know a bit about St Roch too, as being an occasional collector of the graves and tombs of the famous, I have met him before so to speak, having visited his resting place in the church that bears his name in Venice. Two out of the four saints in the painting isn't bad going I reckon for someone who doesn't deliberately go in search of these things but which I just happen to come across in the course of my travels.

But what does it all mean? Could it possibly be a knobbly knees contest and perhaps Jerome is checking the rulebook for guidance and could St Helena possibly be the prize for the winner? If so, she is supremely indifferent to the whole thing: she has her own troubles.

Alas, the truth is a little less interesting. In case you are not too much up on your saints, St Jerome was a pretty brainy geezer who translated the Bible into the so-called vulgar or vernacular Latin, not from the Greek, not because he couldn't, but from the Hebrew because he felt it was more accurate. St Sebastian, despite having more arrows shot into him than the quills on a porcupine, nevertheless survived to tell the tale – only to be beaten to death by Diocletian's thugs and his body thrown into a sewer. He is merely showing St Roch that he is no longer one of the Untouchables, that he has had a jolly good bath since then and has even scrubbed his knees which tend to get overlooked unless your mum reminds you to do them. Likewise, St Roch, who was a great healer of plague victims, but ironically fell victim to the disease himself, though perhaps not, since he was in their company so much.

He was miraculously cured however, and here he is proving it by showing a leg to Sebastian.

And talking of plagues, just by the front door is the original of the *Madonna and Child* by Matteo Civitali, who although he does not have half as good a name as the other artists I have mentioned, is widely reckoned by those who know about such things, to be Lucca's greatest artist and sculptor. The sculpture however, does have a more ringing name – the *Madonna Salutis Portus* and it was commissioned as a sign of thanks for deliverance from the Black Death which was rampant in the city in 1476. The copy, you could scarcely miss, is on the right-hand corner of the façade.

Outside again, in the full glare of the sun, Iona sits down on the steps by the side entrance to put new batteries in her camera, but there appears to be a problem.

"They're dead!" she announces in the sort of tone that makes me feel as if she wouldn't be too upset if I were in the same state. Past misdemeanours not withstanding, I have added another sin to the list, so it seems. The batteries are, strictly speaking, not "new" at all. Before we left, I had borrowed them for my life-support when my batteries ran out. My "life-support" is my Walkman which I use to get me through the sleepless nights, listening to Radio 4, or to programmes I have recorded from it.

Iona gets abruptly to her feet, furious with me that she is unable to capitalise on all these photo opportunities. She is just about to dispose of the worthless batteries in the nearest bin when I stop her. It's just not possible that I could have drained that much power in just one night.

"Just a minute! Can't be! Let me see."

When I put the batteries in, the camera works perfectly. She must have put them in with the wrong polarities. The storm clouds that had been gathering on the brow of my German wife, Frau Ning, have now lifted and she is restored to her normal sunny self. Phew! That was a close one: those batteries were nearly in the bin! They are good for hours yet in my miserly Walkman after they are too weak to take another photo in her power-hungry digital camera.

But, unfortunately, it is only a stay of execution. My next sin is just about to make its appearance. We are now standing in front of the incredible mosaic on the façade of the church of St Frediano. That would be Fred for short. Not the best-known star in the saintly galaxy I would have thought, but a sign to all of us that just because you have a humble name doesn't mean that you can't aspire to higher things.

So who was St Frediano? Well, he lived in the 6th century and was of Irish extraction apparently, who passed through Lucca on pilgrimage to Rome and never left. Eventually the pope made him bishop. When the river Serchio flooded the countryside, bringing death and devastation, the peasants asked Fred to help. Right, said he, and on bended knee got straight on the hotline to Heaven. Then, thus inspired, he single-handedly changed the course of the river. No wonder they made him a saint. It was a very good deed indeed and I don't know why he is not the patron saint of engineers, but he is not.

The incredibly impressive and eye-catching 13th century mosaic of *The Ascension of Christ the Saviour* on the topmost part of the façade, with its peacock blue and glittering gold colours, was designed by Berlinghiero Berlinghieri. It seems to me he has come on a bit since his Crucifixion. The huge figure of Christ being borne aloft by a couple of angels in what looks like a wicker basket, rather like the presentation pot plants you get in garden centres, appears more realistic - at least from this distance. Having said that though, the expression on His face still seems rather wooden and not, as you might expect, full of joy at the prospect of seeing His Dad again - not to mention bidding good riddance to all those beastly Romans.

It is a bit of a shame really that the mosaic is so splendid because it rather detracts from the rest of the façade. I really like it for the slim Ionic pillars; for its symmetry, the main door flanked by the two smaller ones with the Romanesque arches above them; for the plainness of the façade, apart from the pilasters.

So much we can see unaided, but naturally we would be able to see much more through the binoculars. I'd especially like to see the Apostles in close-up. Would they have expressions of joy on their faces as they waved Him goodbye, wishing Him bon voyage or would they be pleading: "Come back! Come back! Don't leave us here alone with those beastly Romans who will persecute us to death!"

Iona seems to be of the same mind.

"Have you got the binoculars?"

From the tone I take it to be a rhetorical question.

"No. I gave them to you."

The first line of defence, as any guilty person will tell you, is denial. But to tell you the truth, I don't actually remember doing that, but I must have, because I certainly don't have them now. For her part, Iona doesn't remember taking them from me. But I must have done because she is the carrier. She carries the guidebooks, the binoculars, her camera, the key to the hotel (in case I lose it) and God knows what else besides in that bag that she carries on her back. I only carry my camcorder which leaves my hands free and which means, should a sudden gust of wind come along, I have a better chance of catching my hat before it becomes airborne and I make an idiot of myself chasing after it.

A search of the bag does not divulge the binoculars, nor does a search of my memory produce anything more than the last I have of looking for duplicates of the pillars on the façade of San Michele which the guidebook says do not exist. Iona has a memory like an elephant, and when she says she does not remember me giving them to her, I am inclined to believe her. It means I must either have dropped them or, a more likely scenario would be, put them down somewhere, probably when

I was filming the façade. They and the camcorder would have been a bit too much for me to handle simultaneously. Or so it seems.

It is only later, when it is too late, so accustomed am I to being the one who does the wrong things, that I reckon I know what really happened. I bet Iona had put them down beside her when she changed her camera battery, when she stomped off in high dudgeon with me rushing behind her before she chucked the "dead" batteries in the bin. That must have been where and when and how they got lost.

Anyway, whatever the truth may be, that is how I came to be back in the doghouse as we go into San Frediano's. But what a far cry from a doghouse this is! It is as big as an aircraft hangar inside – something that takes me completely by surprise, although it shouldn't really, as only yesterday we had walked its entire length from the rear to the front with Carla's case. That had seemed very long but it is the height, rather than the length that takes the breath away, not forgetting the breadth, which out of the three is the least, but not in the least insubstantial.

There are several attractions in here, but the principal one for me is the supposedly incorrupt corpse of St Zita. She is lying in state here: it is promised you can actually see her in a crystal coffin and this promises to be the best thing I have seen since the body of Pope John XXIII in St Peter's in Rome. I must admit he looked pretty good, if rather waxy, but then he has only been dead less than half a century and I confess to being a tad on the sceptical side about the state of St Zita's remains and I am prepared for a disappointment. Having said that, I can hardly wait to see her but I must be patient and I'm in enough trouble already as it is without going haring off after another woman's body, even if she has been dead for 730 years.

Apart from that, there is a certain deliciousness in denying yourself a pleasure which you know you will certainly have, but by putting it off for just a little bit longer, it makes you anticipate the moment, whets the appetite, so that when the moment comes, it is all the better for the delay.

So, instead I do what all the guidebooks say you should do, have a look at the baptismal font, just by the entrance. You can hardly miss it. It's called the *Fonta Lustrale* and looks more like a fountain than a font and it's a bit of a laugh really, a reaction which might have offended the anonymous sculptors had they got to hear about it.

But I am appreciating their work really, all those hours they must have spent chiselling away. I can't help however, but be amused by the sight of Moses and the children of Israel fleeing from Egypt kitted up in full Crusader gear. It must have been very hot under all that chain mail and pretty hard going for the horses ploughing through all that sand with all that weight on their backs. If I had been around then and a betting man, I would have put all my shekels on the Egyptians catching up with them and recapturing them. But that's where I would have been wrong: they are depicted crossing the Red Sea with the water no higher than the horses' hocks and we all know what happened next.

There are other Biblical scenes as well, all very interesting I'm sure, but Moses and his troops were the best. Duty has been done, homage paid. Zita is meant to be somewhere near here. It's time I went in search of her.

She's not that easy to find right away, but that's because I thought she would be tucked away in some quiet and dark spot. Not a bit of it: in the second chapel to the right, there she is all laid out and lit up. I can't get as close to her as I would like as she is high up and roped off, but the zoom on my camcorder means I can get a pretty close look at her.

And pretty she is most certainly not. How anyone could imagine that her body is incorrupt beats me, though I suppose she must look better than most would do after being dead for nearly seven-and-a-half centuries. She is a wizened, shrunken creature with a skin like leather. The mouth, with blackened lips, is obscenely open, as if her jaw is agape with her last breath. The tip of the nose, jutting prominently heavenward, is also black, as are her eyelids, which mercifully, are closed.

And although she has nowhere to go, since she is already in heaven, she is all dressed up in rich green brocade with gold trimmings and yards and yards of what appears to be net curtain is swathing her from head to toe. At her head they have placed pink plastic roses in the net curtain, giving her the appearance of wearing a bride's veil, though it is pretty safe to say no-one ever asked for her hand in marriage if that is what she looked like in life. Not since Miss Havisham has anyone been so inappropriately dressed.

Both hands are on display, poking out from lace cuffs, crossed, and resting on her lap. At least they seem to be in a better state of preservation than her face. The hand, or both of them, prospective suitors may have asked for, but definitely not the rest of the body.

The coffin rests on a black marble plinth. In the centre, a gilt laurel wreath is inscribed with the words: CORPUS S. ZITÆ VIRG. LUC. I am glad I have seen her and glad I prepared myself for a disappointment. Of course she was 60 or so when she died in 1272, a pretty ripe age for those days, but surely to goodness she looked better than this when she died!

Of course she did work very hard for a living, by all accounts working tirelessly and living the life of an ascetic. No command, no matter how unreasonable or unpleasant, was too much trouble for her. She did everything asked of her without complaint and with humility and servility. Nor did she cost a lot to feed, for she was on a permanent fast, surviving (for it could hardly be called living) on bread and water alone, and even that she sometimes donated to those worse off than her. She didn't even have a bed, but slept on the bare wooden floor, which maybe explains why she got up so early, before everyone else, stiff as a plank, so she could say her prayers which she threw herself into with as much fervour as she did her work.

She impressed her employers, the Fatinelli family, so much that they promoted her to head housekeeper. All very admirable I'm sure, but I'm not so sure I approve of how she insisted one of her fellow servants was sacked immediately just because he uttered a wee sweary word. He might have hit his thumb with a hammer for instance, or burnt himself on the stove. But no, he had to go, and at once, for she was mortified and could not bear to be under the same roof as him. And the Fatinellis, realising what a little gem they had, acquiesced to her request – or should that be demand?

Strange to tell, her fellow servants didn't like her very much for some reason, and one day, when she was out helping some poor person instead of slaving over a hot stove as she was meant to be doing, they cliped on her, hoping *she* would be the one to get the sack this time.

Her employers rushed into the kitchen, expecting to find her in flagrant dereliction of her duties, but instead, found to their utter disbelief, (and subsequent belief) not a host of angels exactly, but at least two of the blighters baking the bread in her absence. No skin off the Fatinelli's noses – as long as there is bread on the table for tomorrow's breakfast, what does it matter who baked it? If it tasted a bit different, or heavenly even, they may have put that down to the new bakers. Or maybe it was the ergot.

Whatever the truth of that may be, because of the zoom on my camera, I have been able to see the saint in closer detail than Iona and although it is a bit far away, I don't need it to read the writing on the tomb. Iona, however, can't make it out so clearly. As so often in our relationship, she tends to see things rather differently from me: where I can make out the less clearly incised ligature at the end of the saint's name, she merely sees a dot where the upstroke of the A starts. In short, she sees S. Zit.

"She'll be the patron saint of teenagers, presumably," she observes dryly.

I have to admit I wish I had thought of that one. She is in fact, the patron saint of domestic servants as you might have already guessed, and by association, you might have supposed, waiters and waitresses – but would you have ever guessed – lost keys? Now I see what I have been doing wrong all these years. Instead of cursing them for losing themselves, I should have been asking St Zit to spot them for me. And now I know, Iona should let me carry the hotel keys from now on, just to lessen her burden a little. Like St Zita, I am always ready to serve in any way I can, for I know my station in life.

At the other side of the church, in another chapel, are Amico Aspertini's 16th century frescoes. On the left is the *Arrival of the Volto Santo*, the so-called Holy Face, said to have been carved by Nicodemus, who I am sure you need no reminding, helped to put Christ in the rock tomb and so this face of Christ is reckoned to be the nearest we have to a true likeness. It is in the Duomo and we will certainly go and see it for real, but for the moment, we have this depiction of its arrival in Lucca, all the way from the Holy Land.

Be prepared to suspend your disbelief. The story goes that the *Volto Santo* came across the seas by an unmanned ship, then a couple of unmanned oxen took over when it arrived in Luni in the neighbouring region of Liguria. Somehow they got it into a cart and found their way to Lucca all by themselves, and according to this painting at least, did it the hard way, not laying the statue down flat, but standing it upright, like a pope in a popemobile. That sounds very impressive for dumb beasts but they weren't all that smart in actual fact. They deposited their cargo in San Frediano's but in the morning, it was found in San Martino's – having transported itself there. They had delivered it to the wrong address obviously. You just couldn't get the staff in those days before St Zita.

But fascinating though that may be, it is the painting on the other side of the chapel which interests me more at the moment, for it depicts St Fred performing his miracle. There he is in the centre back with his rake, laying out the new course the river is to take. That's right – with a rake! But Fred is really an obscure figure; you would scarcely notice him but for the eye following the path which his rake has traced out from the upper right of the painting. What you notice first are the blokes in the front, stripped down to their underpants, driving log piles into river. It looks as if they may be building a dam.

So much for Fred single-handedly altering the course of the river! Him and a cast of thousands more like. And he thought all it took to alter the course of the river would be a rake!

No wonder they didn't make him the patron saint of engineers after all.

CHAPTER SEVENTEEN:
IN THE FOOTSTEPS OF THE
VOLTO SANTO

There are many other attractions in this marvellous place. The grave of San Frediano himself is supposed to be beneath the altar. I stroll across to it but don't see any signs of a marker. Maybe he's beneath that big table they have up there. I suppose that counts as another famous grave I have been to, and another saint. I am beginning to build up quite a specialised collection of them, just like some philatelists restrict themselves to collecting a theme such as birds or some other subject that interests them, there being so many stamps from so many countries, it's impossible now to have a collection of every stamp in the world as it was once possible to do.

Then, apart from the Aspertini frescoes that I haven't mentioned and which are a bit difficult to see properly as they have roped the chapel off for some reason, there is the monochrome sgrafitti on the arches which act like a frame to the frescoes. It really is incredible how the eye can be deceived, but you would swear that the outermost sgrafitti are on hexagonal columns, but they are in fact, quite flat. Amazing! Arguably, they are of more artistic merit than the frescoes themselves, but of course, the eye is drawn to the much more colourful frescoes and no doubt, they go mainly unnoticed by the majority of tourists, in much the same way that the generation brought up on colour television would never waste their time watching a black-and-white film as it would be just too incredibly boring and consequently they miss countless numbers of classics.

Another thing I can't help but admire is the polyptych by Jacopo della Quercia in the Cappella Trenta. The polyptych is what first arrests the eye with its gothic spires. It features the Madonna and Child flanked on either side by a pair of saints in their niches, like sentries in their sentry boxes. Beneath this and beneath the altar (which looks like a dining room table) is tucked an elaborate stone sarcophagus and in front of that, inset into the marble floor, are the twin, white bas-relief marble slabs where Lorenzo Trenta and his wife lie sleeping the Big Sleep side by side, their heads poignantly inclined towards each other, just like professional photographers make you do today when they take the portrait of you and the dearly beloved together.

He is wearing a heavy gown. I can tell because it does not have so many folds in it as his turbaned head which is resting on a richly-decorated pillow, while his ankles are supported by a cushion. Her head rests on an even more elaborate cushion from which drapes are hanging down so you get the feeling you could draw them over her as if she were sleeping in a four-poster bed. Then there are the folds from her headdress that are so long they are draped over her arms and knotted at the waist. When you add to this the voluminous folds of her gown, it really is as fine a bit of virtuoso sculpting as you ever would ever hope to see out or in of an art gallery, and it is hoped that Lorenzo and Lisabetta saw what they were getting for their money before it was too late.

Trenta was a wealthy merchant who commissioned the chapel in 1412. Work was a bit on the slow side however, as Jacopo, the sculptor, had to flee the town charged with theft, rape and sodomy. He fled to Siena where he found gainful employment creating the Fonte Gaia in the city's splendid scallop-shaped Piazza del Campo. His assistant, however, was not so lucky and got two years in the jug and Jacopo only came back to Lucca in 1416 with the promise that a similar fate would not befall him and he could get on with finishing the job. And a very good job he made of it too.

Of lesser interest is another tomb, that of Lazzaro Papi. Who, you may ask? And so did I. To get to the old city we have to walk along a part of the road named after him – L. Papi. Not the road of the Fifty Popes, or the road to hell, as you might well dub that racetrack that forms a giant roundabout round the ancient city, but a mere man's name. But not so "mere" since he earned the distinction of being buried in San Frediano. He was an early 19th century writer, physician and, somewhat surprising to relate, commander of the Bengal Lancers. So now you know.

"David."

A sibilant whisper reaches my ears but there is no-one to be seen. It sounds a bit far away. There it is again. It can't be from Up There, can it? Is this what sudden death is like? Surely my time can't be up yet! It's far too soon for me to be called home. When I hear it for the third time I realise it is only Iona calling me to the exit.

I had been aware of a little man going about ringing a bell but hadn't paid him much attention. I just put it down to something that Catholics do and mine not to reason why. They are always ringing bells, lighting candles and wafting incense about the place, so how was I to know that this was the signal, like a school bell, to announce the church was about to close – or would do just as soon as I get my skates on and get down to the other end of the church where the wee man with the big key is patiently waiting along with the wife with the red face.

We have decided to visit the Duomo next. It seems the natural thing to do, to transport ourselves there, like the *Volto Santo*. No oxcart is waiting outside unsurprisingly enough, and we make our own way there, threading our way through the narrow streets, which is a pleasure in itself. In the Via degli Angeli, for instance, where the street takes a bend, the roofs of the houses almost seem to touch, leaving only a slit of sky where they appear to have been rent apart.

Lucca was not made for vehicular traffic as I already pointed out if you remember, and we stop and watch in fascination as a small van reverses up a side street. But first the driver must get out and remove a bicycle from the corner and reposition it further down the street. The tyres screech in protest on the polished cobbles as the driver turns the wheel and reverses a few inches, very slowly, then comes forward again another few inches and so on until the van is perfectly aligned with the narrow gap and at last, he can reverse into it.

If he was put off by his impromptu audience, it doesn't seem to show. He has probably done it hundreds of times before and that is why he is so skilled at it. But hundreds aren't. I show Iona where the sandstone has been worn away to the depth of my forefinger by less skilled drivers. It even appears to bleed where a layer of red paint has been left behind.

Ah, here is the Liceo Classico N. Machiavelli with graffiti on the wall. Well, what else would you expect? I mean the graffiti could be expected, but not a school in his name, which seems as unlikely to me as the Adolf Hitler synagogue. It sounds all very grand and he may have been a brilliant writer and philosopher, Machiavelli I mean of course, but it worries me what they may be teaching the future generation in there. You won't find any of his immortal words in the Oxford dictionary of quotations, (unlike my *pab* or *pabby*, one day I hope will be) but I will never forget this phrase which I came across when I was studying the Renaissance and which seems to me to sum up his philosophy: "It is better to be feared than loved, more prudent to be cruel than compassionate."

Of course he was advising his Prince, and always had an eye on the main chance for himself, but if that is what they are teaching the future generation in there, then that is not graffiti on the wall but the writing on it. A depressing thought, even if I don't really believe it is true. I have hope and faith in the modern generation and I had better believe that because I am relying on them to pay my pension.

But for some, the pension has come to an end. Here, pasted on a wall, and of interest, at least to me, because we don't have such a thing, are six of those funerary announcements in appropriately big black letters of which the most prominent is the name of the deceased, followed by such details as age, the relations left behind and the funeral arrangements. I wonder if advertising like this ensures a bigger turnout to send you off. I, for one, never read the despatches in the local paper on the basis that if there is a funeral I should be attending, I would have heard about it anyway.

I do happen to notice however, that at the very time we were hauling Carla's case about in search of a box and brown paper, according to this, two people lay dying and that the funerals will be held tomorrow and the next day in Santa Anna's, the church opposite the Scilla. It hadn't seemed likely at the time, but it does seem to prove the truth of the saying which my daughter's father-in-law never tires of trotting out – there is always someone worse off than yourself – though in his case, it is hard to imagine of whom that could be true, unless you are already at death's door.

But life, like us, goes on and presently we come to an altogether more cheery prospect. Here it is in a shop window, the only sort of shopping I normally approve of Iona doing. Remember it is November: Christmas is still more than a month away, so it is not that surprising to find Christmas decorations in the shops, is it?

Of course not. And the centrepiece of this Christmas display in this shop window definitely isn't Rudolph, because he doesn't have a red nose, his snout looking more like that of a moose than his cousin, the caribou. I don't know what sex Dasher and Dancer and so on are, but this is definitely a lady deer, so I am pretty certain that this must be, as the song says, "Olive, the other reindeer."

Her feet have been daintily shod with bootees tied with ribbons in a big bow (so that proves it must be a girl); on her back, a Royal Stuart blanket has been spread, and on her tail, a festive wreath has been hung like a quoit in a hoopla stall.

But the thing that appeals to me most of all is her hat. As far as hats go towards making you look ridiculous, this has to be the worst, far worse than that favoured by the likes of the Mad Hatter earlier. It is a helmet really, with two holes at either side from which Olive's ears stick out at 90° which is already comical enough, but better still are her antlers which don't come out of her head but from a pad on top of the helmet, like a *kippah,* (there's an irony for you) and which have been transformed into a candelabra, complete with candles.

Now, if they had used little Olive here as a carrier for the *Volto Santo, that* would have been much more miraculous than a couple of oxen slowly wending their way o'er the lea, would it not? And it would have arrived a lot quicker by airmail too. I'm surprised they didn't think of that, but perhaps whoever was in charge of the despatch at the time was a bit like me and maybe was not quite *au fait* with the new technology and didn't quite trust it to deliver. Poor Olive.

I would have hired her myself for the parcel I had to send, had I thought of her, but if there is one thing of which I am certain, it is that Carla would want her bag long before Christmas.

CHAPTER EIGHTEEN:
BEGGARS AND BEGGARS BELIEF

By the much more pedestrian method of shanks's pony, we plod our way to San Martino by a long and winding road, which included a fruitless quest past San Michele which happened to be closed, just in case, by some miracle, there was any sign of the binoculars, plus a stop at a *pasticceria* to pick up a sandwich for a walking lunch.

The logically named (for once) Piazza San Martino has finally been cleared of the marquees and a squad of workmen are at work clearing up the litter. Well, actually, one young bloke is going about picking up the mess while his older mates are standing about having a laugh. He'll be the one with the zits, and he's possibly doing community service.

Like San Michele, the façade of San Martino has a variety of columns, but that is not what strikes you first. What you can't help but notice is the asymmetry, how the right appears to be squashed by the campanile so the last of the three arches is much smaller than the other two and the angle of the roof is much shorter on the side abutting the campanile than on the other side, so it looks more like a dart than a triangle. That's because the campanile was there first and what you can't help but notice right away is that it is composed of two halves, so to speak, the lower red brick part and the upper two tiers of white marble with the crenellations. But it scarcely seems to matter because in spite of this obvious contrast, it is not displeasing to the eye, even if it does look rather like the icing on a cake. But it is not over-decorated or striped like a zebra's pyjamas as I could say of some other hideous campaniles which I have also written about elsewhere.

But what I fail to understand is how they got it so wrong. Anyone capable of building this in the first place should surely have been capable of scaling down the arches to fit, or if they had started from the campanile, and built from right to left, like reading Arabic, they would have got it right. But that, I suppose, would have been next to heresy.

Nevertheless, for all the asymmetry, the arches do add to the appeal of the building as a whole, and do I suppose, mark the exterior as being superior to that of San Michele, though there do not appear to be any of those interesting busts of real people nor any of those fascinating animals. On the other hand, the decoration above the columns is much more ornate – perhaps just a little too much for my taste. I don't know if there is, or was, a beauty contest between the two churches, but I know on balance, which I would vote for.

Further contributing to the asymmetry, and this looks strange, there are couple of brackets between the two largest arches on the left, as if it had been intended that a statue should be placed there, or there had been one there once which has since disappeared. On the matching brackets on the right, but smaller and lower down, stands another sculpture executed by Lucca's favourite, Matteo Civitali.

This one is of San Martino mounted on his horse, with the two forelegs on the left bracket and the hind two on the right. From this lofty height the saint (though he wasn't then, just a Roman soldier) is dividing his cloak with his sword to give to a needy beggar. Very noble, I'm sure, but it seems to me it would have been more noble still if he had dismounted from his horse, come down to the same level as the beggar, so to speak, and presented it in a less dramatic and patronising manner.

But what right have I to criticise? I am not a saint – far from it, and I certainly don't want to patronise you, dear reader, but just in case hagiography is not your specialist subject, just in case you are not a devoted Catholic, or a philatelist who specialises in saints, may I gently remind you that of all the saints, St Martin is of particular interest because he was the first saint to die of natural causes, rather than achieving his sainthood through martyrdom. He died in 397 or thereabouts, aged about 80. Not in too much of a hurry to join the fraternity in heaven, evidently.

Subject matter apart, this sculpture does have a connection with the *Madonna and Child* on the corner of San Michele because, like that, it is only a copy. It is considered too valuable a work of art to be left to the vagaries of the mild Lucchese weather and so the original has been removed to the safety of the interior, which you are likely to miss unless you are specifically looking for it, or you happen to catch sight of it on your way out, as the interior is rather dim.

One advantage that San Martino does have over San Michele (and this is what might ultimately decide my preference for it) is that those arches form a portico that is very pleasant in its own right, but to set foot in it is to enter an outdoor art gallery, or more specifically, a sculpture gallery for there are some marvellous carvings within. It is also a bit like the moment in *The Wizard of Oz* where it bursts into colour, for the marble here, as well as the white, is also of a restrained pink and green. Here too can be found the black-and-white intarsia that I had liked so much on San Michele and naturally, there are some scenes from the life of St Martin, as you might expect, and round the doorways, carvings of religious scenes, including some early work by the celebrated Nicola Pisano. But most intriguing of all is the frieze that depicts the months of the year and the labours that have to be done during each of them.

Life is full of toil right enough; no-one said it was going to be easy and neither is the path to heaven either, symbolised by the labyrinth carved on the pillar next to the campanile. Circular in shape, it has a maze of lines etched into it and that is exactly what it is meant to represent – the many false turns, side turnings and blind alleys that lie betwixt us and salvation as we make our way through life.

And life, as we know, is harder for some than others. Life is more full of temptation for some than others, especially if you have a bit of money to splash about, and outside the smallest of the three doors and the only one that is open, a beggar has stationed herself. She has been patiently waiting for us as we made our way along the art gallery, admiring the frieze and it is only as we are about to enter that she extends her pitiful hand and says something in a voice to match. This is the first beggar we have seen, and like the one I remember outside the Duomo in Florence, she is an Asian. That one had been blind or half-blind; this one looks perfectly healthy and seems to me, speaking as one, you may remember, who gets all his clothes from charity shops, to be better dressed than me. For the moment at least, we ignore her and step into the Duomo.

The first thing you see, off to the left, is Civitali's *tempietto* or little temple, to house the *Volto Santo* and I must say, like Bernini's *baldacchino* that covers the altar in St Peter's in Rome and which I think hideous, I don't care for this at all either, however heretical such a view may be about Lucca's favourite son and this, his masterpiece.

It looks so big and heavy with its sturdy Corinthian columns, its ornately tiled roof, the porphyry on the base, its solid sides and it is certainly not helped by the metal grilles that give it the appearance of a prison cell through which you can see, but certainly not touch, Lucca's most revered relic. I suspect the *tempietto* would not look half so bad if it were outside in the garden of some stately home, like some sort of fancy gazebo, but in here, in the dim light, it looks extremely depressing to say the least.

If that is heretical, wait till you read this. (Please don't let me be struck down!) I have even less of a favourable opinion of the sacred relic itself, the best that Lucca can offer, and remember that Lucca was chosen out of the whole of Italy, though of course, Italy as such, was not even a glint in the eye of Garibaldi's ancestors back then. So this is the face of Christ is it? Carved by Nicodemus himself, was it? Well, no, not exactly.

For a start, the legend goes that Nicodemus, after having completed the body of Christ, had a bit of a nap. It did worry me somewhat, I have to confess, while it was all very well to say that Nicodemus, having more than a nodding acquaintance with Christ so to speak, and who would have recognised Him like a brother if he had happened to pass Him on the street – it doesn't necessarily mean he could carve His exact likeness out of the trunk of a cedar of Lebanon any more than I could. So, I am a bit relieved to learn that after his forty winks, he woke up to find that the face had been carved for him by – you'll never guess… That's right – angels!

Now they may know how to bake angel cakes for Zita, but I would have expected angels to be better at carving than this. I for one, on this evidence, would not let them anywhere near the Sunday joint. Or maybe Christ was not that handsome a bloke – after all, all those images we see of Him in art are just someone's idea of what He looked like, and I will say this for the *Volto Santo,* it probably is a lot nearer to showing His actual skin colour than those images with the pale, white skin and the red hair that you see so often depicted in Western art. How many people like that would you expect to see in the Middle East, before cheap air travel made it possible for the Scots to get there? And even then, their pale skin would not have been the dominant characteristic and their children, the fruit of all those ladies they impregnated who had found their freckles irresistible, would have been on the darker shade of pale.

So, if the skin colour is right, then maybe the face is too. Well the hair colour is certainly right, black as the ace of spades, but Christ, being about 32 or so, and with all His worries, you might have expected a little greying about the temples, but perhaps not. But what I notice first, what anyone would, is not the brown skin, nor the hair, luxuriant black growth though it may be, nor the bushy black beard – but the eyes, which seem to be popping out of his head. If I were a medical man, (which I am not) I would say that those horribly bulging protuberances suggest He has a problem with His thyroids. I am not quite sure if it is a symptom of the over or the underactive, but that is what it looks like to me. Or maybe, (and it wouldn't surprise me in the least) your eyes *would* tend to go pop when beastly Romans drove six-inch spikes through your hands and feet.

A couple of more things need to be said. Firstly, the cross on which the carving is hung (or should that be nailed?) is a later addition, though it is true that that must have been the intention of the original artist, whether or not that was old Nick, for the head is protruding forward from the shoulders and slightly downwards, suggesting it was designed to be viewed in an upright position, from below.

Secondly, and be prepared for a shock – this is *not the original carved by Nicodemus and friends*! I'm not sure how they know exactly, carbon dating, or the expert testimony of art historians, or just plain scepticism, but this carving is a mere eight centuries old! That *may* sound old, but it is a mere blink of the eye compared to when Nicodemus was a man and carved his masterpiece. After his death, the *Volto Santo* disappeared for centuries until Bishop Gualfredo, who was visiting the Holy Land, had a dream in which its location, in a cave, was revealed to him. The rest you know.

That is one disappearance, and a mystery solved, but there is no mystery to the second disappearance, or rather there is, as you will see. But first you have to understand just what an object of reverence the *Volto Santo* was in medieval times (and still is today for a great many Lucchese). It was known widely throughout Europe and people regularly invoked it in prayer. For instance, the second king of England, William Rufus, or

William the Red, because of his complexion, not the colour of his hair, and who was rather inclined to swearing oaths (as medieval folks were prone to do, being good Catholics all) regularly used to swear by the Holy Face of Lucca.

Anyway, in the extremely superstitious 8th century, and after all, what is religion but a form of superstition – people wanted to own a piece of this venerated relic and, so it is told, the original *Volto Santo* disappeared, bit by bit, splinter by splinter, until nothing was left.

Well, you can believe that if you like, and you may call me naïve if you want, but I really don't believe that religious people would do a thing like that because they are good people, are they not? I'm not religious, but I don't steal because my mum taught me not to, because it is bad. But religious people have another reason not to: they would go to hell if they did, wouldn't they?

Not half would they steal, because in those days they were really, really superstitious, and if a little bit of the *Volto Santo* could help them to procure whatever was vitally important to them at the time, such as curing a disease or making the object of their desire fall in love with them – why not just nick a little bit of the *Volto Santo*? If a splinter might work a miracle, just think what a bigger chunk might achieve – you might even become a medieval babe magnet.

So that is how the *Volto Santo* disappeared for the second time. But the mystery to me is this: you might have thought, might you not, that those in charge of this Wonder of the World, might just have noticed that it was beginning to fade away before their eyes and might have put a stop to it before there was nothing left?

No wonder then that this 13th century copy is locked up the way it is today. They are taking no chances with today's secular society.

CHAPTER NINETEEN:
A LITTLE LIGHT SHOPPING

The *Volto Santo* it was, by removing itself from San Frediano to San Martino, provided a sign that it should be the Duomo in preference to any other church. Remember of course, that this was long before the present churches were built. And I too have now definitely decided that I prefer the Duomo to San Michele.

I have arrived at this conclusion because on coming round to the rear of the Duomo, I see that it too has a gallery of famous faces, or at least the ones who got ahead in their day. Being not so high up as they are in San Michele, it is possible to see how lifelike they are and they look even more intriguing when I see the individual features through the zoom lens of my camera, in the absence of the much-missed binoculars.

From here we can go on the wall. Iona is in need of her drug again and out of all the cafés in Lucca, there is one that deserves to be patronised more than any other - the supplier of brown paper and the words *nastro adesivo grande*, By Appointment to The Lunatic in Lucca.

But when we get there, to my disappointment, neither the waitress or the boss appears to be on duty, so as far as anyone could tell, we could just be any ordinary couple of tourists, even if one of them is wearing a rather eccentric-looking hat.

So there we are, Iona with her americano and I with a new kind of beer, writing up the notes as usual, when I am not unduly surprised to spot Dinah and Rod coming through the piazza, obviously heading towards San Frediano. Simultaneously, they catch sight of us and come over to hear the latest in the case saga. That has to be the reason, because that is the first question they ask, even if it may merely be out of politeness rather than a burning desire to be put out of their suspense.

Spotting Iona's fleece with the logo of the Linlithgow Jazz Club on it, (which she has had to put on again, for it has turned rather chilly after the sunny start to the day) they divulge, by an amazing coincidence, that that is where they come from and they are getting married in St Michael's in the summer. What a small world! Since it is not a very big place and Iona goes there quite regularly, I would not be at all surprised if she were to bump into them again there. Stranger things have happened.

In answer to my question, they report that their meal last night was only average and if they are not already glad that their short break has been enlivened by having met such an interesting person as me, then they should be, because not only do I recommend the Baralla, but also I insist they go into San Frediano and, with careful directions, tell them precisely where St Zita is to be found.

"You know, not everyone is as weird as you," remarks Iona after they have left.

"Why, what have I done wrong now?"

"Not everyone is as mad keen on seeing the shrivelled-up corpse of an old woman as you, you know."

Strange but true. I remember how in St Peter's neither she, nor the friends we had made on that trip, expressed the slightest curiosity in seeing Pope John XXIII and he was in very good condition indeed, all dressed up in red and ermine and who would not have looked out of place in that shop window with Olive.

"You're right," I reply. "There *are* some very odd people about."

To this she makes no comment, but maybe that is because the wind that had been getting progressively stronger, suddenly produces a gust that sets the tablecloths flapping wildly and threatens to make the canvas canopies over the tables take to the air. It is time to go. The sky is like an ugly bruise and we are miles from the hotel and while Iona has nothing waterproof at all, I wouldn't care to put my jacket to the test.

The plan had been to go to the Guinigi Tower, which is to Lucca as the Leaning Tower is to Pisa. It looks dilapidated because of the trees growing at the top like weeds, but in actual fact they are holm oak trees which were planted there on purpose to provide shade. It is pretty much in the centre of town and from the top there should be a bird's eye view of all those tiled roofs and those narrow streets meandering their way between them. But in view of the imminent rain, it seems better to postpone the tower to another day. Plenty of time. After all, this is just our second day, but it won't be tomorrow as we intend to revisit that other tower, probably the most famous one on the planet, the one in Pisa.

But as we make our way to the hotel, the squall that had threatened so much, fails to produce anything more than a few scarcely noticeable drops of rain and the wind dies down just as suddenly as it had arisen, leaving the sky clear and blue again. St Michael's wings are as still as the rest of the statue, I happen to notice, as we pass through the piazza, but by this time, Iona is too tired to return to the tower, so we decide to do some shopping instead.

Of course you will have instantly realised what a lie that is. I did not decide anything and if I had, it would certainly not have been to go shopping. You're right: it is Iona who made the decision, attracted by the leather bags that hang like haemorrhoids just about everywhere on the Via Paolino. It doesn't seem to matter which shop you go to, they all seem to stock the same bags and are the same price for the same size and style. She knows what she likes, but she doesn't know whether she should get this style or that, in that colour or this. Good grief, she's even asking me for my opinion, as if I knew anything on the subject.

Well, since she's asking, I tell her I don't think she needs one at all. Hasn't she already got one, if not two, or three even? And it's not as if any of them is worn out is it? But that is not the sort of advice she wants to hear; in fact she rather despises it, pointing out that they are not the same as these and you could not possibly get this quality of bag at this sort of price back home. Oh is that a fact? €18 or €23, depending. She rather likes this dark one. What do I think? What do I know about women's bags? If I knew anything about bags, I would not have picked up Carla's would I? Surreptitiously, I look at the price tag.

"It's horrible!" I tell her. "This one is much nicer."

And without a word of a lie, so it is. It is a much lighter colour, more natural-looking and lighter on my pocket too, as it happens to be a mere €18. We are all pleased: the shopkeeper who has made a sale; the wife who has bought something; and the husband who has got off with damage limitation to his wallet.

Until such time as we get our case back, there are two other things that would contribute to Iona's feeling of wellbeing. The first would be some more mascara for the one we had paid for but somehow inexplicably lost and the second, which would give her even greater pleasure than that is if she didn't have to go around with a tramp all day – if I would shave that awful fuzz off my face. The first seems achievable, just as soon as we can find the Upim store and at a time when it is not closed, but I am reluctant to buy a new razor when I will be reacquainted with my own tomorrow.

But as it so happens, Iona's prayers are answered when we happen to find a €1 shop. Now *that* is my kind of shop! €1 won't break the bank and I'll probably get a whole packet of them for that price. It could be an investment in fact.

But although we find the mascara relatively easily amongst this Aladdin's cave of wonderful things you can buy for that princely sum, the razor blades prove impossible to track down.

I conclude that they must not stock them but Iona is convinced they must be in here somewhere. The only thing to do is ask.

"Er…scusi do you happen to have something to…" and here I screw up my face and make an upward scraping motion meant to convey the idea that I am shaving.

"Razors? You mean razors?"

I stand amazed, wishing I had gone a little nearer and not demonstrated to everyone within hearing range, which is to say everyone in the shop, that I didn't know a simple word like "razor." But that is not what I find so astonishing and it is not because of the colour of her hair either, though being vermillion, it does have the power to transfix. No, it is her accent that I find so surprising.

"I know I've got them here somewhere," she says and I follow her about as she searches shelf after shelf. "They're in a blue packet," she adds helpfully.

"You're a long way from home."

"Yes."

"And where was home originally?" I prompt.

"Canada."

"Really! That's what I thought! What part of Canada?"

"Near Toronto."

"Is that a fact! I have a couple of friends near Toronto. Burlington and Norwood, near Petersburg," I inform her, giving the latter its transatlantic pronunciation.

It would be too much of a coincidence if she came from either of those places. You can travel for a whole day just in Ontario alone and never get out of the place. And sure enough, they don't seem to mean anything special to her.

"How long have you been here?"

"In Italy – thirty years. I came to do an art course and never left."

"Thirty years! You've certainly not lost any of your accent."

There is no telling how long this interview might have gone on had she not had to go and serve someone.

"They are definitely here somewhere," she says as a parting shot. "Keep looking!"

"For heaven's sake! Have you got to know *everything* about *everybody*?" La Belle Dame Sans Merci chastises me. "It's a wonder you didn't ask her what course she was doing and how many marks she got. Your mother was right!" she concludes feelingly.

I know what she means. My mother was often driven to distraction by my questions and on such occasions could be heard to remark: "That's enough! I am not answering any more questions! You always want to know the far end of a fart!" For a convent-educated girl, I thought that quite shocking. I never thought that nuns would do such a thing, let alone admit it.

Eventually we do manage to track down the elusive razors and I'm sure my new Canadian friend is very grateful for the information when I show her where they are to be found, just as I am sure Iona will be delighted when I put one of them to use later. But in the meantime, I am going back to see my new German friend, Beate. I would like to know where the nearest supermarket is because it is always interesting to walk round foreign supermarkets and see the sort of things they sell that we don't have back home. Besides, they are bound to have the necessities of life, such as wine and other alcoholic beverages. Besides, she will be interested to hear the latest in the bag saga – which indeed she is.

If we go out the Porta San Donato to our right, we will come to Esselunga on the Viale Carlo Del Prete. No, it's not that far Beate assures us, though it does look a long way on the map she gives us but she also shows us how we can take a short cut back to the hotel from there without having to come all the way back again.

It does seem a long way to us however, and an even longer way back burdened down with our purchases, but it is amazing how sustaining the thought of a stiff gin and tonic can be. It is dark now and following Beate's directions and in a further bit of lunacy, we find ourselves walking along the Viale Del Prete, otherwise known as the Wall of Death, not on the pavement mind you, for none exists at this side of the road, but actually sharing the road with juggernauts as they thunder past us just inches away.

This was definitely not what Beate had intended. At the other side of the road, I had seen what I had thought were the mansions at the end of our street and took the chance, when there was a gap in this almost ceaseless tide of traffic, to cross over. Only the mansions turned out to be funerary monuments and if we didn't get off this road pretty damn quick, that is precisely what we will be needing.

I wouldn't mind coming back here in daylight though, as any cemetery with tombs the size of houses has to be worth investigating.

CHAPTER TWENTY: STUFFED

The previous occupant of the room, some saint or other, had made ice cubes, so we can enjoy a nice cold gin and tonic, superior by far to the warm variety which, until I make my own ice, I normally have to make do with in hotel bedrooms since an over-zealous maid, probably called Zita, has emptied the ice tray.

It is very nice to take the weight of one's feet, nibble some *arachidi* or peanuts, and write up my notes. Not so satisfactory however, for Iona, as she is sorely missing her sewing. Furthermore, she has finished the book she was reading on the plane and the rest of her travelling library is, of course, in the case. Fortunately, another saint had left a book lying about in the communal room next to us and although it would not be a natural first choice of reading material for her, at least it is in English and it does give her something to read – and it does save my life for the second time that evening after the failed suicide attempt of walking along the Vialle Del Prete, this time from being strangled by idle hands.

Since neither of these methods had procured my premature demise, after my shower, and before the first gin, let me state that absolutely, so there can be no confusion about it – I tried my best to cut my throat. It wasn't depression – it could never be that with the gin to look forward to. No, it's just that when I use a new razor for the first time, it tends to make me bleed. My skin, like the rest of me, is very sensitive. So, with a new blade, I might expect a bit of bleeding anyway but without a brush to apply the soap, and the whiskers being a bit longer and thicker than normal, it has resulted rather painfully in rather more of the red stuff than usual. More than that, it proves particularly difficult to stop. The only way is to stick pabby paper on the lacerations. My throat and chin look like a barber's pole when I finally emerge from the bathroom and Iona can't help but laugh out loud at my appearance.

I am not offended. I like to make her happy and if it takes cutting my throat to ribbons to do so, so be it. But after this loss of life's precious elixir, like a blood donor, I need some restorative refreshment and I pour myself a gin. Iona would probably call it a treble if she could have seen it before I added the tonic, but I cunningly manoeuvred my body between her and the bottle while I performed this operation. Having said that, if she hadn't realised what I was up to, I was probably deceiving no-one but myself.

"Don't eat too many nuts," she advises, as I settle myself on the bed with my notes and the nuts within handy reach.

I hear what she is saying, and I can also hear what she is *not* saying. She doesn't want to be stuck in here all night with a book she is not particularly interested in. She wants to go out for a meal, wants some stimulation, whereas I am perfectly content here, with my food and drink. She knows I know that peanuts contain more protein than steak and the bottle of wine I had bought (mercifully they sell them with screw tops these days, for people who have left their corkscrew in their luggage) would be a very acceptable way of washing them down, after the apéritifs. And the grapes will provide one of the five essential fruit and veg that the nanny state is always bleating on about. Actually all five in my case if Iona has only one glass and I have the other five which means that not only will I be much healthier than her, and I mention this only as a brief aside – we could dine in for less than €10 for both of us, better even than Marks & Spencer's *Dine in for £20* promotion. Well, admittedly that is a bit of an exaggeration but in the absence of any M&S stores here, this is about as good (and as cheap) as it gets. This is all the food I need and I would be perfectly happy to spend the entire evening here, especially if I were allowed a little bit of popular culture and could catch one of those TV programmes where bored Italian housewives take their clothes off, or so I have heard.

There is fat chance of that however, and after the gin is finished and after I have peeled the toilet paper off my face – for she is definitely not going out with me "looking like that" we set off in search of what she calls "proper food."

Once again there is no sign of Gisele, nor any other receptionist for that matter. Perhaps there is some truth in the reviews I had read about the hotel after all. It is rather disappointing to note that the little plant I had bought her in thanks for her help is on the desk still, as is the card I had left with it, so she would know who it was from. There is an office right by the entrance and I thought she might have at least moved it in there even if she had not taken it home with her. We had combed the streets looking for flowers yesterday after our visit to Upim and this little cyclamen, already gift-wrapped in shiny red paper was the best we could find. I stick my finger in the top. Quite dry. If it doesn't get a drink soon, it will die. I have often found myself suffering from the same predicament.

And that's how Iona feels quite a while later, except in her case it is food she is lacking. Fuelled up on gin and peanuts, when we arrive at the rustic restaurant we both thought we were making for on the Via Paolino, I have a modest change of plan to propose.

"How about trying to find that restaurant Dinah and Rod went to?

"Why? Why do you want to go there?" Iona asks suspiciously.

"Well, just to see what we think of it. They must have liked the look of it. Maybe we will like it, even if they didn't particularly. Maybe it's got a bit of ambience about it or something."

"We don't even know its name or where it is."

"I know, but it should be easy to find if we go along the Via Fillungo to where we met them, then it should be down one of the streets to the left."

"You're not really hungry are you?"

How does she do it? I know for a fact that my father was not a glazier, but she can see through me as if I were made of glass.

"I told you not to eat so many peanuts, didn't I?"

There is nothing I can say to that, so I don't. Guilty as charged. But in my defence, she just doesn't see the world in the same way as I do, and there is no point in pointing out that if she had eaten as many nuts as me, and if it had been washed down with a bottle of the blushful Hippocrene, we might, in all probability, be consummating Lucca at this very moment, having an early night, ready and refreshed to enjoy the delights of Pisa tomorrow, instead of wasting all that energy by tramping all the way up here, just to spend more money on food we wouldn't have needed, if she had chosen the *menú del día chez nous*, so to speak, if I may mix my languages.

I dare not look her in the eye but study the flagstones on the street instead. It's amazing how interesting they are! Each one is different. I wonder how many tourists to Lucca have noticed this fascinating fact, even the Lucchese themselves, and that there are strange hieroglyphics on every other flag, like the marks medieval masons used to carve on certain stones when they were building the cathedrals, like a sort of signature.

"Oh, all right then! But I'm warning you now, I don't want to spend all night looking for it! I am hungry even if you are not!" And off she sets so abruptly on the quest, I have to run to catch her up like a little puppy dog.

But when we get to the Via Fillungo neither of us can agree where it was precisely we had met Dinah and Rod and so the restaurant could be on any of the streets off to the left, or the right, depending on your point of view. We are both agreed however, it was nearer the amphitheatre end than where it meets the Santa Croce. But after trying the most likely looking street without success and finding ourselves instead in an ill-lit backstreet amidst a maze of others and again after choosing the most promising, we come again to the Via Fillungo, we have to admit that we haven't a hope in hell of finding it.

We know there are some restaurants in the amphitheatre but that is a long way back, and not coming across any other eating places, we end up where we started in the beginning. Predictably, Iona is not in the best of moods. She is my Chinese wife, Scow Ling, which is a few degrees worse than my German wife, Frau Ning. It wasn't all wasted time though, I point out. I believe I could eat a little something now I tell her.

"Well that's bully for you! My stomach thinks my throat is cut!"

I suppose I can take the credit for making her come out with that particular expression.

Back where we started, there is no difficulty in getting a table, really more of a bench. It is at the rear and this time it really is like Jack Horner because it is right in the back corner. Furthermore, I would call it the plum position in the restaurant as from here I can see every table in the place.

Unfortunately, there is no chance of overhearing any conversations this time. Next to us is the dresser where the waiter cuts the bread with the dexterity of a surgeon, but one hopes, the latter uses a great deal less speed. It's not like any bread I have seen before: crusty and square and fairly flat. Iona informs me it is *focaccia*. This done, he places it in a basket, all done without so much a naked finger being anywhere near it and places it in front of us, poised to take our drinks order and like a good boy scout, I am prepared.

It is always one of the pleasures of being in Italy to eat the bread accompanied with the wine while the main course is being prepared and so it is important to make the decision about the food as speedily as possible, so a quick read-through of the menu is necessary in order to see whether the red or white would be more appropriate. There is no doubt as to whether it will be a half-litre or a litre. Iona leaves the decision of colour to me. I think it will be the red tonight. And to make it go further, and since it seems to be an Italian custom, I order a litre of sparkling water to go with it.

That important mission accomplished, it is time to get down to studying the menu with serious intent. What had attracted us the night before no longer seems so appealing, at least to me, once the boar and the rabbit have been removed. After much thought, for starters, I decide to have tomato and basil soup with bread, while Iona has chosen a different kind of soup, a Lucchese speciality. As a main course, I have settled on the "filled beef in red wine" while Iona, commendably, still in a while-in-Lucca theme, is going to have meatballs à la Lucchese.

"You won't like it," the waiter, who is still some time off his thirtieth birthday, advises me, his pen hovering, but not prepared to commit itself to paper. "It is very bloody."

He is absolutely right. I wouldn't like it, if it is as bloody as he says, but how did he know I wouldn't? Normally it is the duty of the waiter to ask you how you want your meat cooked; not his job to tell you not to touch it with a bargepole. Had he asked, I would normally have said "medium" but I know that on the continent, that means no more than it has been wafted over a medium heat for a few seconds, so I would have said "well done."

"Oh, is it? All right!" is what I hear myself saying instead.

Why did I say that? Why didn't I ask to have it the way I want it? Or even better, tell him that's how I want it done. I may not be the master at home, but surely here, I am? I am paying his wages after all. I suppose it was a combination of shock and being so used to doing what I am told that it was just an instinctive reaction.

"I'll need some time to think. You'd better come back later." There. That's telling him.

Before he goes, the waiter takes away the nearly empty basket of bread and to my delight, refills it. This is the moment when I should have come out, told him I am a man of simple tastes. Like Omar Khayyám, I'd be perfectly happy with the wine and bread, in that order, and if the book of verse were not for dessert, then that wouldn't worry me too much.

Of course, as an ex-teacher of English, I am not averse to the occasional poem now and again, but it would be a bit rude to stick one's head into a book when dining out with the love of one's life, or one's wife even. As a matter of fact, if she, the "thou" of Omar's poem had not been there, more *focaccia* and more wine is what I would certainly have ordered – if the waiter had let me. Iona would certainly have not, which is a great pity. Since a carafe of wine here is only €8, we could have dined out for €20 between us, which, for two litres of wine and the best bread on the planet, has to be the best bargain in Lucca.

This bread really is delicious. I can't leave it alone.

"It's all right," I explain to Iona when she attempts to paralyse my hand with a Gorgon stare. "I won't eat the bread that comes with the soup."

But when it comes, the bread, like I am very often, is actually in the soup. And not in lumps that you can take out either, but part and parcel of it – the thickest soup in Italy. I hadn't been too sure about it but I am glad I had chosen it now – it's not like any basil and tomato soup I have ever eaten before. Iona's soup, on the other hand, turns out to be thin and watery with bits of cereal, probably barley, floating in it, or rather, lying dead at the bottom.

Something rather strange is happening in this restaurant. The sausage and beans I had chosen for my second course, although it did not sound too inspiring, turns out to be delicious, and Iona's meatballs, though tasty, like her soup, are not nearly so nice as my mine. I am unaccustomed to making correct decisions like this, even if I did have the help of the waiter.

Both meals are very filling. Well, you might expect me to say that considering I wasn't very hungry in the first place and after all the bread I had eaten, but the proof of the pudding lies in the eating – so runs the adage, but the proof of how filling the meals have been lies in Iona's non-eating of the pudding. This is unprecedented. When choosing a restaurant, Iona normally reads the menu backwards, from the sweet to starter. But now, despite her thin soup and having consumed much less of the bread than me, she declares she is unfit for what she sees as the most important course. You certainly know you have been fed when you have been here – the very antidote to nouvelle cuisine – a mouthful of food prettily arranged on the plate to tempt the eye but which leaves your stomach rumbling and your husband grumbling when the bill comes – if you are married to Iona anyway.

And although I do not expect our bill to be of such eye-watering proportions as that, nevertheless it still comes as a shock – €46.27. Why that is more than last night, considering we had, or Iona had, a sweet, and then there was the extra side plate, to say nothing of everything costing just a little bit more than here. There has to be some mistake.

Not according to the waiter.

"No, no, signore, the bill is correct." And patiently he takes me through it. It is a bit difficult to follow, as I can't read what he has written. It appears to have been written in early Italian, the sort of Italian that a six-year-old would write. Everything accounted for and added up correctly. Maybe it is because of all that bread. But even another coperto couldn't account for the discrepancy between what I expected to pay and what I am being asked to pay. I could be persuaded that I was wrong – but when Iona feels there is something wrong too, then I know I must be right because she always is.

"No, it's still not right," I insist. "Something is wrong."

"Momento." And he busies away to see the manager. I can see it all from where I am, like watching a silent movie or the TV with the sound turned off. I hope it does not turn out to have scenes of a violent nature. After all, it is well after the 9 pm watershed now.

The manager, who has better things to do than deal with troublesome customers who can't count, such as serving drinks behind the bar and chatting to his mates, is now abandoning his bailiwick and advancing at a fearsome pace, looking swarthy and grimly determined. I don't go around picking fights with people at the best of times, but say I did, he is definitely not the sort of bloke I would choose to start one with – but it may be too late, I already have. Biceps like a heavyweight boxer, hair in a ponytail and the tattooed dagger on his forearm all have the power to delicately suggest to me before he opens his mouth that I might be persuaded that I have been in error after all and for all the trouble and hassle caused, it would be appropriate to leave a larger tip than usual.

He is a man who means business – a real big bruiser, determined to spend as little time as possible sorting me out. He comes armed with the waiter's pad in one hand and a blank one of his own in the other. He sits down at the opposite end of Iona's bench, facing me. His acolyte, our waiter, hovers at the end of the table.

Coperto 2 X; soups as starters, ditto; two main meals, this price and that price; one litre wine; one litre sparkling water. The pencil flies over the page. It's a matter of simple addition. With a flourish, he underlines his total and passes his hieroglyphs across the table to me: €38.27. All quite simple really. His expression says: "argue with that if you dare."

Of course I wouldn't dare to, nor even presume to. With relief that this is not going to deteriorate into another humiliating scene with me crawling out of here with my tail between my legs like a mongrel cur, rather than any sense of elation or sense of one-upmanship at being proved right, I merely wordlessly present my copy of the bill for his inspection – the one with the €8 excess. QED.

His eyes fairly bulge. In fact, I am convinced it is only because they are bulging so much that that prevents them from disappearing into the recesses of his cranium where they would have come to a sickeningly splattering stop against the hard bone.

Profuse apologies. The mystery is explained. We have been charged for two litres of wine. The waiter had been reading my mind again but I had only been thinking of ordering another one. A happy ending. That's what most people like, and so do I – on this occasion at least.

Having paid the new, improved bill, it is time to go. Coats on, hat on, I am even counting out a tip, which just goes to show you how much of an incurable wimp I am. My soup had been too cold and I had had to send it back. But catching the eye of the waiter in the first place, then waiting while it was heated up and brought back, then waiting again while it cooled down to a temperature I could eat it, all took time. Iona had finished her soup long by the time I could begin mine. Then there was the trouble with the bill. And for this, like Shylock, I should pay them this much moneys? But nevertheless, this I am still prepared to do, even if they do not seek it, nor, I would imagine, expect to receive it.

Then the surprise. Had I not been sorting out the tip, it might have been too late. The surprise comes in the form of the waiter bearing gifts – two liqueur glasses containing a yellow liquid. I haven't spent years travelling in Italy not to know what this is. It is limoncello, Italy's best method of disposing of its lemon mountain, and which just happens to be Iona's favourite fruit. (No comment.)

I had noticed earlier, with a little bit of jealousy I must confess, the two diners at the bench in front of us, two men leisurely finishing off their meal with a glass each of the delicious nectar. By contrast, the young couple across from them, sharing a pizza, looked rather awkward, as if this could be their first date. They would certainly not be having the liqueur and neither would we, but for this unexpected windfall. Since it had not occurred to me to indulge myself in this way, I had not checked to see what it might cost, but I would have thought for both of us, certainly not less than €5.

And so we remove our outer garments again. Hat doffed in respect. Liqueurs can't be hurried. And then comes the next surprise. It is ice-cold – and it is extra delicious. This is a new experience. We had had it in Sorrento and had it in Sicily but never had it cold before. And what a difference it makes! It is nothing less than an epiphany.

So that's what I have been doing wrong all this time! When I bought a bottle of it in Sicily I was convinced I was on to a sure thing. Iona's favourite flavour mixed with 20% proof alcohol could not fail. But when I got the investment home, there it remained, an ornament in the drinks cabinet, along with various other alleged aphrodisiacs from other holiday destinations such as Crete and Corfu.

Whoever would have thought that to arouse that red-hot passion, one should first reduce the limoncello to subzero temperatures, or just about? I am mad to think of it, but methinks a trip down to Esselunga again and a bottle of the yellow elixir rapidly cooled in the freezer compartment, might work wonders for the consummation of Lucca.

CHAPTER TWENTY-ONE:
TO PISA AND THE SINÓPIE

Breakfast at the Scilla as usual and then to the bus station for the 9.32 to Pisa. Why not 9.30? But I like the way timetables do that and it is a practice I have copied when I am arranging to meet people – never on the hour or the half-hour or the quarter-past or quarter-to, but for example, 9.02 or 9.34 and so on. It seems to me these are neglected times and it is high time people used them more often.

We know where the bus station is of course, but finding the bus to Pisa is a bit more problematic. I have not had a happy relationship in the past with Italian buses and it looks as if this not going be any different. Admittedly, the Italians have not yet single-handedly developed a rocket capable of putting a man on the moon, but you might have thought it within their capabilities to have thought of putting up bus stops with the destinations written on them so travellers would know where to queue. It beats having to walk round each and every bus looking for a sign on the front. From this exercise, I would deduce most appear to be going nowhere. It seems their destinations are a closely guarded secret only to be revealed just before departure. Which, out of all these buses is ours? What if we don't spot it in time? On the other hand, maybe it is not even here yet.

"Pisa?" I ask of one driver about to board his bus.

He shakes his head. Wherever else he is going, he is definitely not going there. Perhaps on a mystery tour?

"Dove?" I am so glad this is one of the six words of Italian I learned.

By way of an answer, he points in a careless way to somewhere over his shoulder. That's very helpful, I must say. If he is to be believed, it narrows our target down to only half the number of buses now. It is getting perilously close to departure and Iona is getting increasingly worried.

Seeing a queue beginning to form, I ask the person at the back, "Pisa?"

"Behind," she answers with a gesture to an empty space behind her. How did she know to respond in English when I had spoken to her in Italian, albeit a little briefly?

"Grazie."

I am not precisely clear if she was telling me to get behind her, like Satan, and not pester her, or whether she means the bus would appear behind the bus she was about to board. If so, it doesn't have much time to do so. Iona, in the meantime, getting increasingly frantic, has set off on an investigation of the buses again. She, for one, plainly does not believe what the bus driver signed.

Just then a bus arrives, a driver alights and goes into the office from where one or two people emerge and then take up a stance by the open door of the bus. This looks as if it might be it.

"Pisa?" I ask one of them. He looks like he may be a student.

"Sì. Sì."

Well, thank God for that! At last! But where is Iona? The Lord giveth and the Lord taketh away. Good God, she is away over there! I would wave madly at her, but that wouldn't do any good as she has her back to me. I would shout but I feel an odd sort of reluctance to draw attention to myself in this way. Fortunately, in the days of my youth I learned how to whistle using my fingers and I now put this skill into practice. You can almost see her ears prick up like a collie's, then she stops and turns and now I can semaphore for her to come to heel. I'll say this for her. She is obedient.

Just as I am boarding the bus, a fat little woman rushes up and breathlessly asks me if this is the right bus for Viareggio.

At least I presume that is what she was asking, but truth to tell, the only word I recognised was "Viarregio" plus the intonation which marked it out as a question.

"No, Pisa e aeroporto."

"Grazie," and she hurries off, not having the remotest idea that she had been conversing with a boy from the boondocks of Banff or the lunatic of Lucca. Whichever way you choose to look at it, I am the last person on whose word she should put an absolute trust in a matter of this sort.

"Pisa?" I ask the driver, just to make sure, and it is more reassuring still to see, as we come to a roundabout, the sign to Pisa, and the road to which we diligently follow.

Time to sit back and relax, enjoy the scenery, at least once we get out of the suburbs. It is a fertile valley with apples the size of oranges and orange nets spread beneath the olive trees to catch this year's crop. The bus, which had begun with only four of us, is now quite full, the majority of passengers apparently students living at home instead of enjoying student life in the big city, due no doubt, more to reasons of economy than a desire to be at home, though perhaps, since this is Italy, they are still tied to the matriarchal apron strings, especially the boys.

Gradually, we are beginning to climb out of the valley, and then plunging into a tunnel, we burst out the other side into bright sunshine from the dullness on our side of the mountain. The trees seem on fire as the evaporating moisture rises like smoke from the warming heat of the sun, and just for a moment, through the trees, we can see a glimpse of Pisa in the distance, shimmering like a mirage on a plain so wide and vast that you could imagine it going on for infinity.

In a series of looping bends we descend to the valley floor and lose sight of Pisa. We know we must be getting near however when first we see the city walls – such puny things compared to Lucca's, though they do have crenellations – and even nearer still, when we see some street vendors in twos and threes all heading in the same direction. Forewarned by this, it nevertheless takes us by surprise when the bus stops and we recognise the Baptistery first of all, its lemon-squeezer roof with its orange tiles peeping above the walls, then the gates, through which we can see the green sward of the Campo dei Miracoli. Help, we have arrived! Beate had told us that the bus would drop us right outside but I didn't expect it to be this near! Last time we had to walk for miles from where we had been dropped off.

Hurriedly, I push my feet into my shoes again and one heel still not in properly, hobble down the aisle after Iona. The bus driver, seeing her coming, lets out his clutch again and like Aladdin, commands the door, which was about to close, to remain open.

We find ourselves stepping over a miniature fleet of cars whose doors can open and shut at the whim of the drivers who, like our bus driver, are controlling them remotely, only in their case from a little black box. Likewise, platoons of crawling commandos are wearing their elbows and knees out on the flagstones, nursing their rifles. These are the vendors and these their hugely resistible merchandice. Or if neither of these appeals, you can buy a little tripod for your camera or what about another handbag, or perhaps a watch?

Up to the left, we can see the stalls we had passed as we came into the Campo the last time and where we had bought our son the worst pair of underpants in the world – a photograph of Michelangelo's *David's* nether regions, front and back, in fetching shades of brown – dark brown at the seat and gradually getting lighter the further away from the accident zone.

Then going into the Campo dei Miracoli itself, much less busy than before, we recognise the phalanx of stalls where, amongst other wondrous souvenirs that unfortunately, I am unable to describe as it would contravene the laws of good taste, we had bought the miniature, glow-in-the-dark, lilac Leaning

Tower of Pisa for our daughter. We resist the temptation to make any further purchases on this occasion, however. A decision which has nothing at all to do with the big A frame boards that warn, in several languages both within and beyond my ken, that it is an offence to buy any imitation goods, punishable by a €1000 fine. To *buy*, mind you – not sell! I never wanted a Gucci handbag anyway and it's not just sour grapes that make me say that. Mind you, having said that, I *could* do with a new false Rolex that some person without a father once relieved me of when I was at the gym. He no doubt mistook it for the real thing, when actually the most expensive thing about it was the cost of a replacement battery.

There is a moral to this tale, and it is not on the perils of possessing flashy jewellery, though I have heard of at least one case where someone was murdered for their false Rolex. My point is that it proves the dangers of taking exercise.

Entrance tickets for all the attractions on the Campo are on sale in the Museo delle Sinópie. On the wall inside, the tickets are listed by price according to the variety of combinations on offer. We decide on the €8 combo that will allow us entrance to the Sinópie itself, the Baptistery, the Campo Santo and the Museo dell'Opera del Duomo. The Duomo is free. We don't feel any inclination to climb the Leaning Tower. You need a separate ticket for that and there will probably be a big queue in any case. Having said that however, there is only one couple ahead of us as we queue up to buy the combo ticket – a bargain at double the price.

The sinópie, if you don't already know, are the preliminary sketches beneath a fresco. Actually they are the most important part. If you were to ask how many people it takes to write a book, most people would correctly answer one, usually. And if you were to ask the same people how many it takes to create a painting, they would probably give the same answer, only this time they would be less correct - the Old Masters were always getting the apprentices to do the colouring in. The initial designs and details are the thing. And that's just what the sinópie were and that's just about all that was left of the frescos that adorned the Campo Santo, or cemetery, after they were tragically burned to a frazzle when Allied incendiary bombs unfortunately rained down on it in 1944.

Before we go in to see these pale shadows of the colourful frescos however, as if to whet the appetite, there is a 3D film of the Campo Santo which, in order to view in 3D, you have to make an exhibition of yourself by wearing those silly paper spectacles with the plastic lenses. There are some headphones so you can listen to the commentary in the language of your choice. And we wouldn't have had a snowball's chance in hell of doing this if we had been here at the height of summer, or at any time in the summer for that matter. Put it this way: let's imagine Jesus had wanted to borrow them to teach his disciples – someone would have had to go without, Judas probably, because there are less than a dozen of them.

It also soon becomes apparent that it was a mistake to come in here. There is only one other couple here, in all the vastness of the two floors of this place, a former hospital. This is for the seriously siniópic and definitely not for the even mildly myopic. Not only are they all around the walls, but they have stored even more siniópe in upright sliding racks that you can draw out, should you succumb to the overwhelming desire to examine even more of them. But even if you were to have the eyes of a hawk, and in spite of being so near to them and despite their enormous size, the siniópe appear, in most cases, only as faint and indistinct monochrome sketches.

The most striking, or so it seems to me, is the one in the corner, on the left, as you go in. It is vaguely mesmerising, with its concentric circles. It appears to have a solid circle in the centre, which represents God, which is fair enough, and is just as valid as any portrait I have ever seen of Him, since no-one knows what He looks like. The outer circles seem to contain certain indistinct figures, but what with them being so faint in the first place and in the second, so high up, God knows what the images between the circles are, but I would guess it lets the illiterate, and especially the poor, see the Way Things Are; that they are at the bottom of the heap, while nearest the centre and God, there are orders of angels in descending order: seraphim and cherubim and ophanim and so on until, finally you get downtohim – the one that could be me.

He would have been the lowest of the lowest order of angels, furthest from heaven and nearest earth, spending quite a bit of time down here in fact, earning his wings and then learning to fly right, because it is a long haul to heaven, as impressive as that of the Monarch butterfly which migrates from Canada to Mexico and back again. Imagine, 5,000 miles on fragile wings like that! No wonder it takes them two or three generations or even more!

And no wonder the Archangel Michael, on top of his church in Lucca needs such massive appendages to get all the way to heaven, for if that does not make *Danaus plexippus'* trip look like a mere short hop, I don't know what does. And, when he got there, by the way, he only managed to finish second bottom in his class. That's right! We tend to think of him as a big cheese, but that's only because as mere mortals, we sort of got to know him a bit better than those really important angels like seraphim, who spend all their time swanning about in heaven and don't bother with scruffs like us.

That's how difficult it is for the likes of you and me to get to the Pearly Gates and even then, you may not be allowed in. And yet, (and you may laugh and scoff if you like) but I can't shake off this feeling that I have been here before, and I don't just mean to Pisa. More and more I am becoming convinced that that persistent itchiness between my shoulder blades must count for something.

Which is a bit strange really, as I keep doing so many wrong things.

CHAPTER TWENTY-TWO:
THE PULPIT AND THE PENDULUM

As a service had been in progress during our last visit, we had not been able to see much of the interior of the Duomo, apart from what we could manage to see through the open central doors and over the heads of the tourists, standing three deep behind the rope stretched across the entrance. All I had been able to make out, on the ceiling of the apse at the end of the nave, was the hulking figure of Christ. But perhaps it was a blessing in disguise as it meant our already limited time could be spent on admiring the exterior.

On our Italian Journey, which had encompassed the cities of Naples, Florence, Pisa, Siena, Assisi and Rome - Pisa's Duomo had been the first we had seen. I was impressed by it then and looking at it again now, I am even more impressed than I was before. That is because I have now something to compare it with. The façades of the Duomos of Florence and Siena are a sight to behold, but too fussy and ornate by far, while St Peter's in Rome is rather like the Grand Canyon: awesome, but in its immense hugeness, difficult to know where one should focus one's attention. Pisa's Duomo, however, or so it seems to me, gets the balance right between ornamentation and restraint and between being impressively large and colossal.

The overall impression of the cathedral is one of white and sober grey but on closer look, the façade does contain a lot of ornamental detail and a great deal of coloured marble and stone too, but it does not smack you in the face like those of Florence and Siena. A feast for the eyes the latter two may be, but there is such a superfluity of detail and colour it is rather like the feeling you get after overeating, like last night, where the sight of more food makes you feel sick. As for size, though it certainly is impressive, it is not so huge that you can't appreciate its overall cruciform shape, and in particular, the curves of the apses in the transepts. Lucca's Duomo, which was built in the Pisan style, is a poor imitation of this. There is no doubt about it - Pisa's Duomo is the best *I* have seen, certainly, and is arguably, the finest in all of Italy.

As for its campanile, the *Torre Pendente*, the Leaning Tower, it wins hands down over every other campanile in the entire country. With its cotton reel drums and innumerable slim columns, it fully deserves its iconic status, even if it were not for the lean that made it famous.

The architect of this masterpiece, by which I mean the Duomo rather than the *campanile,* deserves to be better known than he is. Buschetto. That's his name; no other name is mentioned or necessary. There is a memorial plaque to him fairly high up on the left of the façade and which probably goes unnoticed by practically everybody amidst all the other much more eye-catching detail. He is said to be buried behind that, though that seems a bit of an odd place to me, but if true, I suppose you could say that is another famous grave I have been to, even although until today I had never heard of him and neither have a lot of other people I am willing to bet. Poor, neglected, Buschetto.

But can this marvellous exterior be matched by the interior? What if it is like the interior of Siena's Duomo – truly horrendous?

But I needn't have worried. Huge of course, but surprisingly light and airy, the only fault I can find is this fondness for Moorish stripes that the medieval Italian architects seem to find so desirable. You will know what I mean if you think of Cordoba Cathedral (or Mosque if you prefer) where it is seen to its worst excess. The pillars and arches there make you think you've discovered the Candy Man's factory. Thankfully, there is nothing as horrendous as that here, although it is a pity that they have used dark grey-and-white stripes on the pillars on the upper galleries especially. But after a time you become used to them and they become scarcely noticeable, being so high up and there being so many other things to offer as a distraction, such as the stained glass windows and the scores of colourful paintings.

The massive pillars of the nave and the aisles (all five of them), seem to draw the eye down the entire length of the cathedral to the huge figure of Christ, where the curve of the ceiling of the apse seems, appropriately enough, to create the impression that He is bending down from on high to look at us little ants. This time I can see He is not alone but flanked by His Mum and His second cousin, John the Baptist, whose face is by Cimabue, the last, great, Byzantine-style artist. His pupil was Giotto and of course, after that things were never quite the same again. He probably did not realise the artistic revolution that he was fomenting and even less, or so it is hoped, that this was to be his last work. He died in Pisa in 1302, probably only in his early sixties. But his time had come, just as his artistic style had had its day. He did not know it, but he had passed on the baton.

There are more Byzantine paintings and mosaics, an art gallery really: you could spend a day in here if you knew what to look for, and if you were a dedicated follower of Byzantine art, I think you could get pretty high on this place. I am not particularly, and don't really know what I should be looking at either, just letting the eye roam wherever it will until it is arrested by whatever grabs my fancy.

One thing I think we, as a whole, generally tend not to do often enough – is look up. We wander down our High Streets through the regiments of shops with their plate glass windows, and we see what the window dressers intend us to see, but what we should *really* be doing is looking up, looking at the architecture in all its infinite variety. Try it and see. And you will see, I guarantee it, something of much more worth than that at eye level. If I had a coat of arms, the motto beneath would read: *Only look up.* (© David Addison 2010. All rights reserved.) What could be more succinct than that - and more inspiring? In the literal sense, that is what we *should* do but don't. Taken figuratively, the message is: Hold your head up high and think positively.

And in the literal sense, that's what I do now. The black-and-gold coffered ceiling with the Medici coat of arms (what is their motto I wonder – Money, Money, Money?) looks rich and magnificent, but I prefer the ceiling of the galleries with their blues and whites and gold, each square panel a miniature work of art, though in actual fact, if I could get up there, they would not turn out to be so small after all. And then there is the painting on the dome which I like all the better because in a departure from the norm, it is elliptical rather than round.

Coming down to earth again, or at least halfway between there and heaven, towards which the Blessed Virgin is floating in Riminaldi's fresco, a huge chandelier hangs suspended high overhead. So what you may ask? Ah, but this is no ordinary lamp. This is a lamp with a history attached to it.

The story goes, as he sat here, bored out of his skull, (as one tends to be in church) Galileo, it is said, noticed the swaying of the huge brass chandelier to and fro, fro and to, to and fro. Mesmerised by the swinging of that arc – no, it's not what you may be thinking – he wasn't hypnotised by God, who commanded him to throw a pound of feathers and a pound of lead off the Leaning Tower, to see which would land first. Nor, more prosaically, was it that he merely fell asleep, his eyes following that hypnotic rhythm, like the eyes of the owl you often see on cuckoo clocks.

No, his mind, as usual, was on much more mathematical things and measuring the swing of the arc against his pulse, and like the lamp above me, this is a bit over my head, but somehow these observations, apart from making him the greatest swinger in town, led to him to think of the pendulum as a way of keeping time and so ultimately, I suppose you could say, he is partly to blame for the cuckoo clock.

Actually this is not really the same chandelier as Galileo saw at all, but something similar and furthermore, it is as steady as a rock. What Galileo noticed apparently was that regardless of the strength of the wind that caused the chandelier to move, the oscillations always took the same amount of time, so the thought came to him that it would be a pretty accurate way of measuring time. He never got round to developing his idea though and it was the Dutch Christiaan Huygens who brought out the first patent for the pendulum clock in 1657.

What I deduce from all this is that Galileo spent a great deal of his time dreaming in church instead of keeping his mind on the mass. Still that was only a venial sin compared to the massive one of his heretical heliocentric view of the universe. His astronomical observations had led him to conclude that Copernicus was right and what's more, he could prove it. As a result he was placed under house arrest for the rest of his life and made to publicly recant. That's what you get for being so smart.

Coming completely down to earth now, we head for what is actually reckoned to be the star attraction of this place – the stone pulpit carved by Giovanni Pisano, son of Nicola, who even if he did have a girl's name, managed to sire a son all the same. Between them they seem to have pretty much cornered the pulpit-carving market in Tuscany. Nicola's pulpit is in the Baptistery, where we will be heading next, so it will be interesting to compare them. This pulpit is amazing and I don't just mean for the wealth of carving on it. It fairly teems with life – it hardly seems possible to carve so many figures on these panels, yet there they all are, vying for space, living, breathing figures or so it seems, they are so full of movement. The panels tell the main events in the story of Christ's life from His pre-birth to His death and beyond – and a reminder of what will happen to us on Judgement day if we are not good.

It is an incredible *tour de force* and literally breathtaking. As you might expect, with all those scenes to depict, it is immense and not just for the girth of the pulpit itself, but its height. I am not incredibly tall it has to be admitted, especially for these well-nourished days, but a combination of being born during the post-war rationing period and heredity, resulted in me being like a tin of condensed soup – full of goodness but rather compressed. I reckon it would take three of me, standing on my shoulders, if such a feat were possible, just to reach the bottom of the pulpit.

The great bowl of the pulpit is supported by figures of Christ, the Archangel Michael and Hercules (who, at least should be strong enough to support the enormous weight) and Corinthian pillars, two of which are mounted on the backs of lions. And that's not all, because round the base of Christ's pillar there is a group consisting of Mathew, Mark, Luke and John. Furthermore, on top of the capitals there are figures of saints and sibyls, prophets and preachers. Then there are the panels themselves, and this is what I especially like, each panel is curved and separated from its neighbour by caryatids and telamons who also serve to link the upper and lower rims of the pulpit. In addition to that, (as if that were not quite enough already) there is a central support on which are the allegorical figures of Faith, Hope and Charity and that itself rests upon a base on which are carved even more figures, though they are much smaller this time. No wonder it took Pisano nine years to complete it!

I have gone into some detail here as I hope I have conveyed an impression, not only of how amazing this pulpit is artistically, but just how big it is. And I haven't even mentioned the flight of stairs that would have been required to get up there, which would not have been insubstantial as you can imagine. Now get this – and be prepared to be amazed. There was a fire in 1595 and the whole place had to be redecorated, though the fresco in the apse at the rear was unaffected, as was the pulpit.

Anyway, this mammoth piece of stonework was dismantled, put into crates, then placed in storage for the duration.

At some time during the refurbishment, someone, or some committee or other, had decided that this masterpiece was not as great as it was cracked up to be (philistines) and it was left where it was, in storage. Then, believe it or not, it was totally forgotten about for three centuries. You might have thought that someone, in all that time, might have stubbed their toe on one of these crates and wondered what was in it, or during the spring-cleaning, it might have occurred to someone to get rid of all these wooden boxes lying about the place gathering dust, at which point, presumably, they would have discovered what they contained.

Incredibly, it was not until 1926 that Pisano's lost masterpiece was rediscovered and reassembled. However, because they hadn't carefully marked the pieces like they painstakingly did when they took Abu Simbel apart, block by block, and built it again on top of the cliff – only just as they didn't quite get the alignment right, so here too, the panels were not put back quite in the right order, so Christ's story is not in the correct chronological sequence. They didn't even try to put the pulpit back in its original position, though that hardly could have been so vital as it was in the case of Abu Simbel, where the sunlight does not quite illuminate the inner tomb in precisely the same way as was originally intended. And here is something else. *The stairs have never been found!*

But now for something completely different. And I like this almost as much as the pulpit and I salute the person, or committee, which commissioned it because nothing could be more different in style. I can imagine it might have caused a bit of controversy when it first appeared on the steps to the right of the altar. It is a late 20th century work or early 21st even, by an unknown artist (at least to me) and although I don't approve of the bronze top, I love the figures of Christ and two disciples, just beginning to emerge from flawless cylinders of white marble.

Of the three, I only recognise Christ as, in this triangular arrangement, he is at the apex and the only one with any colour about him – his yellow (!) hair. As a group, they look like candles that have melted and have flowed down the steps, so that when you look away for a moment and then look back again, you half-expect more of the figure entombed within the wax, hinted at by a hand or an arm, which you can just make out beneath that incredibly smooth, pure white pillar of a body, to have emerged. The heads, seeming to emerge fully formed from those slim, white, narrow bodies, look like wicks, which, once lit, could shed a little light on a naughty world, especially the one on the right, the slightly dodgy one, the hoodie, whose head looks like a flame already. In its understated way, I think it is just as skilful as Pisano's lively figures. Well, maybe not quite, but I still like it a lot.

And there must be, in the greatest cathedral in all of Italy, (I have now definitely decided) some famous dead people, some famous sons of Pisa who have been honoured by being laid to rest here. For a start, there is poor neglected, what was his name again, the guy who designed the best cathedral in Italy, something beginning with B? That's it, Buschetto, who lies within the walls instead of being given a place of prominence on the floor here, where if he had been, he might have been better remembered.

Galileo, I know, is in the Santa Croce in Florence, which, with the possible exception of Westminster Abbey, has probably got the greatest concentration of really, really, not just famous dead people, but people who have been really influential in shaping the planet. I have been there, naturally, which although it was thrilling to come across so many famous dead people and although it considerably augmented my collection, it was a bit unsatisfactory in the sense that there was no sport in it, no serendipitous discovery, nothing of the excitement of the chase. It was, in short, rather like shooting fish in a barrel.

We go our separate ways, Iona and I, she to find what interests her, me to seek out what interests me – famous dead people. There are meant to be two in here, but one I know I will not find is the tomb of Pope Gregory VIII. I have been closer to more dead popes than you can shake a stick at when I visited the crypt in St Peter's so it doesn't matter a docken to me that Pope Gregory VIII used to be planted here, but no longer is.

The reason is there was a fire in 1600 (what – another one?) and he went to the everlasting bonfire, where, I bet, he would have met a great many of his predecessors. In fact, since he was only pope for 57 days, he would have been at the back of the room, nowhere near the fire in that crowded room. He was only buried here rather than Rome because he happened to die of a fever when he was up here on business trying to persuade the Pisans and the Genoese to bury the hatchet. So that means he was a good guy, does it? A peacemaker, a conciliator? Not a bit of it! The only reason he was on this mission was that he wanted these enemies to kiss and make up so they would join forces and he could start a bigger war, launch the Third Crusade. The George W. Bush of his day. The road to hell is paved with good intentions, so they say, and I am sure Gregory thought his intentions were good.

Right, he is no longer here. So who is? This is one of them. It is a bit late in the day now for me to regret having flung my first Latin primer across the room in frustration at having to learn a dead language. I couldn't see then what possible use it could be to me: I had no intention of being a lawyer or a doctor, nor had I any intention of visiting Latin America, so like Dan Quayle, saw no point in learning a language I thought I would never use. Besides, if I ever did go there, I was sure that the natives would be able to speak English.

How wrong I was! Here I am in the very place where they really did speak Latin in the olden days, standing before the tomb of Henry VII, Holy Roman Emperor from 1308 – 1313. Unfortunately, my Latin is not quite up to deciphering the inscriptions. You may not have heard of him, but you don't get to be Holy Roman Emperor without quite a few people knowing who you are. Dante was a big fan, regarding him as a bit of a champion against the popes' meddling in temporal affairs and gave him several mentions in *Purgatorio*, Part Two of *The Divine Comedy*, hence the quotation from that on the tomb which my medieval Italian is not quite up to either.

Despite Dante's admiration, Henry must have done something wrong if he needed a bit of scrubbing up in purgatory before he got into Heaven. Anyway, as far as I am concerned, he counts as one of the famous people I have met, but only too late in his life. But how do I classify him? He could go down as the only Holy Roman Emperor in my collection, or he could be another entry in my list of famous dead people whom I didn't know were famous until I had visited their tomb.

And here's another one.

This has to be someone special, all lit up, glowing in an eerie green light, in another of those see-through coffins, though, in this case, disappointingly, there is nothing grisly to see, as it is too high up and too far away to see anything. It looks as if a mask has been placed over the face, so perhaps there is something pretty grisly under there after all, but that doesn't normally prevent them from displaying relics in various stages of decay, such as St Zita. There is nothing to say who it is, but since there are only two famous people buried here, and one having already been identified, it is a fairly good bet who this suspect must be – the corpse of San Ranieri, the patron saint of Pisa, no less, but another new saint for me. He can therefore either go into my saint collection or the collection of famous people I'd never heard of before.

Right, that's quite enough of death and gloom. I've seen all I want to in here and I go to find Iona. It's time to look at the other end of life's spectrum and visit in my opinion, the best building on this field of miraculous buildings – the Baptistery.

CHAPTER TWENTY-THREE: A MYSTERY AND A MAGICAL TOUR

Outside, in the warmth of the sun, and with our back to the Duomo, we pause to let the sunshine soak through to our poor, old, cold Scottish bones and admire the Baptistery. It really is splendid. I love it most for the tracery of the white marble mullions in the Gothic pointed arches which don't look the least out of place with the rounded Romanesque blind arches on the lower levels. Our appreciation isn't helped however, by a couple of distractions, right in front of us, between us and the Baptistery.

The grass is being given its last cut of the year – or maybe not. Perhaps these acres of green sward have to be mowed all year round. It's the price you have to pay for living in a temperate climate. I should remember that next time I moan about our weather – at least I get a break from having to cut the grass for six months. Still, if I had a vehicle like his to cut it with, something that looks like a mini combine harvester, I would gladly do it in exchange for a better climate.

The other distraction is a group of workmen who are digging up the paving although, from what I can see, it looks perfectly all right the way it is and who are creating an obstacle course, not to say an eyesore, in the process.

And seen from this angle, I can see another eyesore and it is something that just beggars belief. I just can't comprehend it. If there were a modern day equivalent of the ancient world's Seven Wonders of the World, this UNESCO World Heritage site would certainly be in that number, but it has one incredible flaw. I am not referring to the fact that not only is the tower leaning, but all the buildings are, as they slowly sink into their inadequate foundations. Nor am I even referring to the stripes inside the Duomo. Some people may even *like* them. The Moors certainly seemed to. No, my complaint concerns something else; something that everyone, bar none, would agree is an eyesore.

Apart from the features mentioned above and the quality of the carving, especially round the doors, what makes the Baptistery so appealing to me is the shape of the roof and its orange tiles. And here we come to it. For some unfathomable reason, it has only been partly tiled, leaving half of it bare so all you can see are sheets of ugly lead. I know nowadays it is fashionable for some young men to consider a completely bald pate preferable to a receding hairline, or the crowning glory receding from the crown, resulting in a hairstyle rather like a tonsure. It is not uncommon in people of my vintage and I am no exception. Actually Archimedes is credited with this style of hairstyle and if it was good enough for him, then it is certainly good enough for me.

Alopecia, or natural baldness, you just can't help. It's in your genes, inherited through the distaff side I believe, but not to hang on to your hair for as long as you can, to deliberately shave it off, right down to the wood, I regard as an act of self-mutilation. Baldness never enhanced anyone and what's more, its proponents would do well to remember the fate of poor Aeschylus who was killed when an eagle dropped a tortoise from a great height on his dome. It had mistaken it for a rock on which it intended to smash open the shell to get at the juicy contents. Still, I suppose, having said that, eagles carrying takeaway meals are not as common now as they used to be in the 5th century B.C.

When I first saw the Baptistery roof, four years ago, I had assumed that they were in the process of retiling it, but this cannot be the case: it is just as it was then all these years later. It seems it must there by design. But why? What possible reason could there be for leaving the roof in this unattractive state? It looks like a building under construction, which of course it was over the course of three centuries until finally, the dome capped it off in the 14th century. But seven centuries later, it still looks unfinished, as if the money had run out and they were forced to stop work on it.

It's not as if that hadn't happened before. In fact, they ran out of money when the construction was barely begun. The original architect was Diotisalvi, which literally translated means "God Save You" and if his parents were not charged with child abuse, then they should have been. When the money ran out, so did the building, naturally, and it was a century before it began again, by which time, in the course of nature, Diotisalvi had gone back to his Maker. Perhaps it was a blessing in disguise, for when the Baptistery began to rise again, the architects were Pisano and Son. It not only explains why there is such a divergence in styles, but why it looks so fantastic. It was bound to with guys like that in charge.

But surely to God, if the money ran out again, surely that is no reason after all these hundreds of years, to leave the roof in this unfinished state? It makes me feel like starting a Friends of the Baptistery Society (FOBS) to raise some money to get the job done. Not the best acronym in the world I would be the first to admit as it suggests that the powers that be would just fob us off with some specious excuse or other. But you can't tell me that there are not barrow loads of euros sloshing around this place, despite the bargain admittance price. It is a UNESCO world heritage site after all, for God's sake, so it must get a grant on top of the thousands of visitors who pay their €8 – so why are they are not channelling money into the roof project?

Now that I am aware of this defect, I can't dismiss it from my mind, for that disfiguring scar seems to utterly ruin what otherwise must be, by anyone's reckoning, one of the most magnificent buildings on the face of the planet. Why, when it could so easily be remedied?

With these questions buzzing about my mind, we step inside the Baptistery.

The first impression is just how immense it is. Huge pillars soar upwards and support an upper gallery before the eye is drawn upwards again to the dome where light comes flooding in from a circle of small windows. Considering how small they appear to be, it's incredible just how well lit it is in fact. The only other source of light comes from the windows all round the perimeter, which on the lower level, are composed of stained glass and which, incidentally, provide just about the only splash of colour in the entire place, though just at the moment, one beam of sunshine, slanting in like a spotlight, highlights a gold plaque of some saint or other with such an intensity that I have to look away as mine eyes dazzle.

While the size of the place impresses, the plainness shocks to the core, particularly when you remember the beauty and intricacy of the carving on the exterior. Even the dome, where you might expect to see some heavenly figures, is as bald as a coot. At least it has that in common with its outer skin I suppose. Not that I am complaining. In fact, I like it all the better, especially as the arches have also been left plain, with none of those hideous stripes to disfigure them. And, come to think about it, if the reason why the dome is not fully tiled really *is* because the money ran out, then I should not have been so surprised at the bareness of the interior, as there would have been none for decoration either.

But there was money for the font – after all, you can't have a Baptistery without a font and there is also a pulpit because you can't conduct a baptism service without a place for the preacher to preach from. There is so little else to see, the attention is immediately focussed on them. Centre stage goes naturally enough to the font, but the star attraction is Pisano Senior's pulpit. On our Italian Journey I had seen his effort in the Duomo in Siena and had been mightily impressed. As a matter of fact, it is considered to be his masterpiece, begun in 1265, five years after this was completed.

It's not that I don't like it, but even at first glance, from a distance, I am disappointed by this earlier work. But that is because I have just come fresh from seeing Giovanni's pulpit. Where that is curved, this is angular and that's what immediately strikes me as disappointing. Sharp angles are just not as pleasing to the eye as curves and even from here I can see that the figures are as still as…well…statues. They have nothing of Pisano Jr's lifelike movement.

Maybe this is not Nicola's masterpiece, but it is a significant work of art nevertheless, and we have a lot to thank him for. Think of him as being the first runner in a relay race. Just as Giotto picked up the baton from Cimabue and turned his back on the Byzantine style and began the painting of lifelike figures, so Nicola Pisano, inspired by the sarcophagi in the Campo Santo, turned the clock back to the glory that was Rome which in turn, got its inspiration from the greater glory that was Classical Greece. Next to receive the baton would be Ghiberti (he of the famous bronze doors on the Baptistery of Florence) who then passed the baton on to Donatello. The last recipient of the baton in this imaginary race would, of course be Michelangelo or Leonardo. Decide for yourself to whom would fall the honour of running the final lap.

After Michelangelo and Leonardo, the baton was not dropped of course but passed on, and gave us, amongst others, the Pre-Raphaelites and the Impressionists and the Scottish Colourists and so on and so on until we end up in Tracy Emin's bed. If that is where progress takes us, then it seems to me that we have taken a wrong turning somewhere.

This pulpit then, marks the start of the Renaissance, as far as sculpture is concerned. The figures have recognisable features, like real people, with real expressions, and Mary is dressed like, and looks like, a Roman matron. And now that I am closer, though it is rather high up to see all the detail clearly, the Nativity scene does teem with life just like Giovanni's panels and I admire the way the folds of the gowns of Mary and The Three Kings in the *Adoration of the Magi*, ripple across the panel like silk. I'm not so sure about the Crucifixion scene however, which looks to me the least successful. It may be blasphemous to say it, but it looks rather comical, the way Christ is portrayed on the cross. There is something about the lift of the shoulders and the outspread fingers that makes it looks more like a Gallic shrug of resignation rather than death by excruciating crucifixion. His face, instead of expressing the agony He must have been going through looks resigned to His fate, as if He couldn't help being there, as if there was nothing He could do about it, which, when you think about it, is no less than the truth. It was His destiny.

The octagonal font on its octagonal dais is but a step away. It is the work of Guido Bigarelli da Como and completed in 1246, predates the pulpit by fourteen years. Now this I like a lot. On each of its sides there are two square panels with black borders in which there are very pleasing circular designs of inlaid marble, each one quite different from the other. At four of the corners, huge holes have been scooped out of the wooden pillars. They are big enough to hold complete babies, while the adults were baptised in the centre. Galileo, in fact, was baptised in one of those basins when he was only four days old, in February 1564. I'm glad it was total immersion, making it worth all the time and trouble of building a purpose-built edifice like this (even if they did not quite finish it off) and the baptism did not consist of a mere splash on the forehead.

In the centre, on a pedestal, is a figure of St John the Baptist – which should come as no surprise to even the most Bible-illiterate. This bronze sculpture is by Italo Griselli. John looks severely malnourished – not the first time I have seen him represented like this, as if he didn't have the strength to haul you out of the water after he'd ducked you under and thus ended up drowning more people than he baptised. But if all you have to eat are locusts and wild honey, and if you've not got a sweet tooth, it's no wonder that he ended up looking like the sort of rake that St Frediano used to divert the course of the river Serchio. In the history of the Baptistery, this is a very recent addition, dating from only 1929.

The stairs did not seem to require much of an effort to climb, yet when we look down at the floor below it's enough to make you giddy and even then, we are only halfway up. And seen from this perspective, the font looks even better. It's like a spider in the centre of its web, an impression that is created partly by its octagonal shape, but also the dais on which it stands with its three broad steps spreading out onto the floor like ripples on a pond. But most of all, it is conveyed by the black marble lines on the floor, radiating out from the corners of the steps towards the walls, but all linked together with lines running parallel with the sides of the font, just like the strands in a spider's web.

And from here too, you can see the floor of the altar and see how it mirrors the geometric panels round the font. Very good indeed. Yes, I like this place, both inside and out, which is a first for me as far as Italian architecture is concerned. It's a pity about that blemish though – the unfinished roof, otherwise this supremely magical building would be quite perfect. Maybe that's it! Maybe it was given this deliberate flaw because only God can be perfect. I know this is an idea prevalent in Eastern art. Turkish carpets are said to contain one deliberate mistake and one of the minarets on the Taj Mahal is supposed to have been built with a slight lean, not that you would notice, at least not that I could see, but God could, and He is the one who matters after all.

As well as being high, the gallery is wide and runs of course, right round the building, which means that as you circumnavigate it, you can get a different perspective of the campo from each window. At the peak of the tourist season, we would never have been able to do this - to stop at every single window at will, to see the Campo from a variety of perspectives, each one just slightly different from the last, but each, by infinitesimal degrees, providing a 360° tour, and seen from this elevated position.

Unfortunately, the glass is rather dirty, and the windows have, in a further obstacle to a good view, wire meshes to deter the pigeons. (They might have removed the droppings first though.) However, in what arguably affords the best view of all, they have, in the window facing the Duomo, thoughtfully cut a rectangle out of the mesh, so you can take a photograph of it through the glass, not darkly exactly, but certainly not clearly, through all the grime.

Here, in the upper gallery, we are alone apart from a small child and her mother. I dare say to her this wide, empty, circular area might well resemble a racing track, a notion which her indulgent parent does nothing to dispel as she is let loose to tear around the gallery, screaming at the top of her lungs. Perhaps she lives in a little flat and she can't resist the urge to stretch her little legs and exercise her little lungs too.

Jesus it was, who said to suffer the little children and after a career in teaching, I have certainly done my fair share of suffering. Another time, another place, I could have cheerfully strangled her but now I am indebted to her for the tinnitus ringing in my ears. The acoustics, I had read, were supposed to be amazing. I am grateful therefore to the little girl for letting me hear just how incredible they indeed are.

CHAPTER TWENTY-FOUR: IN DEATH'S DOMINION

And now, though the Baptistery may be impossible to beat, and it is always dangerous to look forward too much to anything as it invariably turns out to be rather disappointing, the gods make sure of that, we are going to what I imagine will be, at least for me, the best thing of all – the most beautiful cemetery in the world as someone once called it – the Campo Santo.

The cemetery has a rather interesting history. It is said to have been begun in the 12th century, when Archbishop Ubaldo dei Lanfranchi, on his way back from the Fourth Crusade, brought with him no less than five shiploads of earth from Golgotha so that the great and the good of Pisa could be buried in Holy soil. That sounds like a really good idea to me – bound to speed your soul to heaven. They said that a body, placed in that soil, would disappear completely within 48 hours.

How did they know that? You can just see them, in medieval Pisa, conducting the experiment: exhuming the body by lantern light after 24 hours and covering the corpse up again when they saw some remains, then the next day coming back to find nothing left. The conclusion: God must have taken the body to heaven. While that is what the superstitious medieval Pisans may have liked to believe, I think the truth is a lot more obvious. In the days before the crime novel, the most, not the least likely suspect, is probably the one whodunit. And who would that be? Well, just imagine that voyage across the sea from the Holy Land. How long would that have taken? Weeks for sure. There is no doubt about it in my mind – the worms done it. Munch, munch, munch. With nothing to eat all that time, they were absolutely famished. No wonder bodies disappeared so quickly.

It was just an open cemetery to begin with, but in the 13th century, Giovanni de Simone began building the walls to turn it into an enclosed space. They were not completed until the 15th century and it was still used as a cemetery until 1779. From the outside, it presents a pleasing prospect as your eye lingers on the long white wall with its blind Romanesque arches – but it is nothing compared to what awaits you when you step into the hallowed interior.

The first thing you notice is the rectangle of rich green grass hemmed in by the four walls. It is like being in a cloister and if there is one thing I am fond of, it is cloisters and this is a cloister to die for – and thousands did so they could sleep here throughout eternity. And there are a lot worse places to spend eternity let me tell you. In fact, I wouldn't mind being here at all, though, I think, on balance, I might prefer a bluebell wood. That would be nice and tranquil. How could you rest in peace in here with all those hundreds of people continually tramping over you every day until they closed the gates?

But the best thing of all about the cemetery is the delicate tracery of the mullions, so fine and intricate, that without any exaggeration, they look like lace. And so many of them! No wonder it took the best part of two centuries to complete! You can't rush mullions like these, even if you had an army of mullion manufacturers. Awe-inspiring in themselves, but looking through them, they enhance the view you get of the Baptistery and the side of the Duomo with the Leaning Tower peeking above it, like someone rudely reading your newspaper over your shoulder, too mean to buy their own.

I was right to suppose this would be a pretty interesting cemetery and I have been to some in my time, let me tell you. Haworth, for example, which could hardly be described as beautiful, like this is, but certainly is interesting in a macabre sort of way, partly for its toppling ancient gravestones amongst which goats roam free mowing the grass, but primarily for the

Brontë connection - for the minute you see the view the girls had from the vicarage, you can instantly realise why the books are so gloomy. Then there's Père Lachaise in Paris which has so many famous dead people in it, you need a map to seek them out and which makes for some jolly good fun.

But Forest Lawn in Los Angeles has to take the biscuit and the cake and the cherry on the top as well. No-one can do death half as well as the Americans when they put their minds to it as anyone who has ever read Evelyn Waugh's comic satire, *The Loved One* knows only too well. The gravestones in Forest Lawn read like a *Who's Who* of Hollywood as well as all the ones who only made it on to TV shows, not to mention all those who didn't even make it that far and ended up pumping gas. Well, maybe not them. They probably didn't make it here either.

Actually, Forest Lawn is a bit like a theme park for the dead where those about to join the angels are grouped according to what seems most appropriate. For example: Babyland (the saddest part) or Slumberland (for those who have worked hard all their lives and just want a rest) or Vesperland (for those who don't have a prayer of getting to heaven) or Graceland (for those with no musical taste) or Borderland (for people like me on the cusp of sainthood or going to hell). You get the picture. And, just in case you don't, how about this. You can choose to have your send-off from chapels with such evocative names as *The Little Church of the Flowers* or my favourite and the one I just *had* to visit – *The Wee Kirk o' the Heather*. Well, in self-defence, I had been away from Scotland for more than a year and it was natural to feel a wee tad homesick, wasn't it? And when I saw it, dear reader, I was. But it had nothing to do with home.

Beautiful Forest Lawns certainly is, with all that grass and trees and statues, (even boasting a complete collection of Michelangelo reproductions) and I am sure it would win hands down in that annual Narcissistic show known as the Oscars, if they had such a thing for cemeteries, especially with it being on the home turf, so to speak, but it's just a little bit...tacky. And while it may suit the rich and famous, it wouldn't suit me. But I needn't worry about that: I'm sure they wouldn't let a scruff like me anywhere near the place.

And I wouldn't get in here either – not being a Pisan for a start, nor a rich one, nor the slight matter of turning up more than two hundred years too late. Having said that, for those who did manage to get in, there can be very few places to rival this as a setting to be dead in. But scarcely worth it, I would have thought, for the slight amount of time you'd be spending there, bearing in mind this is reckoned to be on the superhighway to heaven.

The walkway is wide, and once again, we have the place practically to ourselves, if you don't count the hundreds of dead people beneath our feet, and the sarcophagi you keep tripping over. Well, that's a bit of an exaggeration really, as there are only 84 of them left now and they are tucked neatly into the sides - the survivors of the Allied incendiary bomb, which in 1944, set the roof alight, which melted the lead, which covered the frescoes, which covered the sinópie that lay in the house that Giovanni built.

Here is the scaffolding where the restorers are working on the frescoes that were mutilated by the conflagration. It's painstaking work, yet it doesn't seem to be causing them too much pain: they are laughing and joking as they go about their business, up there on high, above the real world, back in the minutely medieval past. It looks nice work if you can get it: much less stressful than trying to control a class of thirty unruly teenagers who think they know everything, don't see why they should be in school and with complete disregard for their futures, do their utmost to make life hell for their teachers.

Here are the sarcophagi, Roman and Etruscan, with their finely executed carvings that Nicola Pisano so admired (and so do I) and which kick-started the sculpture revolution. They were never meant to be planted, these works of art. What a waste of time and money that would have been! No, they were meant to be left above ground so people could see how rich you were. They could come and visit you, walk around you, chat to you even, if they didn't mind a one-way conversation. Or your widow could come along and nag you to death for sins committed or omitted. But what you'd wish for more than anything is that she and they would just go away and leave you in peace.

And in the end, you were the one who went. The lid is off this one so I can see you are not in there any more. And, look! See those holes in the bottom? That's where your decomposed bodily fluids drained away after the stone ate you. What? You mean you didn't know that? You thought that you would be safe from the worms in here, safe and dry forever? So they never told you, did they, that that's what "sarcophagus" means in Greek – flesh-eating stone. Bone takes a bit longer, but they reckon that this limestone could polish you off within weeks. Not as fast as the Holy soil mind you, but still pretty quick. The idea seems to be that after you die, the sooner you get to the Elysian Fields the better. Right enough, I suppose it would get you out of earshot of the wife and out of sight of your enemies dancing a jig.

Here on the wall are the massive chains with which they used to seal off the harbour in times of strife. After the Genoese beat the Pisans at the battle of La Meloria in 1284, they took the chains away and gave half to their allies, the Florentines, and then, after they all made up, they gave them back again as a gesture of friendship: "Here are your chains. You are free." In my opinion, it doesn't seem such a good idea to hang them up here like a trophy when, in actual fact, they are a symbol of defeat and enslavement. But if that is the way they want to interpret history, then that's their affair.

And here, tucked into a corner, as it was in the Sinópie, is the fresco of the concentric rings, not in Technicolor exactly, more like a faded rainbow reflected in water. Next to that, more frescoes, enormous in size. It is enough to give you a hint, regardless of how impressive you may already think this place is, just how much more amazing it must have been when these frescoes were here, in their original vibrant colours. Wall to wall art. Yes, certainly then, if not now, it surely would have deserved to be known as the most beautiful cemetery in the world.

And graves, graves on the floor everywhere. (Tread softly, because you tread on their dreams.) The ones carved in high relief are the ones you notice most. Like this one here for instance, which my skill in deciphering Latin numbers informs me is dated 1428. More precisely than that, I can work out that he died on the first day of July in that year. And I can tell he must have been a pretty educated guy, especially for those times, as he is clutching a book. Maybe he even wrote it.

Nearly six centuries later, it is still as legible as the day it was carved. Not being exposed to the vagaries of the weather, even the mild Pisan winter, the thing most likely to damage this tomb would be the scuffing of scores of shoes and sandals over the centuries. But the figure is so deeply etched into the pavement that that is going to take a long, long time and could possibly even last as long as the planet. That is another way to make yourself immortal I suppose. Unfortunately I can't make out this poor geezer's name as it is so stretched out around the perimeter of the slab that you need the neck muscles of a contortionist to read it. If immortality was his goal, it looks as if it was just wide of the target, but a good effort nevertheless. But just because you are dead, it doesn't mean that you have to write your name and all your details in a dead language too. Mind you, if it had been in medieval Italian, it would not have made any difference as far as I am concerned.

Apart from the tombs below your feet, if you look about you, there are much more elaborate tombs above ground. Tombs with carvings round the sides, in emulation of the Roman model; tombs with the deceased lying in peaceful repose on the top; tombs with mournful maidens in various stages of dress and undress, draped in dolorous poses over the deceased's last resting place. They are obviously missing him a lot. They must be his former girlfriends or more probably his current mistresses, since they look so grief-stricken. Of course it might be the loss of the lifestyle that's upsetting them more. But I must say it is very considerate of his wife to let his admirers dance attendance on him like this.

Not all the monuments are funerary however. Here is a statue to another of Pisa's famous sons, Fibonacci, also known as Leonardo of Pisa, or Pisano, the 12th century mathematician famous for the sequence that bears his name though he was not actually the one to discover it: 1, 1, 2, 3, 5, 8, 13 and so on which is achieved, as I am sure you will have noticed, by adding the sum of the two previous numbers. It has all sorts of practical applications that I won't bore you with, except to say it is reckoned to be a pretty good way of calculating if you happen to have a couple of rabbits, let's say, how many you will end up with over a given number of years, should you ever want to know such a thing. Maybe if you are think of starting a glove factory or something.

In those days, far removed from now, when people were not half so numerous as rabbits, you would be known by just your first name and Leonardo only got *his* new name, which means "son of Boccaccio" (itself a nickname) posthumously, there being just too many other famous Leonardos about, like that one from Vinci for example. Anyway, Fibonacci's main claim to fame was, (though he wouldn't have known whom you were talking about) as an Arabic scholar, he did more than anyone to make redundant the Roman system of numerals and spread the use in the West of what we call the Arabic system, not to mention that very useful number that tells me, for example, how much chance I have of ever understanding differential calculus – zero. Yes, this is the guy I have to blame for my lack of numeric skills. Those Latin numerals that look like letters would have been a lot easier to manage, at least in my book.

Some black-and-white photographs show you what the cloisters looked like before the practically all-consuming fire of 1944, but off to the side, is probably what is for most, the highlight of the Campo Santo – the frescoes that were saved. It is a big room with what look like Parker Knoll squishy seats where you can rest your weary legs and pretend to be engrossed in your guidebook, and not in the least listening to the guide who is giving an exposition to a group of some twenty or so who look in the last stages, most of them, of terminal boredom. We were there before them, it so happens, and we have just as much right to be sitting there as anyone else.

The fresco she is describing is *The Triumph of Death*. A big brass plate (and she) tells us it was executed by Buonamico Buffalmacco, though our guidebook tells us it is not known who did it and the artist is known simply as The Master of *The Triumph of Death*. In the bottom left-hand corner are three bodies in open coffins, in various stages of decay, while to the right of them are some very rich people (just look at their clothes, the guide points out) who seem to be expressing a morbid interest in the deceased, which is more than could be said for the guide's charges.

One is pointing dispassionately to the first corpse as if to say: "This was my last Duchess." His companions are coming as close as they dare, one knight on a fine roan holding his nose and just about passing away from the stench. Curiously, it doesn't seem to affect his horse at all who has its neck stretched out as far as it can go towards the Duchess as if to get a better view, while at its feet, a mangy dog with ribs like a xylophone, loiters with intent of grabbing a tasty bone to gnaw. Meanwhile, in another vignette, to the right and centre foreground, bodies are piled up high, while above them, devils with wings and talons like dragons are disembowelling the dead, ripping out their souls, depicted as naked, new-born babes and despatching them headfirst to hell.

By contrast, at the right of the fresco, a party of young knights and ladies are disporting themselves in a garden, or orchard, without a care in the world, as if *they* were the ones who were going to triumph over death – inconceivable that ones so young and beautiful as they could conceivably get old, let alone die. Indeed they seem to be the anointed ones, for over their heads, fly not demons, but angels, safely gathering to their bosoms the souls of the saved.

You might have been forgiven for thinking, with so many bodies about, that the Black Death was raging, but in fact, it seems this predates this grim reaper by some ten years. No, it is an old, old story. The whole fresco simply seems to be a reminder, as if you needed any reminding anyway, that death is inevitable and you had better be good, or just look and see what will happen to you.

And don't think that just because you were top of the heap on Earth that you will be spared death – or hell either. Just look at that figure on top of the pile of corpses, him with the tonsure – his soul is being dragged out of him not by an angel, but a demon. A friar who, when his number was up, had placed his chips in the wrong place evidently.

Buffalmacco had a reputation as a bit of a joker and this looks as if it might have been one of his jokes, or else, as I like to think, he was making a serious point about the clergy. He liked to give the figures in his frescoes words, coming out of their mouths in balloons like characters in a comic strip. They are missing now, but the knight gesturing to the newly-dead body of the richly-dressed lady in the coffin might well have been saying what I thought he was saying after all and it was not just my imagination putting words in his mouth after all.

CHAPTER TWENTY-FIVE:
TREASURES, TROUBLES, TOURISTS AND A TOSSER

All morning, I had had my phone switched on and my mind switched off to my current problems. Actually that is being a little bit economical with the truth. While I had been distracted by the attractions aforesaid, a bit like the toothache, sudden pangs of depression, like a dagger, would stab at my entrails and remind me that I was not here purely for pleasure: I had a more serious purpose and mission to fulfil here in Pisa – the liberation of my case from the airport authorities, but some premonition was giving me a sense of foreboding that all was not going to be well.

It is a Friday, not the thirteenth, but it may just as well have been for the feeling I have lying like lead in the pit of my stomach whenever I remembered Carla's case. Not while we had been going round the Sinópie had I expected to receive a message, nor the Duomo, nor the Baptistery, but by the time we were exploring the Campo Santo, my hopes began to build that surely anytime now, that message would come to say we could get our luggage out of hock. And as time passed without it coming, I consoled myself as best I could with the thought that it was still early in the day and there was still plenty of time for it to arrive. But the longer time went on, the stronger my sense of foreboding increased that Carla's case was not going to get to Elba today. And if it did not, with the weekend beginning and a public transport strike scheduled for Monday, the prospect of not getting our case until Tuesday, the day of departure, was beginning to loom larger in my mind. In fact, the spectre of having to fly home without it, and the consequent fortune it would cost to repatriate it, was beginning to form an ugly shape in my mind.

But a moment of light relief is on hand in the form of a Japanese woman who has her digital camera on a tripod and is posing in front of the Tower – one of those poses that some people feel compelled to do, as if propping the Tower up or toppling it over, depending on whether they have destructive or conservationist tendencies. She is on her own, and has adopted a very dramatic pose. With one arm fully extended and the other flung back and her head tilted back as far as it can go, she obviously has no inhibitions about making an exhibition of herself. Apart from revealing that she has destructive tendencies, the pose suggests that she is accustomed to being looked at by an audience, possibly as a member of a chorus line or corps de ballet. Having taken the photograph, she nips back to the camera to examine her handiwork.

Not quite right and so the process must be repeated again and again. I would offer to take it for her, but I don't, as she looks perfectly capable of managing by herself. Besides, it is amusing me, watching her. Finally, however, she seems satisfied, and apparently having virtually over-toppled the Tower, collapses the tripod for good measure and with it slung over her shoulder, goes jauntily on her way.

To get to the Museo dell'Opera del Duomo, we must pass between the curve of the apse of the Duomo and the Tower at the point where the lean is most pronounced. Here are the back doors of the Duomo, so to speak, the Porta di San Ranieri, the great bronze doors that, in former times, were the main doors through which people used to pass to gain access to the Cathedral. Like a cartoon strip, the panels depict the life of Christ. They were made from 1286 onwards by Bonanno Pisano, another local lad, born and bred and dead in Pisa. They found his tomb at the foot of the Tower in 1820. How about that for a headstone? Whatever he was paid for his work, he could scarcely have been paid any greater tribute than that.

It would be nice to have a closer look at the panels, but there is a bit of an obstacle. A man is sitting on the steps, smoking and showing not the slightest inclination to move, to let us have an unimpeded view of the doors. Furthermore, unlike the Japanese lady, who showed not the least embarrassment at us watching her antics, I find the perfectly normal procedure of looking closely at the panels distinctly unnerving with him looking at me looking. It is just as well that I know the story, especially how it ends.

His thick skin also seems to be incapable of being penetrated or his conscience pricked by the quiverful of arrows that Iona's narrow eyes are slinging in outrage at his boorish behaviour. He is just not going to move for us or anyone else in the foreseeable future, for he has just lit another fag.

I know when I'm beaten, so I turn my attention to something else. On the wall of the Duomo, I can see some blocks with writing on them. Closer inspection reveals it to be in Latin – clear evidence that the Pisans were not averse to "borrowing" some stones lying around from the ruins of Roman buildings such as temples and adapting them to create a temple to *their* God. What you might call taking a chip off the old block.

I am curious to know what this inscription says but I know it is bad to read other people's letters. I learned this unforgettable lesson one day when Iona gave me a terrible row for reading one addressed to our son, which I knew came from Central Scotland Police as it was emblazoned all over the envelope in red ink for anyone and everyone to see. But I knew it was really for me because I had borrowed his car. Well, wasn't I entitled to? Who do you imagine paid for it in the first place, and the road tax and the insurance, not to mention most of the petrol? I also knew I had been caught in a speed trap and I couldn't wait to find out if it was just a warning or a fine.

But despite that lesson, I can't resist trying to make sense of these letters, but alas, once again, my schoolboy Latin is not up to the task. One block, in block capitals, appropriately enough, reads "ARTE," but carelessly, it has been placed upside down and for all I know, could quite possibly be only part of a word. On another block above it, the lettering is a bit fainter, but I can make out the word "HADRIAN" which gives us an idea as to where it might have come from and how old it is, but I can't make head nor tail of the rest, for the vandals who nicked this stone, showing scant regard for their architectural heritage, have cut it on the slant, cutting off the tops and bottoms of letters, willy-nilly, with complete disregard for future generations who might want to read the writing on the wall.

And here is another interesting block, this time on the Tower. My old English teacher, Norman Emanuel Faid, (may his name be praised) was very fond of addressing us and quoting from *Julius Caesar*: *Oh, you blocks, you stones, you worse than senseless things*! And no doubt we were, in those far-off, half-remembered days, but blocks can be very useful indeed, apart from being mere materials in the construction of a building. Like this one for instance.

It bears the date 1173, which tells us that this was the date when the Tower was begun. It is a pity that they did not put the name of the architect there as well, since no-one knows for certain now who he was. His was a name that should have lived hereafter. It is a word that would have echoed for all time. The most likely contender is he of the most unlikely name – Diotisalvi, who began the Baptistery. But he usually signed his works, as he did the Baptistery, (look for it on the left as you go in) and no such signature has been found on the Tower.

And here is yet another useful block. It depicts two stately galleons upon a seasick-making sea, with more waves than Marcel ever dreamt of in his hairstyle, and which serves to remind us that the Pisans were far from peasants, but once a powerful maritime city – a fact which the memory might well be in need of jogging, considering how far Pisa is from the sea, via the Arno. In fact, it was once a maritime power whose influence once extended to the Eastern Mediterranean, Greece, North Africa, Sicily, Sardinia, and the Balearics. In short, these block and stones are not worthless things at all. They do indeed speak. Well, some of them anyway, if you can interpret what they are saying.

We head now towards the last of the places on our ticket, the Museo dell'Opera del Duomo. For my part, it is taken with leaden steps. For a start, the Museum of the Cathedral Works doesn't sound all that inspiring (we are only going because it was part of the ticket package we had bought) and now that I have begun to hope that my phone will ring, the heavier that knot of anxiety in my stomach seems to weigh when it doesn't. So much so in fact, it is becoming increasingly difficult to take my mind off that and concentrate on anything else.

When we get there, it turns out that it is also the Tourist Information Office. Perhaps I can get them to phone the airport for me. What a difference it would make to the rest of my day in Pisa if we were to be told that yes, Carla had received her bag and we could pick ours up any time we wanted.

But there is no-one in the little kiosk which I take to be the Information Office. In the end, I have to resort to asking a woman hanging about the entrance hall if she knows where it is.

"I am it," she says. "Just a moment." And walking past me, she slips into the kiosk and now installed, is professional and wants to know how she can help.

"…and so, if you would be so kind to phone the airport," I end up by saying.

It's a long tale but a small request and she does it willingly and without asking any questions, only to tell me a few moments later that it is an automated voice announcing that the office is closed and if you want to speak to a real person then you must phone back later. Good grief! Is that what they call progress! Helpfully, she provides me with the number so I can call back on my own and my heart feels heavier than ever as I suspect I'll never be able to cope with that. The Post Office experience is all too fresh in my mind and I feel a strong sense of *déjà vu* coming on. I wish now I had waited until after lunch. I can scarcely go back now and make the same request. But how was I to know the "lost" luggage department would be so modernised that you could only speak to a machine?

It is the condemned man therefore and his wife who have their tickets clipped and pass on in to the inner sanctum of the Museo dell'Opera del Duomo where the first thing the visitor sees is another condemned man – an enormous wooden figure of Christ on the cross. It is by an unknown artist from Burgundy, from the second part of the 12th century and I must say I like it a lot. It takes me a moment to realise why. It isn't just the way Christ's head is tilted to the side, nor is it for His naturalistic expression, as if He has just passed out from the pain that was too great to bear. He has the same elongated arms as Berlinghieri's crucified Christ in San Michele in Lucca and maybe they would stretch to His knees, especially if they were pulled from their sockets.

And that's it. In a sudden epiphany, I realise in fact, just why this Crucifixion is different, unlike any I have ever seen before. Christ's right arm is not fixed to the cross, but has been torn away. No wonder He has passed out. This sculpture catches that elongated arm poised in air, just the moment before it fell, helpless, to His side. I never read of that happening in the Bible, but the things you read there are not necessarily to be taken literally. Sportin' Life in *Porgy and Bess* put it a bit more tunefully but whatever way you put it, it is probably enough to give fundamentalists a fit. In any case, I give full marks to the anonymous sculptor for his artistic interpretation. It is a very fine piece of work indeed and outshines Berlinghieri's carving like a halogen light bulb does a candle. It is just a pity that he did not take the time to carve his name at the base of the statue. Had he taken the time to do so, his name would also have lived hereafter.

In the same room, tucked into a corner, is a brass griffin of interesting provenance. It is an arresting bit of sculpture. I can see why they placed it here beside the Burgundian Crucifixion. There is nothing else quite like it. A notice next to it informs us that the griffin was venerated by the Greeks, and being half-eagle, half-lion, it symbolised Christ's half-earthly, half-heavenly status. It was captured by the Pisans, probably when they defeated the Muslims in the Balearic islands, and they used it as in incense burner before they had loftier thoughts and stuck it on top of the cupola of the Duomo to create another symbol – a Yah Boo sign to the Arabs of the Pisans' dominance over them and there it stayed until 1828.

Nor is that the only Islamic influence here. As well as a capitol from a pillar, there is a 12th century marble slab from the choir, which, with its intricate swirling loops, is unmistakably inspired by Islamic art. It comes from the school of Guglielmo, so the notice beneath it says. Willie's school. His parents must have had no ambition for him otherwise they would have given him a name like Diotisalvi, which *his* parents must have thought was a sure recipe for fame, if not a fortune, just like the present generation of parents do with their weird and wonderful variant spellings of names new and not so new. What was wrong with Archibald and Alfred and Ethel and Edna I would like to know? And how much more colourful life would be if we were known by our nicknames as they were in Fibonacci's father's day. Not "Your tea is ready, David" but "Come and get your tea, Slobberchops."

I am struck with another curious thought. While the griffin was up there on high, waving two fingers so to speak, at the enemy, here below they were singing his praises: for what greater tribute can you pay to your enemy than to imitate his art as they did in the Dumo, to name but one? And meanwhile, as we had just seen, Fibonacci was adopting the enemy's mathematics. Remind me – who was the victor again? The Pisans or the Muslims?

This is turning out to be much better than I had expected and we have hardly started yet. Many of the figures and statues on the buildings of the Campo dei Miracoli are copies: the originals are here. Like this for example. It comes from a capitol from the Tower and it features a human head, a lion, a wolf and a donkey. Animals were used in medieval times apparently, to ward off evil spirits. Isn't that an amazing thing? Admittedly, the human face, with his poppy eyes, is enough to give any evil spirit a fright unless he thought he was looking at his own reflection in a mirror, but those animals look more like pets than having any ability to petrify any evil spirits. Just think about it for a moment. The whole of the Campo bristling with saints and a host of other heavenly residents, all the way up the hierarchy to Jesus Himself, and who do the Pisans put their faith in for their protection but Lenny the Lion, Dobbin the Donkey and Virginia the Wolf!

There are wooden models of the buildings on the Campo Santo, cut away so you can see their innards, showing, for example, the concentric rings of the Tower and the staircase between them which will take you 294 steps nearer heaven. You can even go down some stairs beneath the Duomo and look up inside it as if you were Alice just after eating the antidote to the drink that shrunk her. It's a weird feeling, this feeling of being not just tall, for once, but a giant.

Rooms and rooms of treasures abound here – and not just the sort of treasure that pirates would recognise. There are enough silver and jewelled items here to fill several chests of even Dolly Parton proportions but one of the jewels in the crown is not a precious stone at all, but made of marble. It is by Giovanni Pisano and known as the *Madonna del Colloquio* so called because you can really see the communication going on between mother and child. Like the Crucifixion by the unknown Burgundian, it is a new dimension in art. Normally, Christ sits on His Mum's lap like a doll, but here He is being held up practically at her eyelevel and they are looking at each other and certainly saying something.

But just what exactly *are* they saying? It would be fun to have a competition where you were asked to draw bubbles coming out of their mouths like one of the figures in a Buffalmacco fresco and see what people came up with. It seems to me that Mum is not best pleased with Him. She is not smiling but looking at him rather sternly, while He is looking at her in an apologetic sort of way, as if He knows He has done something wrong. He didn't mean to do it, but He just couldn't help it. My suggestion is there has been a setback in His toilet training, but I'll leave the words in the bubble up to you.

There is another *Madonna and Child* by the same Pisano and it appears that the same models posed for the Master. What is really interesting about this statue is it is carved out of a single piece of ivory which is why the Madonna's back is curved, as if He has become such a heavy child to support, she has to lean backwards to counterbalance His forward-thrusting movement towards the viewer. As anyone who has ever held a child of that age knows, they can suddenly lunge in any direction and you must be on your guard. Here it looks as if Daddy, or Joseph, or someone else has just come into the room (it might even be us) and the child wants to solemnly make a present of the orb that He just happens to have in His hand. It looks a bit like a cartoon bomb and you could, I suppose, regard it symbolically in that light, as after He came along the world was changed forever.

The eye contact here is between Him and the viewer, and none between mother and child, though she is looking at Him, again, you would have to say, without any great sign of affection. There is no doubt about it, for all His diminutive size, He is the dominant figure, and you can see, even at this tender age, there is no doubt about who is in control. I know you are a young and inexperienced mother Mary, but if you don't mind me saying so, and speaking as a parent and grandparent, you should show them who is the boss right from the start. Of course, yours were exceptional circumstances and you were never in control right from the start, were you? Not even birth control.

The Museo dell'Opera del Duomo might just as well have been called the Giovanni Pisano Show. Many other examples of his work abound, though like his *St John the Evangelist*, *Christ giving the Benediction*, and *Madonna* from the second gallery of the Baptistery, they are rather the worse for wear and have been put in here to protect them from the further ravages of the weather. Too late, as it happens, as any subtle detail that the figures may have originally been given by their creator have been badly eroded: details such as, for instance, the luxuriant folds of the Madonna's robe, and especially the tasselled fringe in the ivory *Madonna and Child*. For my money, that is the best thing about the entire statue, apart from its overall curved shape, which is what attracts your attention in the first place.

But, I have to admit, there are so many rooms here and so much to see in all of them, that I pay scant attention to the clerical robes and vestments and silverware by the score and only a little more time to the illuminated manuscripts and books and paintings. In fact, what is more interesting to me in those rooms is not so much their contents, but the painted ceilings of the rooms themselves (always look up remember) and the use of trompe l'oeil that you would just love to touch to make sure that the paintings really are flat and not three-dimensional as they appear to be. But even if I were as tall as

Alice, I wouldn't do it because they are bound to have cameras in here, watching you, to make sure you do not run off with any of the smaller, more portable exhibits.

I am arrested, however, by a very interesting artefact in the Roman room. It is a broken piece from a sarcophagus and shows a naked man lying face down between two naked ladies who are lying on their backs. His arm is flung over the breasts of the one on his left, while he is squeezing the other by the waist, the one whom he is facing. That's how I would like to be buried, with a bit of female company to while away eternity: like suttee, only twice as good. But since I couldn't have that, the next best thing would be to have something like that on my headstone.

I begin to speculate on what the missing bits of the sarcophagus would have looked like. What if they were on the same theme, like a cartoon strip, with the emphasis on the strip, more and more revealed as you walk round it? That would be a good way of making a stranger pause as they were passing by, wouldn't it? Then they'd read your name. That would be a good way of being remembered, long after you had departed. But I can't see my merry widow agreeing to that. Besides, I expect there is probably some EU directive against having tasteful pieces of art like that in cemeteries.

And on the subject of taste, what about this? It is known as the *Cintola del Duomo*. There is only a fragment of it here, and we have to imagine the rest but that is easy as it would have been very much on the same theme. It is made of red damask and encrusted with jewels, and silver enamel, and gold, and in this panel that has particularly caught my eye because of the way the light has caught the iridescent colours of the mother-of-pearl: blue and pink and yellow and green – and colours that do not remain still, but keep changing according to how you incline your head. It defies description, but if you hold your head still enough, try to forget about the colours and concentrate on the scene itself, it depicts a seated figure on a throne who could be anybody from Christ, to some saint or other, or just a bishop on his chair. But the subject matter doesn't matter; it is a miniature work of art by anyone's standards and this is the thing – this belt stretched *right round the Duomo*! Yards and yards and yards of it, and every inch sumptuously decorated in this manner.

They used to bring it out on holy feast days. Which raises certain questions: How much would just a foot of this be worth? And why would you want to make such a thing in the first place? Where did the money come from? Could they not think of something better to do with the money? Why not spend it on the poor so they didn't have to tighten *their* belts? I bet this belt around the Duomo was not tight – because that would have looked mean. I can just imagine it going right round in big, expansive loops. It beggars belief and no doubt the beggars looked in disbelief also.

And you may not believe this either, but let me tell you a secret. If you were to ask me, what, out of all the interesting, the curious, the fascinating and the wonderful things I had seen in this museum, (that I wasn't particularly interested in coming to in the first place, remember) – what did I like best? My answer might surprise you. As a matter of fact, it is not, strictly speaking, in the museum itself, but outside. In short, the answer is: the cloisters.

I am a bit partial to cloisters as you know, but what is so special about these is not the breath of fresh air after all those stuffy rooms of exhibits, (actually, they are not in the least stuffy) nor is it the guard of honour provided by both the Pisanos' sculptures of saints, evangelists, and prophets, (you can get a bit Pisanoed-off in this museum, as a matter of fact) nor is it the light green of the grass which harmonises with the dark green of the conifers and laurels. Yes, they all play their part in making this place special, but the best thing of all is the view you get of the Tower.

On the ground floor you can see it looking over the back wall – just the Tower, no people at all, and it looks alarmingly close and it looks alarmingly in danger of keeling over at any moment. But more than that, you can get a more elevated view, not only of the cloisters and the Tower, but an unusual perspective of the Campo if you go up to the top floor and wander about the terrace. In my view, I submit, it is worth the price of the ticket alone just for the privilege of seeing these iconic buildings from this unusual perspective.

We return to the ground level of the cloisters again, for one last look before we leave. We know now the Tower is safe after the years of remedial action in which tourists were treated to unsightly displays of the engineering works, of weights and wires. But if we didn't know any better, from this vantage point we could easily be forgiven for the instinctive reaction, flight being impossible and however futile it may be, to turn our backs, to cower away, cradling our craniums in our arms. In former years, of course, there was no such assurance that it would not suddenly come crashing down and crush skulls like eggshells.

In one of the rooms they have some memorable quotes from famous writers who have been here. Coleridge, in his diary of 1804, for example, wrote that what he called the "hanging" Tower, by moonlight, had "something of a supernatural look." There is no chance of my hearing the chimes at midnight here but I am sure he is right, especially in his day, when there would have been no other significant source of light. But the quote that really resonates with me is from Dickens who expresses in his *Pictures from Italy* (1845), the opinion that the natural inclination of most people would be not to lie on the grass on the leaning side of the Tower, as "it is so very much aslant."

I hope they planted that lesser-known Pisano, Bonanno, on the non-leaning side. Imagine spending half a millennium with the thought of that Tower hanging over your head, never knowing when it was going to land on you. The sword of Damocles must have seemed such a slight blade by comparison.

Poor Bonanno. How could he ever have got a wink of sleep, let alone rested in peace?

CHAPTER TWENTY-SIX:
PROTESTS AND A PRINCIPLE

That was the Campo dei Miracoli. If we had had only a fleeting impression of what the Campo was like on our last visit, we had absolutely no idea at all of what the town itself looked like, nor what it had to offer. Now I want to put that right too. But first Iona says we must have lunch. My stomach is in such a tight knot, I don't feel like food, but here we are, on the Via Santa Maria, searching out the best deal.

I am doubtful, on the law of averages, that the first place we look at is likely to be the best, but in the end that is what happens but not before we had spent a lot of time and walked some distance with me still unable to make up my mind - which does nothing to improve Iona's patience or her temper, to say nothing of appeasing her hunger pangs. She tends to let her stomach rule her. When it says it needs food, she doesn't tell it: "OK, I get the message. I'll feed you soon, just wait a moment," she just allows it to bully her into giving in right away. What's more, like a spoiled brat, her stomach is telling her that it wants fries and she tells me that the only place we have seen them is at the first place we looked at, so that is how it comes to pass that we are sitting at a pavement café at an Italian version of McDonalds with its own version of hamburgers which they call Papaburgers for large stomachs and for slightly less large stomachs, Mamaburgers.

From where I am sitting, facing up the street with my beer and notebook in front of me, there is nothing to suggest what lies literally just around the corner. Starting just across the street from the Museo dell'Opera del Duomo, the Via Santa Maria wends its sinuous way down to the sluggish Arno and before you have gone very far, where we are now in fact, the first curve of the street hides the Tower and the Duomo from sight completely. Imagine stepping ashore from the Arno and ambling up this street with no idea of what lies ahead, only to be confronted with the Campo dei Miracoli! It would indeed, seem to the astonished traveller, not like just one miracle, but a whole field of them. And it would be another miracle altogether if, in the whole wide world, the traveller exists who did not know what sights to expect in Pisa.

I explain to Iona that I'm not really wanting anything to eat, that my notebook will provide me with all the food I need (for thought that is) and all I really want and can manage, is a beer, but Iona sweeps aside my protests, saying I must eat something as it is not good for me not to eat anything, so I am forced into ordering a Mamaburger. Iona is having a Hot Dog with sauerkraut. We are sharing the fries, or to put it another way, I am having an occasional one or two. Even although I am not too interested in the food, it is pleasant to be able sit outside, have an ice-cold beer, take the weight off my feet and bask in the unseasonable sunshine, well it is to us, at least.

But this little idyll is about to end. To our dismay, someone comes out of the restaurant, stands by his machine, fits his helmet and a moment later, our food is tainted with the added flavour of the fumes from his Vespa that linger in the air long after he is out of sight and sound with his infernal machine. That, alas, is one of the hazards of dining alfresco in Italy. The others, as they are everywhere, are the winged rats, otherwise known as pigeons, which Iona has a particular aversion to, boldly pecking at crumbs around our ankles and the black vendors who pester you by trying to offload their wares. One even tries to *give* me a bangle when I refuse to buy one, but I don't accept it, just in case, in his culture, that might mean we are officially engaged and he thinks that gives him the right to a *ménage à trois*.

I can't put it off any longer. My stomach will not settle until I phone the airport. But it doesn't matter how often I try,

I get the same result – no result. I just can't get through. As I had discovered in Lucca, and which had somehow escaped my memory, my phone does not seem to work here. I am barred, I remember, with some relief.

There is nothing else for it: I am going to have to go back to the Tourist Information lady and fall upon her mercy. Thanks to the omnipresence of the mobile phone, payphones are few and far between here and those that do exist are more of the card type rather than those that take coins. I am not going to enquire too diligently where I might acquire such a card, but I suspect that that multi-tasking institution known as the *tabacchi* is the most likely source. If it were not for the smokers, life in Italy, I am sure, would grind to a halt, but as a non-smoker and an ignorant tourist, how could I be expected to know that?

Thanks to Dorothy I know that I can receive calls although I can't make them, thus giving the lie to the aphorism that it is better to give than to receive. No point in going back to the Tourist Office just yet – better wait until the lost luggage office wakes up from its siesta. So my heart somewhat lightened, but at the same time heavy that no phone call has yet come, we set off: fed, watered and refreshed to explore the parts of Pisa that the majority of package tourists never reach.

There are some fine buildings on the Via Santa Maria as long as you remember to look up and ignore the shop windows, and presently we come to the Via dei Mille whose width seduces us into thinking it might lead somewhere important. It was a correct decision because it brings us to the Piazza dei Cavalieri, and you can see right away that there is much to admire here.

Pisa is a university town of course, having produced a couple, to say the very least, of the most influential alumni on the planet. And here it is, their alma mater: the University of Pisa. This is probably where the majority of the people on our bus were headed, well, maybe not here exactly, but to the

University in general. Could it be that I was, for a brief time, in the company of some future Galileo, or some mathematical genius like Fibonacci? Quite possibly, if my capability to understand anything they might have said to me was anything to go by.

Of course it looks a lot different now than it did when those bright boys were shedding light on our planet's place within the universe and radically altering the way we conducted our lives upon it. What we are looking at now is the HQ or what people think of as "The University," just like that breathtaking edifice, Marischal College, with its Gothic soaring towers and pinnacles, the second largest granite building in the world and which, in my time, symbolised Aberdeen University, my alma mater. Now, alas, it is part of the University no more and was sold to Aberdeen City Council. And if that fills me with dismay, it is a lot better than what might have happened to it. Believe it or not, if the Nazis had won the war, Hitler had it earmarked for his private residence. Which just goes to show you that Hitler, excrescence though he was, wasn't all wrong if he had such good taste in architecture.

The Scuola Normale di Pisa, originally the Palazzo della Carovona, used to house the Knights of St Stephen. Sgraffito covers the façade from top to bottom and from side to side. Not an inch of the façade has the artist left bare, apart from the windows. I'm not sure if I like it or not. It reminds me too much of tattoos and I do not like tattoos, bad enough on men, especially bad on women. I do however, like the double staircase and even the statue of Duke Cosimo I in front of it and which adds a certain grandiloquence, though he does look a bit silly at the moment with that pigeon squatting on his head.

The piazza is obviously Renaissance in style and if you don't like it (and why ever should you not?) then don't blame me, but Vasari, who designed it. Vasari, artist and author of *Lives of the Great Artists* is one of my heroes, which of course you know, if you have read my earlier work *An Italian Journey* so I will not digress on the merits of Vasari here. It is a huge square with less interesting buildings facing the Scuola Normale and with the church of San Stephano in the corner, next to it.

The most remarkable building in the square however is the Palazzo dell'Orologio which stands on the other side of the piazza, to the right of the Scuola. It is eye-catching because of its unusual shape, like the hands on a clock pointing at twenty to four. There is in fact, a huge clock high up on the top of the building above an arch. Not much use as a clock though. It seems to be broken. Time stands still. But that is better than running fast or slow as it means it is telling the right time twice a day.

The part in the middle is a later addition, uniting two separate towers once belonging to the Gherardeschi family. I prefer the tower on the left as it has some rather attractive Venetian-style windows, while the one on the right, though impressive, has no special distinguishing features. Taken as a pair, the non-identical twin towers look much more appealing as a single construction. I suppose, now I come to think of it, this middle section, uniting but at the same time dividing, performs the same function as it does in a bra and, as far as I am concerned at least, provides an uplifting experience.

It has, however, an interesting, if grisly history, which Dante relates in *The Inferno*.

Set against the background of the warring rival city states of Pisa, Lucca, Florence and Genoa, and all the wheeling and dealing that involved, Count Ugolino had a bit of a chequered history as far as his relationship with the Pisans themselves were concerned, having more of an eye to what was in his interests rather than theirs. In 1288, the Pisans rioted in protest at sharp price increases and food shortages and in the course of these riots, Ugolino killed the nephew of the powerful and influential Ruggieri degli Ubaldini, Archbishop of Pisa. The

Archbishop incited the people to rise up in arms against the Count and when he surrendered, the good Archbishop had not just the Count, but his sons and grandchildren incarcerated in the tower on the right and the key thrown into the Arno, leaving them to die of starvation. The Archbishop obviously taking no risks as far as this family was concerned.

In Dante's version, with a bit of artistic licence, the Count's sons pleaded with him to prolong his own life by eating their corpses:

> *...you are the one*
> *Who clothed us with this wretched flesh: we plead*
> *For you to be the one who strips it away.*

It reminds me of those "improving" tales for Victorian children who willingly sacrificed their lives for the "author of their being." And quite right too. If you can't die for your parents when you are a child – who else can you lay your life down for? Not that there would have been a lot of eating in his sons I suppose, by the time they had starved to death. Still, for raw drama, you can't argue with Dante, and regardless of whether Ugolino decided to eat them or not, he would have had no means of cooking them first.

The Via Ulisse Dini (the not so well-known mathematician and politician) leads us to the Borgo Largo, Pisa's smartest street. But along the way we come across an unusual sight. In front of a church, a score, or somewhat less, of students are sitting on the steps. So what, you may say? What's so unusual about students dodging lectures? Nothing. But this is different. They are displaying a banner, a white sheet actually, on which has been written in bold, black letters: "Studenti Scienze Per La PACE" and underneath, less large: "Università di Pisa."

Actually, they are not on strike, but attending a lecture. Their protest, supported by their lecturers, evidently, is very admirable, I'm sure. But for the life of me, I can't see how this handful of students imagines that attending lectures alfresco is going to make any difference to world peace. A million and more, to mention but one example, marched through London to protest against the war in Iraq, but Blair and Bush, two of the most committed Christians you would ever not want to meet, were determined to wage their latter-day crusade – and they did.

The Borgo Largo is not my kind of street. The arcades are pleasant enough, but there is nothing to interest me here. Shops, especially those who specialise in designer names, such as they are here, are a complete and utter anathema to me. Another thing that I cannot get my head around is the thought that people would be willing to pay those inflated prices just to be considered trendy. Their brains, it seems to me, must be in inverse proportion to the amount of money they have.

And so, we come, in due course, to the Arno. Our side, the left side, or possibly the right side – it's impossible to tell, because, no matter how hard I stare at the water, there is not the remotest sense of a ripple to give a clue as to the direction in which this lazy river is flowing, if it is at all, though I suppose it must, to meet its destiny before it expires. And it is then that I have one of those moments, one of those Damascene epiphanies that makes the meaning of life clear to me. With all due respect to Douglas Adams, he was wrong. It's not what he said at all. The Arno is the answer and it has been staring us in the face for centuries. This is it. This is the Arno principle:

Flow gently through your life. Do not rush to get to the end. It is your destiny to be swallowed up by something greater than you. Why should you hasten to get there? Slow down. Before you are swallowed up in that great anonymity, remember this: the longer the life force flows through your veins, the more you influence those around you. Your banks are the course which you have set for your life; your tributaries, your legacy. They all flow from you. Therefore, be careful where you go and what you do – for you are the future.

From where I am standing, on this side of the river, the winter sun is bathing the buildings in a golden light as if Midas had just run his fingers along them. It looks warm, rich, peaceful, tranquil. On the opposite bank, deep in shade, another message has been inscribed in big, white, block capitals: "PALESTINA LIBERE." It has been imposed upon a much longer message in red, which it has obliterated. You can read any symbolism you like into that, but I suppose it is par for the course to see such graffiti in a university town.

Somewhere off to right, on the other side of the river, but hidden from view by a bend, is the Santa Maria della Spina. Unfortunately, it is just too far away for our timescale and anyway it is probably closed as it is just a tiny little church, or so I allow myself to be consoled by that notion, because this little church with its aptly designed Gothic spires houses an interesting relic – a thorn from Christ's crown of thorns, believe it or not! Now that would have been something to top off our visit to Pisa, but even if the church were open, there would be no guarantee of seeing the relic anyway. Alas, it is not to be, so we retrace our steps across the bridge to discover that two more alfresco lectures are going on.

One is quite well-attended and the lecturer has come prepared because he is at his ease in a comfortable-looking chair, holding forth on something or other. He is wired for sound, speaking into a microphone so his intended audience can hear him, or anyone who has a mind to stop and improve the mind. Even those who don't, who are merely passing by, have no choice but to hear before they pass out of range again. Ironic, if you stop and think about it: this is meant to be a protest for peace and here he is disturbing it.

Not for the first time, I reflect on the difference between lecturing and teaching. Lecturing means delivering your stuff to students who attend through choice; their responsibility alone, to absorb your pearls of wisdom. You don't even have to be articulate in my experience – merely mumble your message and shamble off the stage when you are finished. Teaching, on the other hand, means you are a policeman first and foremost. You must keep discipline amongst those who don't want to be there in the first place. Your responsibility is to make sure, to the best of your ability, that the not-so-always-willing recipients of knowledge absorb it.

So, lecturer or teacher, what would you rather be?

I have never been much of a one for going back the same way I have come and so we take the street that runs parallel to the Borgo. It reminds me of a back street in Naples: all it needs is the washing hung out to complete the squalor. Incredible that this is in the Borgo's backyard! The contrast could not be more striking. It does not take long for us to decide that whatever the lack of attractions in the Borgo, it has a lot more to offer than this.

Our shadows are long as they accompany us across the Piazza Cavalieri, the tattoos on the Scuola looking better in this golden light, just as I look better in a soft light, or by the light of a single candle. We thread ourselves through the eye of the needle that is the arch of the Palazzo dell'Orologio and come in due course to the Via Santa Maria again.

Next stop the Tourist Information Office, unless my phone should ring before we get there, but I have really abandoned any hope by now that it will and my travel through hell is not over yet but just about to enter the next phase...

CHAPTER TWENTY-SEVEN:
MORE MISFORTUNES

The gods never have been on my side. When we get to the Tourist Information Office, I am told that it is not available at present. I think that means, in my parlance, that she is in the pabby, or it might just mean she is out the back having a wee puff.

There is nowhere to sit inside and so Iona and I sit side by side on the steps outside and look at the Campo for what will probably be the last time, since I tend not to revisit places, no matter how much I have enjoyed them as there are just too many other interesting places I have never been. And sitting where we are, it is impossible not to notice, as it is right in front of us, that incredibly ugly blot on the landscape – the untiled dome of the Baptistery, bald as a coot, as blotchy with rust as my son's Metro, the one that I was caught speeding in. If it were a person's skull, he would be taken at once to the isolation ward of a hospital for rare and infectious diseases. Why, oh why, oh why, have they left the dome in this state? It is beginning to get under my skin.

It occurs to me that this is another photographic opportunity. I don't suppose that many people have filmed the Baptistery from here, from this angle, with its unphotogenic side towards you. However, whilst I am waiting for the Tourist Information Office to come back from the call of nature, or something more addictive, I may as well take this unusual shot. Except I can't. Suddenly the screen goes blank. Dead. Death of a battery.

Not to worry, I have another here: Superbattery, bought within a stone's throw of the Brooklyn Bridge and twice as big and half the price it would cost in the U.K. Only, when

I go to the pocket of my jacket where I know it should be, it isn't there and neither is it in any of the other pockets either. In short, I must have lost it. And it shouldn't come as such a great surprise either as, since it has been so hot, had I not been carrying my jacket over my arm, then when that got too much of a burden, tied it by its sleeves round my waist? And now it turns out it had all been a waste of money, for this is its first outing since New York and it has hardly been used. No-one deserves to be this unlucky, I think bitterly.

"What is it? What have you lost now?" Iona asks, more in resignation than rebuke.

I tell her and she puts her head in her hands, her elbows supported on her knees. I can't see her face but the slump of her shoulders tells me the strength has been sapped out of her. She is beyond anger, beyond words of reproach, beyond tears and beyond belief.

This would be bad news at the best of times, but we are in the worst of times. Unless I can get my case out of hock that means an end to filming altogether – for in my case is the charger that I need to recharge my now one and only and ailing battery. It gives the phone call to the airport an even deeper significance, for my camera is also my memory should I ever want to write a book about this trip and judging by the number of things that have gone wrong so far and with us barely halfway through it, I might just want to do that. I didn't think things could get much worse, but they just had.

At last the Tourist Information lady comes and I regretfully explain why I can't phone the airport myself. She is happy enough to phone again, and I wait, holding my breath, hoping against hope that a miracle will be announced. But it isn't. It is still the answer machine. Whoever invented that infernal machine deserves to be cast into hell – along with it.

There is nothing else for it – we will have to go to the airport ourselves. Funnily enough, I am not as disheartened by this as I would have been had I received the news over the phone that the case had not arrived. It would have been difficult to ask supplementary questions through a third party, but face to face with a real person and despite my lack of expertise in the language, I feel I might have a better chance of expressing myself in some way to achieve something, somehow. That's how confident I feel.

"Is there anything else I can do for you?" the Tourist Information wants to know.

"Where do I get a ticket for a bus to the airport?"

"From the *tabacchi* over there. See the yellow umbrellas? Go down that side street and you'll find one there."

"And where do I catch the bus?"

"Just outside the Campo. Cross the street and the stop is right in front of the hotel."

"Thanks. You've been very helpful," and I turn to go. Then, struck by a sudden thought, I stop and turn back. "Tell me, I don't suppose you know why the dome of the Baptistery is like that, do you? Why only one half of it is tiled?"

"As a matter of fact, I do," she beams, as if she has been waiting all her life for someone to ask her that question, just so she could answer it, because so few ever do.

For the next moment, our eyes are doing the communicating over the gap that exists between she who has knowledge and he who does not. Her eyes are sparkling; she is toying with me, milking the moment. My eyes are saying: "Well, go on then, tell me! It's been bugging me. Put me out of my misery." And at last she relents.

"Well, they say it was a sort of lighthouse, that the moon shining off the dome was like a reflector, to guide the ships into the harbour."

Can that really be it? Is that fact or mere speculation? I know that in Roman times, the harbour was where the Piazza Cavalieri is now. I also know that the Romans built purpose-built lighthouses and surely to God, a fire on top of a tower would have been more efficient than moonshine glancing off the lead of the roof, even if it were a lot more shiny then and you could almost guarantee cloudless skies for most of the year. But, I have to admit, using the Baptistery dome would stop you having to lug firewood all the way up the steps of a tower and then having to go all the way down and back up again when you discovered that you had forgotten to bring the stupid matches with you.

I thank her and go on my way, like the Ancient Mariner's wedding guest, who, after the former's little homily, arose a sadder and a wiser man. Wiser perhaps, but certainly sadder at the prospect of having to spend time at the lost luggage office; time that could have been far better spent in Pisa. I think I'll only ever be happy again when I get my case back. And maybe I will within the next hour – but I'm not counting on it.

"Is this where you catch the bus to the airport?" a handsome young man wearing a Royal Stuart tartan scarf asks me, as we stand waiting at the designated place, a few moments later. I am beginning to get the hang of this lingo, for although he is speaking fluent Italian, (as he should, being a native) I have absolutely no doubt as to what he is saying. In fact, I am getting quite used to helping the natives with their travel enquiries. I could even tell them, should it occur them to ask me, why the Baptistery dome is bald.

The bus is packed. No chance of a seat, until little by little, as we go on and on, the passengers begin to thin out and we manage to scramble into a seat at the back. Opposite us happens to be one of those vendors who ply their trade on the environs of the Campo. I can't help but notice him as our knees are practically touching.

His skin is as black as ebony. His trade is in umbrellas. He is carrying one; the others are in a huge holdall that he must haul, like a hunchback, through the crowds who must be as impervious to his sales on a day like today as his umbrellas are impermeable. I doubt if he has sold a single one all day and you must question how many he does sell on a good day for him, which would be a bad day for us.

I can't help wondering about him. Where has he come from? I expect he is going home now, having given up the fruitless task for the day. What would his "home" be like? What kind of a living does he make from this? Even if I knew his language or he mine, or had we one in common, it would be too intrusive to ask these questions, and it is frustrating not to know the answers, even if it was just to confirm or contradict my expectations. Once again, I am forced to question the wisdom of my choice of career. Given my life over again, I would not have been a teacher, nor even a lecturer, but a journalist, methinks. My mother had lower sights for me: she thought I should have been a night watchman because of my nocturnal habits and my fondness for sitting around doing nothing more strenuous than reading.

It's quite incredible: we have been going through the suburbs for miles now, though they would be kilometres here of course, and then, when you least expect it, since there's nothing to warn you – no fields or open places anywhere in sight – we suddenly arrive at Galileo Galilei airport. I think that is such a good name, even if it does sound a bit like a Latin declension. No wonder he made such a success of his life with a name like that, even if he did spend the latter part of it under house arrest.

It is a nice little airport with a jazzy sort of mosaic on the façade and an enormous bird on the lawn in front of it, where passengers in transit take some time off to be photographed next to it. I find it rather frightening myself. At two inches long it might be a sweet little bird, like a sparrow or something, but a fifteen-foot-high sparrow is a scary thing. Imagine if all the little birds were that size - just think what the seagulls would be like! And as for the guano...

Because it is such a nice little airport, apart from Big Bird, it is easy to find the lost luggage office. In the entrance, turn left and there it is in front of you. It's only a few steps but in that time, I have already decided how I am going to play it. I'll act the innocent, play the idiot. I'll assume that Carla's luggage must have arrived by now and I have merely come to pick mine up.

Behind a big glass window I can see about ten people sitting at desks doing something very calmly. They are so cocooned in tranquillity that it takes a bit of time for them to even notice I am there. I could have rapped on the window but I didn't want to irritate them. At last, an attractive young lady looks up from her absorbing work, notices me, comes to the window and slides it open.

"I've come to collect my luggage." I tell her. That's enough for her to know and all she needs to know for the present. As I speak, I pass across the little bit of paper that you get with the barcode, so they can trace your luggage in the event that it should get lost.

She looks at it briefly, then at me, much longer, more suspiciously.

"What flight were you on?"

"Edinburgh to Pisa."

"When did you arrive?"

Bugger! While it is a relief to find that she speaks English, I can see where this conversation is going next. She probably knows the answer already.

"Er…er…Tuesday."

"This is Friday," she informs me, unnecessarily, as if I were the sort of idiot who didn't know what day of the week it was. "Why are you only coming to collect your luggage today?"

I realise the game is up. They are not as stupid as I hoped they would be. But it was worth a try I suppose.

"Well, you see, actually, I picked up the wrong bag at the airport and you've got it here and I have come to collect it."

She picks up the luggage receipt. "Just a moment."

I can see her walking across the room and talking to an older woman who I assume must be her supervisor, who isn't even curious enough to throw a glance in my direction, as if this sort of event were an every day occurrence. Meanwhile, Iona seeing this is not going to be straightforward, tells me she is off to the pabby.

I watch as the supervisor goes across to a filing cabinet and takes out a card. Next she disappears from my sight and when she reappears again a moment later, she has my bag with her. It has a piece of A4 attached to it, which she removes. I realise now that I never had a hope of ever carrying out my deception.

She leaves the bag where it is and with business-like steps, she turns her attention towards me. This looks like trouble, like the shootout in the Western re-enacted, only speeded up, where you need to be quick on the draw. But this is where I have the drop on her. While she had not known I was going to drop in unexpectedly like this, I had anticipated a confrontation and from my holster I have already withdrawn my weapon of mass communication – the proof of postage document. My hostage has been released; will they release mine?

Before she can shoot, I pass the flimsy piece of paper across the window towards her.

"This is the proof of postage. To show you I have posted off the other case."

Wordlessly, she takes it and scrutinises it.

"I'm afraid it is a bit faint," I apologise. I realise I am babbling. She can see all this perfectly well for herself – that the vital names, addresses and signature are all so faint as to be practically illegible.

She looks up. "Just a moment." And with that, she walks away. Now I have no proof of ownership of my luggage or proof of posting the other. My throat is dry; my palms are clammy. I suddenly realise it is very hot in here and slip out of my jacket.

I watch as the supervisor hands the flimsy to the girl who had first come to the window and has a brief conversation with her, then goes away again. For a while nothing seems to happen and then the girl picks up the phone and dials. After a long while, she puts the phone down and goes to have a word with her boss. They have a brief consultation and now they are both coming towards me. This does not look good. They are going to let me have it with both barrels.

"The case is in Livorno," the supervisor announces.

"*Livorno!*" I don't know where that is exactly, except that it is on the coast somewhere. What is it doing there? Surely, if anywhere, it should be in Piombino, where we were to have got the ferry? It sounds as if it has a long way to go and it seems very unlikely that it will arrive before Monday now and Monday is the day the public transport strike is due to start. It looks as if it will be Tuesday at the earliest, before Carla gets her case back. Tuesday, the day we leave.

What's to be done? There is only one thing I can think of – to throw myself on Carla's mercy.

"Er, do you think you could possibly phone signora Cremona and tell her that you have seen the evidence that I have posted the case and ask her if she would be prepared to let mine go?"

Maybe it's because I look so crestfallen they agree to accede to my request. Well, it looks as if that is what they are going to do. They are not the best of communicators; just leave me standing there without telling me anything while they have another of their little consultations. A decision appears to have been made. They split up, again without so much as a glimpse at me over their shoulders, as if what they were about to do were no concern of mine. I can see the supervisor studying the card and presently, to my relief, she reaches for the phone.

She is having what looks like a deep and meaningful conversation, while I wait with mounting suspense. I notice that I am gripping the edge of window ledge as if my life depended upon it. In *Macbeth*, King Duncan found it impossible to *read the mind's construction in the face* and if he couldn't do it, how could you expect a mere peasant like me be to be able to? I can get no clues as to how this conversation is going or its likely outcome.

Now, every so often, the supervisor is looking in my direction. It is unnerving knowing you are being discussed right there in front of you, without any idea of what they are saying. Perhaps Carla is asking: "What kind of an idiot does he look like, or would you not be able to tell just by looking at him?" And the supervisor is telling her.

Wait a moment. This looks like a development. She's getting up and coming towards me and, oh no – she has the phone in her hand. Oh, God, help me!

"Signora Cremona would like to talk to you," the supervisor says, holding out the instrument towards me.

CHAPTER TWENTY-EIGHT: A CASE OF STRESS

It's just as well I was not prepared for this – there was no time to feel terrified. What could she want to say to me, other than berate me for all the trouble and anxiety I had put her through? That's why I am so worried. I had better get in first, try to take the sting out of her attack.

"Hello. This David Addison here. The idiot who picked up your bag at the airport. I am really, really sorry."

"Yes…"

Well, that's a lot better than some of the things she could have begun with and she sounds prepared to listen rather than launch an outright offensive.

"I am really, really sorry for the inconvenience I have caused you. I have posted the bag to you. It should have arrived today, but apparently it is in Livorno. The Post Office people assured me it would arrive today."

"You should have come to Elba with it."

"Oh! Actually, I did look into that but it was too complicated for me to do that."

"It is not so difficult. It is not so far."

Her English is impeccable. She sounds young. And she doesn't sound like a pushover. How can I tell her that I was too scared to meet her? How can I tell her that apart from being too complicated, it was a lot more expensive? It didn't seem worth it, just for the sake of a day, as I had been led to believe.

"Well, you see, it is difficult for us. We don't know our way about and there were so many changes. It looked very confusing. And besides the Post Office told me –"

"If you had told me which ferry you were on," she cuts in, "my husband would have met you at the ferry terminal."

"That would have been very nice of him."

Silence. This is not going very well. She is clearly annoyed that I did not come to Elba and if I had, I would not be in this predicament now, so I have only myself to blame. Under the circumstances, it seems unlikely that my tongue, even if it were made of pure silver, would have much chance of persuading her to release my case, but I can but try.

"Er… you know that the ladies at the airport have seen the proof of postage. I was just wondering if you would be so kind…I know I have no right to ask…it's all my silly fault anyway…but you do know your bag is on its way…and I wondered…er…would consider letting my bag go?"

My ears are straining to pick up any reply but all I hear is a resounding silence.

"You see, I have medicines in my bag that I need to get…" Still silence. "I know you don't know me, but I promise you that I have not taken anything from your bag. I am asking you to trust me, and you *can* trust me, I promise you… Will you be so good to let me have my bag back, please?"

More silence, then: "Let me speak to the ladies."

"Yes. Yes, of course. Thank you. And sorry again for being such a nuisance. Bye."

"Bye."

I make a gesture with the phone to show I am finished with it and the supervisor comes to retrieve it.

"She wants to speak to you."

Just at that moment, Iona comes back. I am shocked to see her – tears are welling up in her eyes. She is doing her best to hold them back, but at the sight of me, her face crumples up and they spill over her cheeks.

"What? Whatever's the matter? What's wrong?"

She has retreated round the nearby corner of the information kiosk so the staff in the lost luggage office can't see her, which means I can't see *them,* just at this vital moment. Whilst one part of my mind is on this new crisis, the other is on what is happening in the lost luggage office. Have I done enough to persuade Carla? She didn't say no and naturally she would have to speak to the ladies herself to issue the release orders. I daren't begin to hope, but I do.

"What's wrong?" I ask again, even more alarmed, since she was too upset to reply.

It's difficult to make out what she is saying between the sobs. "There are full-length mirrors in the toilets (sob sob) and I saw myself (sob sob) and I look such a fright (sob sob). My hair…(SOB SOB)."

"No you don't," I try to reassure her. "Besides, I've been talking to Carla and I think there may be a chance that we might get our case back." And I tell her briefly what has been happening during her absence.

"*Livorno!* Why that's *miles* away from Elba! That's not even halfway!" She sinks into an empty chair and then in adds in tones of abject despair, "I can't see us getting our case back before we leave."

I have a feeling she may be right, but this is the one time when it is better not to agree with her.

For her part, apart from trying to avoid her reflection in the toilets, she has been asking about buses to Lucca and has ascertained that there is one due to leave in ten minutes. If we don't catch that, we will have to wait an hour for the next one and I certainly don't want to have to do that in this place that harbours so many bad associations. It sounds far too short a time and it adds another element of tension and anxiety to an already fraught situation.

"Where does the bus leave from?"

"I don't know. He wasn't very helpful. He just pointed to the entrance and said 'Out there.'"

That effectively cuts more minutes off the few we have. I notice I am sweating profusely and remove my hat.

"Come on, come on!"

Back at the window, I am urging the supervisor under my breath to finish her conversation though at the same time, I am afraid to hear the result.

Ah, I'll know any second. The supervisor has hung up and is coming to deliver the news. I swallow hard.

"Signora Cremona says she does trust you, but she wants to make sure. She wants to wait until her case arrives."

In other words, she doesn't trust me at all, but I wisely refrain from pointing this out. It's a bit of a blow to find that the nightmare is not yet ended, although I had not allowed myself to build my hopes up very high. Then a hysterical voice pipes up at my side.

"Well, she should have had a lock on her case!" Iona is near to tears again. "If she had a lock on her case, we wouldn't have been able to get into it, would we?" And with that, the tears come again and she turns away.

At once, the supervisor who had been so helpful and obliging, visibly stiffens.

"No, no, it's quite all right," I chip in hastily. "I quite understand."

The supervisor appears to be mollified.

"Signora Cremona says you may take your medicines out of your case, however."

I thank her, and turning to Iona I ask, "Have you got the keys?"

I don't expect her to. Why should she? We either expected to get the case back, or not at all. And yet, women carry all sorts of things about with them in their bags, so you never know. But the answer is no, she doesn't.

"I'm afraid we don't have the keys with us," I relay back to the supervisor. "Do you think that you could break into the case for us?"

Once again we are left to our own devices and left to ponder what is going to happen next as she turns away without saying anything. I wish I'd added: "And make it snappy!"

It is frustrating to see the bag sitting there only a few yards away, but it might just as well have been in Elba. Meanwhile, the minutes are ticking away like seconds. Iona has gone to sit down in one of the seats in front of the information kiosk where no-one can see her. My fingers are instinctively beating an impatient and nervous tattoo on the ledge. Infuriatingly, nothing seems to be happening.

Ah, finally, something is. The supervisor and her lovely assistant have picked up our bag, there is a click and to my surprise, the panel beneath the window turns out to be a door and the supervisor slides our bag through, followed by herself and the lovely underling, crouching down on their hunkers to get through the gap.

It's a long time since I saw such an expanse of sheer nylon thigh and it is an even longer time since (in my dreams) I had an attractive young lady kneel at my feet. The lovely assistant is offering me something, and my eyes light up. She has not just come to worship apparently, but has come bearing a gift in the form of an old coffee tin. Not much of a gift, and much more than I deserve you may say, but this one is filled with keys. I've never seen so many in my life before. That tin must be some sort of incubator for there must be hundreds of them in there! And, by the law of averages, one of them *must* work. Only which one? So many keys and so little time!

Having made these deliveries, the ladies back out and to my astonishment, lock the door behind them. I am left alone with our bag and hundreds of keys. I run round the corner to get Iona. Being the one in charge in our house, she has a better chance of recognising the most likely suspect, but by the time she arrives on the scene, with trembling hands, I have already rejected three.

"Out of the way," orders the custodian of the keys. "It's got to be one like this," and she chooses one that has a bit of black plastic on the top. That will cut the search down by a few hundred. I leave her to sift through them and stand up to see what is happening at the other side of the glass. Nothing. The lost luggage staff are merely getting on with their work, as absorbed in it as they appeared to be when I first saw them.

What is to stop us just taking the bag and scarpering? In fact, the lovely assistant and the supervisor are showing such a complete lack of concern or interest that I begin to wonder if what they had done was not intentional. Are they hinting to us that we should just take the bag? Have they felt so sorry for Iona, either because of her dishevelled state or her tears, that they just want us to take the case and go? Or, have they looked at my honest face and trusted me not to run off with it?

I had better not betray their trust if that is the case. Besides, what would happen once they did realise we had run off with it? All hell would probably break loose and it would be all too easy to trace us in the unlikely event that we did make it as far as the hotel. A more likely scenario is they would apprehend us before we left the airport. They are certain to catch us on CCTV and a confrontation with police with pistols is too much like being in a real Western for my taste. On the other hand, I had proved the bag was ours. Can you be arrested for liberating your own property? Would the Italian authorities even care? Surely they have much more pressing matters to be getting on with? Can I afford to take the risk?

I can't. I'm a wimp. And it's no good. The right key has still not been found and we've run out of time. I haven't time to wait to wait to be noticed, so rapping on the window, I attract the attention of the attractive one and explain that we have to go. She unlocks the panel and it is one of the hardest things I have done in my life, to push the case back again but I have no time to dwell on it.

We rush out of the building, our eyes probing the darkness, just in time to see the taillights of a bus disappearing round the bend. Was that our bus? Have we just been too late? If nothing else, it gives us an idea of where the buses might leave from and far down to our right, we can see an empty space where there seems to be some people foregathering, and even more encouragingly, a parked bus, although it has more of an abandoned look about it with no lights on and with no-one standing anywhere near it. Nevertheless, that is where we direct our steps.

In the Italian fashion, there is nothing to tell us where these people are bound: no bus stops, no signs, nothing. The only thing to do is to ask them, and there is no time to faff around trying to speak Italian either.

"What bus are you waiting for?" I ask the nearest person who looks as if he might be able to speak English.

He can't but someone who can, intervenes, and tells us they are going to Livorno.

"Livorno!"

I can't believe it! Now *that* sounds as if it might have been an easier way to get to Elba. Bus or train to Pisa, then the express bus to Livorno, then the ferry. It might well have been a cheaper way of doing it too – if only I had known. I can see Carla's point, but it's not so easy when you've just arrived in a foreign country and can't speak the language. Anyway, it's too late now. I have a more pressing problem at the moment.

"Do you know where the bus to Lucca leaves from?"

By way of an answer, he points to a driver who is just coming down the steps of a bus that has just driven up. "Ask him," he says.

The driver points to where a big white advertising hoarding is gleaming palely like a ghostly face in the dark. "There," says he.

"*There?*" I repeat incredulously. Is he pulling my leg? It seems extremely unlikely. He nods, so off we trot, towards that huge whiteness like two ships being guided to port by the dome of the Baptistery and sure enough, before we get there, we find a bus stop.

It is so dark that I can only read the timetable by switching on my phone and playing its feeble beam over the small print. It keeps going off and I have to keep switching it on again which means I keep losing my place, but finally I manage to make out the word "Lucca." That's what we want. The figures are harder to read, but contrary to what Iona had been told by the unhelpful man in the information kiosk, it seems we have not missed a bus at all, but the next one is due at 6.12. We have fourteen minutes.

"That's long enough," I say to Iona. "I'm going to ask them to break into the case. What do you think?"

"We'd better be quick!"

Surprisingly, the case is still where we had seen it last. Not so surprisingly, the lovely one remembers me, or has not yet had time to forget me, which is good, as it saves moments which might be vital. Breathlessly, I explain what I want her to do, which she then relays to the supervisor. As usual, we are not party to the discussion, and in any case, I scarcely expect them to refuse, given their helpfulness so far. All the same, it is a heartening sign to see the attractive assistant pick up the bag and disappear with it stage left. My spirits have not felt so uplifted since I sent Carla's bag on its way.

But as time passes without anything appearing to be happening, panic begins to mount again. What can be taking so long? By now I feel that I could have broken into it myself, with my bare hands, by brute strength. My nerves are stretched as taut as violin strings and I fight the irresistible desire to look at my watch every twenty seconds. But at last, phew! Here it is! The door is unlocked, the case is pushed through and the assistant is transformed into a goddess as the reason why it took so long to open the case is revealed – they must have found a key, for there is the padlock hanging from the zip by the open hasp.

We fall upon the case like ravenous lions. I've even forgotten to check if the goddess's thighs are on display again, such is my intent on disembowelling my prey. I am meant to be getting out my medicine, so that had better be first, and I may as well take my shaving brush, and a shirt and a pair of pants while I am at it, but before any of these – the battery charger.

Meanwhile, Iona has her own set of priorities too. And if you thought that the hair dryer was the first thing that she removed, you would be wrong: for greater than her need to do her hair, is the need to sew, and after that, the need to read. The hair dryer is next, followed by knickers, next and last.

"Would you like a bag?" asks the goddess.

I look up to find that as she kneels beside us, she is indeed displaying a yard of slim, nylon-clad, heavenly thigh and for that alone, if not for these words, she is promoted to Queen of all the goddesses.

It seems to me, at that moment, that since she is prepared to aid and abet us in this way, they would not have cared in the slightest if we *had* run off with our luggage after all. She returns with a plastic shopping bag for me, accompanied by the supervisor who, befitting her superior status, has a paper carrier bag from some posh shop or other for Iona. I think we might have emptied the entire contents of our luggage into those two bags while they stood and watched us. I suspect the Queen of the goddesses might even have folded my shirt up neatly for me, had I asked her, had there been time for such niceties.

We thank them profusely as they take our bag away. It doesn't matter now if we don't get it back tomorrow. In fact, if it doesn't, Monday is ruled out because of the strike and even if it weren't, we probably wouldn't have bothered anyway as we would be leaving the next day. Please God, let Carla's case have arrived by then.

The bus has certainly not arrived anyway, which is good. But when it has not arrived by 6.15, I start to get worried. Perhaps we have missed it after all. For all I know, what I had managed to read by the light of my phone might still be the summer timetable and they haven't got round to putting up the winter one yet. I have almost convinced myself that this must be the case when, more than ten minutes after the bus was due to arrive, there is still no sign of it. I know that Italian trains work like clockwork, but is it safe to assume that the buses do too?

What are we going to do now? If we can't trust the man in the information kiosk and we can't apparently trust the word of the timetable, then whom can we trust? What makes it even more doubtful that a bus is due soon, is no-one else is here, waiting. How much longer must we hang around waiting in this dark and lonely outpost of the airport? It would be much more pleasant whiling the time away in a café, but how can we do that when we don't know when to expect the next bus? The fear begins to mount that we *must* be waiting in the wrong place. Whatever it says on the timetable attached to the bus stop, it still seems the most obscure and unlikely place to put a bus stop. And yet, if my theory about bus drivers having more lucrative jobs as taxi drivers is correct, this is the very place where you *would* put a bus stop, where only the locals, after a lifetime of living in the area, know where to find them.

And then, after a few more minutes, when the spirit has had a chance to plumb the depths of hopelessness even lower, we can see a bus finally coming along. But is it ours? It doesn't come to a halt until it is well past the stop where it should, if it *is* the bus to Lucca. Two passengers alight, followed by the driver with whom they seem to be on exceedingly good terms just to be merely passengers.

Going round to the front of the bus, there is nothing to tell me where it may be bound. It seems rude to interrupt their conversation. I feel bad enough when I have to butt into the conversation between two shop assistants just long enough so I can persuade one of them to sell me something. All I want this time is information, but I still try to make it as brief as possible.

"Lucca?" I ask, gesturing towards the vacated vehicle.

"Sì," he replies with hardly a glance at me and disappears with the passengers in the direction of the terminal building.

Fortunately, he has left the door open and it is with relief that we sink into the first two seats in the bus, and not without a certain amount of elation. No-one else comes. We sit in the darkness for what seems like a long time, until eventually the driver springs aboard, (probably making up for lost time) and reaching down by his seat, brings out a board which he props up facing the windscreen and in the reflection of which I can read "LUCCA" backwards. It might have been a better idea if he had done that *before* he had left the bus; he might have attracted more customers. But then probably, that is not the idea.

It is good to know we are definitely on the right bus and we can finally relax. It has been a stressful and exhausting day and just to put the finishing touches to it, I remind myself I have lost the new, hardly-used battery for my camcorder. But there are some positives too: I will be able to charge up the old battery and Iona has her sewing and her hair dryer and a book. What more could she ask for? As for me, back at the hotel, I have a bottle of gin waiting. What more could I ask for?

These are all very comforting thoughts as the headlights of the bus cleave the darkness as we head towards Lucca, not the way we came, but through a series of somnolent little villages.

And after a day like today, I will be glad to get to my bed too.

CHAPTER TWENTY-NINE:
A CLOSELY-OBSERVED STATION

"What was the weather like thirty years ago tomorrow?" asks Iona, apropos of nothing, as basking in the bright sunshine, we sit over our croissants at the Scilla.

Her memory is a prodigious as an elephant's and she likes to test me with questions like this every so often, but this one seems particularly perverse. She usually says things like: "Where we were two years ago today?" or three or four years ago, but I don't recall ever being asked to cast my mind back so many years before and never where we were the *next* day. Why not this day for heaven's sake? And why this variation on the theme? It seems such an impossible task that I am not in the mood for indulging her. In any case, it takes me a bit of time to come to in the morning and pointless conversation is just too much effort and just too annoying at this time in the morning. She, on the other hand, is unusually bubbly. That's because she feels like a new person with her hair washed, dried and styled.

"Haven't a clue!" I reply in a tone that is intended to convey that I couldn't give a monkey's either.

As ever, she is exasperated by the feebleness of my memory.

"Oh, for heaven's sake! Think about it! Where were we thirty years ago?"

Oh, God! She wants me to *think* as well as speak. How tiresome. Right, let me think. Ah, yes, I remember now! Put that way, it is quite easy really. We were in Missoula, Montana when I was doing my year's teacher's exchange.

That is acknowledged with a nod of approval. "And what day is it today?"

"The 8th of November of course!" I mutter grumpily. How much longer is this going to go on?

Not the answer that was desired. An exasperated shake of the head this time.

"And what else is it?"

"Hélène's birthday of course!" Really, she is treating me like an idiot with this step-by-step questioning. Hélène is our daughter.

"So?"

"So what?"

"What was the weather like the day after her birthday?"

"Oh, for God's sake, how I am expected to know that?"

"Montana? November? Winter?"

"Could it possibly have been snowing?"

"Right! You see, you knew all along!"

She is triumphant. It's amazing what you know if you only stop and think about it. It's just I don't very often. There are more important things to think about, surely?

"And your point is, exactly?"

"Well, look at us here in this glorious sunshine and thirty years ago tomorrow it was snowing!"

Good grief!

Well, we'll just have to see what the weather brings tomorrow, but we will not be here; we'll be in Florence. After the stresses of yesterday, we are going to take it easy today and stay in Lucca, but first of all, we are going to the station to find out when the trains leave.

It's easy to get there: all we have to do is follow the racing track round until we come to it. Well, that is my plan, but Iona has another. She wants to go through the town and then cut through at right angles. I think it is always best to begin the day with an argument: it means the day is not spoiled – it was bad from the beginning.

So, here we are at the railway station. How we got there, you will have to decide for yourself.

Trying to make sense of the acres of timetables plastered to the wall next to the ticket office is like my reading of the Rosetta stone: I know it means something significant, but I can't understand a word of it and if I did manage to decipher anything, I wouldn't trust my translation enough to put any faith in it. There is another option however: you can buy your ticket from a machine in the foyer. Speaking as someone who can't even make the machine in my local Asda's cough up my parking ticket when I feed a couple of pound coins into it, that is a non-starter. Even if I worked out the right buttons to press, I just know, with my luck, it would swallow up my money without producing the goods and trying to explain to some official or other what had happened so I could get a refund would be just too tiresome, to say the least. No, the only thing to do is speak to a real person and hope to God that of the two clerks on duty, I get one who speaks English.

While I join the queue, Iona goes to sit outside in the sunshine. She has an encyclopaedic memory for the past, but I suspect, she has the gift of foresight also, for it soon becomes apparent that this is not the queue for people who just want to buy tickets to local stations. These are buying tickets to God knows where – to the ends of the earth it looks like, to judge by the length of time it is taking them. It involves a great deal of looking at the computer screen and a great deal of what looks like the exchanging of the passengers' and clerks' life histories before a ticket is issued, only for the process to begin all over again as the next passenger steps up to the confessional.

Counting the number of people who are ahead of me and multiplying by the estimated number of minutes it is taking each person to be served, then dividing that sum by two (since there are two clerks) takes up much of my time, given my lack of arithmetical skills – only for my painfully arrived at conclusion to be thrown into complete disarray by the sudden shutting up of shop by the clerk at the booth on the right, probably the one who speaks English. That would have been enough, had I been near the end of the queue, for me to have given up in despair, but having invested so much time here, I am not giving up now and resolutely stand my ground. That's the problem. I have been standing on this same piece of ground for some five minutes now.

Iona appears to find out what is keeping me, sees my place in the queue has hardly advanced at all and goes out again to further her tan. Not that she is really interested in such a thing. It would be a far, far better thing with her fair skin, if she stayed in here and allowed me to absorb some of those radioactive rays, for my thick skin is much better adapted to dealing with them. But no, she prefers to bask in the glory of the sunshine than loiter palely in the cool shade of the interior here, a place that would suit her much better.

By interminable inches, I draw nearer the head of the queue, but that is nothing compared to how the queue is lengthening behind me. I can see, though apparently the couple in front of me can't, having apparently fallen asleep on their feet, that the vacated ticket office has now reopened and the clerk, having safely stowed his handbag, is now ready for business. A little nudge and a gesture from me and they get the message and move forward. That means I am next for the chop even if the one on the left should suddenly shut up shop.

But actually, I am wrong again. I am not. The rapid click-clack of high heels on the marble floor draws my attention to a young woman who has breathlessly just come into the station. She says something to me in the passing and rushes up to the ticket booth, which just at that moment, has become free. It wasn't a question – like did I (not to mention all the others behind me) mind if she went in front of me? No, she was merely apologising for what she was just about to do. Not that I mind. She's a comely enough wench and her arrival has brightened up the proceedings. I can't speak for the others though. But in any case, it doesn't take very long anyway before her heels are click-clacking smartly onto the platform.

Whatever other kind of mistress she may or not be, she is a mistress of perfect timing – for no sooner has she set foot on the platform when a train draws in. That may be cutting it a bit fine, but that is my idea of when you should turn up for trains and boats and planes.

It only takes me a minute, too, after so many spent waiting, to purchase the tickets, something I could have done in a matter of seconds from the machine if only I had known what I was doing. The people behind me in the queue will have been surprised, if not delighted, by my speedy despatch. In fact, I am rather surprised at the degree of patience shown by these prospective passengers, given the Italians' hot Latin temperament, and as far as I could tell, not even objecting to the way the young lady in a hurry just ignored the queue in much the same way as their government ignores EU legislation. But it is maybe only behind the wheels of their cars that they can't bear to be behind you, because that is an affront to their manhood.

There was one good thing about my long stand in the queue, however. The English-speaking clerk did provide me with the benefit of his advice, something a ticket machine could never have done: I must make sure that I catch a train before 8 pm as that is when the strike is due to start. Not Monday, but Sunday evening.

I'll be leaving long before then; Iona will make sure of that. In any case, she needn't worry anyway. There is no way that I want to pay for a taxi from Florence to Lucca. I'm going to leave plenty of time just in case of any mishaps and the way I've been having them this week, I want to leave a wide margin of safety so there can be no possibility of missing the last train.

The sun, still streaming down for all it is worth, beckons, and I, in dire need of resting my legs and Iona having come back at last to reclaim me, we wander onto the platform to soak up the heat. It is nice just to sit in the sun and relax. But if any trains should happen to come along, so much the better, just for interest's sake. In fact, there is one at the end of the platform now, not the sort of train that I would have thought that even an anorak would be interested in; a bit of a wreck in the locomotive sense of the word in fact.

I saw a film once, in the Sixties, called *Closely Observed Trains*. I can't remember the first thing about it now, except I think it was Czech and in black and white, which is not all that surprising – that I can't remember it I mean. If I can't remember what the weather was like thirty years ago, how am I expected to remember what a film I saw, only once, forty years ago, or more, was about?

Having said that, I do obviously remember the title, perhaps because I have a certain fondness for trains, or rather train journeys in particular. I like the motion of them and the way that the landscape constantly changes before your eyes and you don't have to do a thing but let it unreel before you. And should that get a bit boring for any reason or other, you can closely observe your fellow passengers – just as long as they don't catch you at it and mistake you for a perv rather than a writer.

At the other end of the bench, leaving a respectable distance for her personal space, I can't help but notice a woman with elephantiasis. Only a few hours ago I had been drooling over the shapely thighs of the Queen of the goddesses (well I presume she had one to match). Now, I try my best to avoid looking at this woman's legs, but the funny thing is they draw my gaze, as powerless to resist them as an iron filing is to a magnet.

It reminds me of my former landlady, (whom I have already immortalised in another book) who typically sat with her legs apart, a position that came naturally to her, notwithstanding the fact the she was virgo intacta and although our lives only crossed in her latter years, I am prepared to go to my grave affirming that is the absolute truth. And what is also true, is that no matter how hard I tried to ignore it, that expanse of pink bloomers, vast enough to sail the *Mary Rose,* kept drawing my eye back as if I couldn't believe what I was seeing, despite the feeling of revulsion it aroused in me.

Because of her elephantiasis, her companion has been designated to queue for their tickets and it is on account of my hat that we fall into conversation with her, on her initiation. She wants to know where I come from. Could I possibly be Australian?

So that is how I come to tell her that I got my hat in Montana and in exchange, learn that she and her companion are from Santa Catalina, California and they are going to Bagni di Lucca to visit an ex-patriot who happens to come from there also. But before we get to exchanging addresses, their train is called, we bid each other adieu and their train shambles out of the station. That was it, the stationary one; the wreck at the end of the platform. Just the local hack shuttling up and down the track between Bagni and Viareggio probably. How dull. How boring. That's not what I call a train journey.

Now this is more like my idea of a train: the antidote to that, just arrived on the other side of the tracks, probably all the way from Florence. Streamlined and smart and not something I have ever seen in Britain, probably because our bridges are too low – a double-decker. And once again, the evidence is before my eyes, why the continentals are so much better at public transport than we are. Wherever you go in Europe, you can buy public transport for a song, a week's transport in any capital you would care to mention for just about as much as it would cost me to make the single two-mile journey into my town, if I were not in possession of my bus pass. And the Government can't understand why they can't persuade us to leave our cars behind…

Hopefully, that will be the same train, only in reverse, that we will take to Florence: an hour-and-a-half's journey through the hills. Sounds delightful. Almost better than Florence herself.

I am really looking forward to that.

Of course, I should have known better than to let the gods get a hint of this keenly-felt desire.

CHAPTER THIRTY:
MAKING A KILLING

Apart from the ramparts, and the amphitheatre, the most iconic structure in Lucca must be the Torre Guinigi and that is where we are heading now. On such a beautiful day like today, we should not only have this bird's eye view of Lucca, but we should be able to see for miles around too.

If Pisa's tower is interesting because of its tilt, Lucca's tower is interesting because of the trees that sprout from its top like overgrown weeds, which, as I mentioned before, give it a ruinous, dilapidated appearance. In fact, while it is not a ruin itself, it is the only survivor of four towers that once belonged to the Guinigi mansions.

Paolo Guinigi was the ruler of Lucca at the start of the 15th century, from 1400 – 1430. In fact he was the King of Lucca, no less, but no despot, who ruled with the consent of the people. In these desperately troublesome times, when cities like Siena and Pisa were falling to ambitious city-states such as Milan, Florence and Genoa, to name but three, Lucca never was conquered. Those massive walls played their part of course, but so did Paolo Guinigi. Thanks to his statesmanship, or wheeling and dealing with the influential connections that he had formed due to his massive wealth, to say nothing of a judicious marriage here and there, Lucca retained its independence.

Unlike the Leaning Tower of Pisa which is a thing of beauty, the same could not be said for the Torre Guinigi, which, constructed of that most unappealing of building materials, red brick, has little to recommend it apart from the trees. There are seven of them in total and the good thing about them is that they are holm oaks, a species of evergreen oak, so the top of the Torre, unlike the dome of the Baptistery in Pisa, will never need to worry about growing bald.

In exchange for €7 we are permitted to climb the 230 steps to the top of the tower. It is a matter of slight concern that we are not issued with any tickets. There had better not be a little man at the very top checking tickets or I am going to get a little bit upset at having needlessly expended all that effort.

We have hardly begun our ascent, when whom should we meet, coming down, but Beate leading a group of tourists. Much to my astonishment, she greets me with a whoop of delight. In fact, I can't ever recall being greeted so enthusiastically before – even by my nearest and dearest. If it produces this kind of effect on someone whom I've just only met, maybe I should spend more time away from them in future.

"Mr David!" she exclaims, and taking me by the arm, steers me into a corner of the staircase, while at the same time, over her shoulder, she instructs her brood, in German, to continue to the bottom and wait for her there. "Tell, me Mr David, what is happening about your case?"

I am very happy to bring her up to date with the latest developments and she is very happy for us too and on this happy note we say our *Auf Wiedersehens.* Has she been lying awake, wondering what was the latest news was, I wonder, like someone who can't wait for the next and possibly the final episode of a whodunit on television? For someone who at first seemed reluctant to take on our case, she is now displaying the most extraordinary interest.

To cheer you on your way as you climb the tower, at the start, there are some paintings of medieval scenes and photographs of medieval manuscripts. Nearer the top, the stone steps give way to iron stairs, narrower and steeper, until you come to the last flight which is narrower still and even steeper, until you struggle out of a narrow trapdoor at the top. Fortunately there is no wee man to check our non-existent tickets, and in the unlikely event that my mother-in-law had made it this far, just as she would not manage to squeeze into the shower in the hotel, she would never have made it up this final flight: she would be stuck fast like a cork in the neck of a bottle. Actually, given her figure, a champagne cork would create the appropriate image and if we *had* somehow, managed to push her up to the very last step, the effect really would have been rather startling when she popped out of that narrow funnel, when you think how far a champagne cork can fly.

And it is a very confined space up here too, with little space to manoeuvre as most of the space is taken up by the so-called garden. A narrow passageway runs round the perimeter, which would be fine if you had the place to yourself, but which I imagine, "hardly ever happens" as Eliza Doolittle aspirated. It is busy enough up here at the moment and if my timing is not quite as perfect as the young woman at the station, at least I avoided being up here at the same time as Beate and Brood.

On the other hand, our arrival coincides with a young couple who seem determined to photograph each other from every angle and from every corner, to say nothing of all the bits in between. It's not a matter of just taking a snapshot either. That would be maddening enough, but what really infuriates me is they are taking so long about it, not being satisfied with one shot, but taking three or four or even more from the same place, with complete disregard for the other people up here who want merely want to move on to another degree of their 360° tour but are held up by this photographic logjam. I suspect they must be in love and love is blind and that is why they can't see the mayhem they are creating up here.

It's incredible isn't it? Here I am upon a monument, like Patience personified, and I've only been in these strangers' company for a matter of minutes, but I already have an overwhelming desire to seize both of them by their legs and toss them over the edge so they could romantically die together. I am sure that is what they would have wanted – to die like that, and by God, I swear, if I have to spend any more time waiting for her to take this photograph, that's precisely what will happen.

But instead, I think better of it and opt for the less drastic option of just walking between them as if they weren't there, without so much as a *scusi,* or a word of apology for spoiling their photograph. It's annoying not to know if they were annoyed or not, or having only eyes for each other, didn't notice this little interruption.

It is fun however, looking down on the roofs of the houses with their variegated tiles of orange and brown, marvelling at how narrow the streets are, how the Fillungo does indeed look like a thread as it meanders its way through the tightly-packed buildings and trying to spot the landmarks. The campanile of San Frediano is easy to recognise, as is the Duomo and San Michele, but trying to spot the amphitheatre is a lot more challenging, until finally, we recognise the convex curve that must form part of the outer walls. The empty centre, surprisingly, is not visible from here, despite our 144 feet elevation.

Lifting our eyes to the distant hills, Iona is the first to notice a curious effect. The peak of a nearby mountain is partly covered by cloud, but it doesn't look like a cloud at all, more like a volcano erupting, a plume of vapour seeming to issue from its side and settling in a dense pall over the summit like the black cap judges used to don before announcing the death penalty. Maybe it *is* a volcano after all, it looks so incredibly like it, though you would expect it to be a bit further south, if it really were.

We are no strangers to active volcanoes in Italy, having been lucky enough to be in Sicily when Etna erupted in October 2002. Then, we were not in any danger, but if this were a volcano just about to blow its top, this would not be the safest place to be. Besides, we have spent sufficient time up here to merit all the huffing and puffing we had had to do to get up here. As we insert ourselves into the narrow neck of the bottle in order to descend, the irritating young couple are at the other side of the tower, still taking photographs. They could be up here for some time yet. If it really is a volcano, they might yet get a chance to die together.

We encounter another young couple as we stroll along the Via Fillungo not many minutes later – Dinah and Rod, who are interested, though not so much as Beate, to know the latest in the case saga. They had enjoyed the Baralla and since they are going home tomorrow, and we will be in Firenze, I imagine this is the last time we will bump into them and if we are to meet again, it will be on our native soil.

Lunch is a leisurely sandwich on the walls as usual, even to the extent of sitting on the same bench. How pathetic is that? We're turning into a staid old couple, sharing a park bench, whiling away a sunny afternoon. Actually, it is just as well that it is not raining, for we are beginning to run out of things to do, and if all else fails, we can always complete our circumnavigation of the walls, going clockwise this time, just for a wee change, to spice up our lives.

"Why don't we visit Puccini's house?" I suggest. Why not indeed? It is the 150th anniversary of the maestro's birth after all and what could be more fitting than that to pay homage to the great man by visiting his birthplace, even if I am not an opera fan. If he had been a famous writer, I would not have hesitated, probably would already have been there in fact. I know I have seen one of those brown signs to it somewhere. But where? In the end, we have to resort to the map, which shows you how we have still not got the hang of all the twists and turns, the meandering streets, lanes and alleys of this maze that is medieval Lucca.

It is elementary, if you think about it. By an amazing coincidence, Puccini's house happens to be in the same rather shabby little square as the seated bronze statue that we had seen on the first day. It's a rather shabby-looking house too – and it is closed. Not just closed for the afternoon or the day;

it looks as if it has been closed since the day Puccini left it as a lad. You might have thought, in this year, of all years, they would have made an effort to have had it open for the public and although it may not be the tourist season, you would have thought that they would have wanted it open for the day of days – the 22nd December, his birthday, so all those Puccini fans could be there on that special date with history.

Perhaps they will. But then again, perhaps we make too much fuss about the half-centuries and the centuries, like we do the minutes. Why not celebrate the 151st or the 152nd anniversary? That would give them time, would it not, for them to get the Puccini house into order, for admirers from all over the planet? And if it is not, well then, the next year will do, or the next...It's just a pity they picked the 150th and made all those posters all over the town, only for this place where the maestro started out on life's fitful fever, to be closed.

While I have had the occasion, in the course of this narrative, to consider my choice of career and some alternatives, it would never have occurred to me to consider being a restaurateur. But this is an option that now occurs to me, as deprived of the Puccini house, I am forced to turn my attention elsewhere. I don't have far to look – only as far as the restaurant across the street.

Like the Puccini house, it is closed, but unlike it, we know when it will open again. A scrap of paper on the door tells us, in English: "Closed for holiday. Open in May." That can't be bad, can it? I've always been more predisposed to holidays than work, but this makes the length of teachers' holidays pale into insignificance by comparison. Imagine being rich enough to go on holiday for half the year! Admittedly, you would have to work pretty hard for the other six months and work long hours, but the late hours would not have presented any problem for me, would have suited me actually. In fact, I can just see me wandering amongst the customers, encouraging custom and building up a clientele by offering a privileged few diners a drink on the house, which of course, in the interests of good business, I would have to drink with them.

Of course, the real secret of having a successful restaurant is to have a good chef and I have that covered. Have I not got the waistline to prove it? Iona is a most excellent cook, who enjoys cooking, who likes experimenting and whose results nearly always end in success. I wouldn't mind being a guinea pig in that respect, if she wanted to try out some new recipes. In fact, the more I think about it, the more I think Iona and I have missed our *métier*. What a team we could have been! While she slaved over a hot stove in the kitchen, enjoying cooking hundreds of meals for hundreds of customers, there would I have been, enjoying what I enjoy doing – drinking, and being convivial. Of course, I would have to remind myself it was work, but I would console myself with the thought that it would all be over in six months and then I would jet off to some place in the sun where I could enjoy a drink or two by the pool without having to butter people up (and trying not to miss them too much).

CHAPTER THIRTY-ONE:
CLOSELY-OBSERVED LUCCHESE

So, what are we going to do now? What Iona and I tend not to do on holiday is sit and relax, sit and let the world go by – we are usually rushing about to see some point of cultural interest or other and we'll be doing plenty of that tomorrow, so maybe it's time for a wee change. Besides, I reckon we have seen just about all we want to in Lucca. Anything I might have been interested in visiting, like the Palazzo Pfanner, like the Puccini house, is closed.

So that is how, from between my lips, comes one of the most unlikely sentences you are ever likely to hear me utter.

"Why don't we go for a coffee?"

It certainly brings Iona up with a start and she readily agrees before the insanity wears off and I have a chance to change my mind. I am not quite the utter nutter she supposes however, for there is cunning in my plan. I have been economical with my suggestion. What I am actually saying is: "Why don't you have a little coffee and I'll have a big beer?"

So that is what she has and that is what I am having along with a huge bowl of peanuts. This is not the sort of bowl that restaurants give you to dip your fingers in after eating a bowl of mussels; this is the sort of bowl that your mother put on your head when you were a boy before giving your hair a trim. And it is practically full!

"Oh, no you don't," says Iona removing the bowl from my reach, after I've only had a few handfuls. "You're not expected to eat the entire bowl and you are not getting any more."

That's what I like about Iona – she knows what is good for me, but actually she's more worried about herself, that I'll end up not wanting to go out tonight – like last night, when we were too tired and too relaxed after a glass or two of gin to venture out again and so we had ended up by dining in and feasting on peanuts and other snacks that we had purchased from Esselunga. I know I have no chance of getting off with that two nights in a row.

We are on the Via San Paolino, sitting outside a bistro facing the massive edifice of the church of the same name. As we passed it in the evenings it had intrigued me, for it appeared to be the hub of Lucca's nightlife. Not that it's that big a place; it only has a few tables and chairs outside. But location is everything, or has a big part to play in operating a successful business and there is plenty of seating available – the steps of the church where the young of the city have plenty of room to spread themselves with their pints. And if ever the Italian government should get around to banning smoking in pubs and restaurants, this place won't lose any custom like some others might do, for it is in advance of the legislation.

After a while it soon becomes apparent that something is about to happen, for in small numbers at first, children aged anything from seven or eight to twelve or thirteen, start congregating outside the church. It's like that scene in *The Birds* where you first see two or three birds on the telephone wires, then when the camera comes back, there are quite a few more and a while later there are hundreds of the blighters. That's what it's like when I look up from my notes for the third time, to see the church swarming with kids. Some are accompanied by parents or grandparents, but the majority are willingly turning up by themselves. Now there's a sight you don't see every day, even in Italy!

Having met up with their friends, they enter the church in their groups and are lost to view. Whatever is going on, it certainly won't be a mass, that's for sure, to attract such masses of fresh-faced, eager children. And just think, if I hadn't been sitting here, I'd have had absolutely no idea that this popular event was taking place, part of the every day life and culture of

Lucca. Maybe it happens every Saturday – a sort of Saturday club where harassed parents can offload their offspring. (As if they hadn't been doing that all week by sending them to school.)

Presently, although I can't see, I can hear what is going on: a young female voice, clearly amplified through a microphone; the responses in unison of scores of young voices; a cheery song (not a hymn) led by the female voice; then silence, or at least nothing my ears can pick up. Maybe they are getting the religious bit now.

Iona's coffee is long since finished, while my beer, being bigger for a start, takes longer. It also takes longer because, as usual, I am writing up my notes. Conversation therefore, as usual, is not of the most scintillating kind. In fact, it is not of any kind at all and Iona takes the chance to do something more stimulating – to do a bit of window-shopping. I seize the moment, and after a quick look round to make sure she is not there, I grab the bowl of peanuts and bring it to within easy reach of feeding my face.

Just then there is an almighty clatter and for a moment I think it a sign of heavenly displeasure, like God clearing his throat in admonishment: "You know you shouldn't be doing that. You know what La Belle Dame Sans Merci said. Well, don't say I didn't warn you…" But it is only the clash of two cyclists who have collided at an intersection and it sounds a lot worse than it is. They pick themselves up, dust themselves down, remount and cycle away. It's the first collision I have seen, but no doubt it happens many a time and oft in these narrow, bike-infested streets.

Another thing I have noticed about Lucca is the weather: it tends to be lovely in the morning but less fine later. And today is no different. It had clouded over some time ago and now, finally, it has started to rain. It's not what we Scots think of as rain, not even a light drizzle, more like a heavy mist. Certainly not heavy enough to make me put my notes away and down my beer hastily before it becomes diluted, but it has the most profound effect upon the Lucchese whose umbrellas suddenly blossom like buds opening out in time-lapse photography. Even the cyclists have umbrellas, steering with one hand; one is even shrouded in a wheel-to-wheel cape as if she were cycling through a monsoon.

It seems to me as if the Lucchese are suffering from collective ombrophobia. I was at primary school with a boy like that, who was so scared of the rain he would make a beeline for cover at the first drop. Perhaps his mother told him he was so sweet he would melt like a sugar cube and willingly, he believed. Somehow or other he overcame his phobia, perhaps when he saw that the likes of me, though short, had not dissolved completely away though soaked to the skin. And I remember too, the day he splashed through the puddles in celebration of his liberation from this limiting phobia shouting, "Look! Look at me!"

Apart from the ubiquitous umbrellas, you have to admit the Lucchese come well prepared to battle against the perils of possible precipitation. Take this other extreme case. I had been attracted to this young, blonde woman coming from the church because of her conch-shaped, lilac hat, reminiscent of something from the Twenties (not a time otherwise noted for its good taste in fashion) before I noticed that she was worth admiring in her own right. And my instinct was right, for noticing a certain dampness in the air, she stops on the steps and from her bag produces a blue plastic Mac which tones perfectly with the hat. It is more of a cape really, the sort of item of apparel favoured by Dracula with a high, wide collar. She zips it right up to her chin and when she turns the collar up, to my astonishment, I can see that it has clear side panels so like a visor, she can see out, safe from any raindrops landing, never mind staying, on her nose and eyelashes.

And it's a tongue lashing I get when La Belle Dame Sans Merci returns. It would have been a much smarter move on my part if I had moved the bowl of peanuts back to where she had left them before she came back, but I hadn't, having been too enthralled by the Lady of the Cape, and now I have to pay the price for all the free peanuts I have eaten. However, the verbal mauling is mitigated somewhat by my drawing Iona's attention to the aforementioned who, fortunately, has been delayed by happening to bump into one of her admirers (there must be many of them) and is engaged in conversation, while, for her part, Iona is struck speechless by the rainwear.

And it is Iona I have to thank for turning my attention to another phenomenon that I might not otherwise have noticed.

"Have you noticed," says The Guardian of the Peanuts, "how just about everyone is wearing boots?"

I hadn't actually. She is referring to the female of the species rather than the male and it's not surprising I hadn't noticed this before, since when I look at ladies, especially the lovely ones, my mind tends to be on higher things. But there's no denying, after just a few minutes' lowly observation, she is right. I suspect it is really just an extension of their ombrophobia.

They come in a variety of colours of course, that is to be expected, but I think that even I would have noticed these, and I am not talking about welly boots here, by the way, but proper leather boots – in a luminous pink. If you are old enough to remember teddy boys' luminous socks, that is the colour. And if you don't, you are lucky. But what about these, with the polka dots? Just imagine two tubes of *Smarties,* then imagine a fluffy pink fringe on top, just to tastefully finish them off.

I might have wandered around Lucca all week and never chanced to come upon such colourful and interesting sights like these. But just by sitting and watching in what the Lucchese take for rain, we are happy again.

Like W. H. Davies attested, and God knows, my life has been *so full of care* these past few days, there is much to be said for just sitting still and staring at whatever passes by. Perhaps the time has come to put my passport into a drawer, get out the slippers, put on the cardigan, sit at my front door, travel no more and just watch the world go by. That would be so stress free – and so boring.

But after the fiasco of Carla's bag, that is indeed what I might find myself doing if I am not careful. I had better make sure I make no more mistakes this holiday.

Just then, it seems to me, a sound rends the heavens. Was that the sound of thunder? The funny thing is the skies are already clearing up.

CHAPTER THIRTY-TWO:
IN DIRE STRAITS

The rain goes off as the Lucchese would say, or the haar burns off as we Scots would put it; the sun comes out again and the umbrellas come down.

We are heading for Esselunga for some vital supplies after the damage we inflicted on it last night, and just after the Tourist Information Office and on our way to the Porta San Donata, whom should we happen to see again but the Lady of the Cape, talking to another admirer. It must take her a long time to get home I muse, every time she ventures out without her husband. I suppose she might make some allowance in her time schedule for that, but she's not making much concession to the weather – the collar has come down, but the cape is still on.

Apart from the gin replacement, thanks to the Rustic restaurant, I am also in search of some *limoncello* now I know how it should be served. In addition to that, we must purchase a less stimulating beverage - Bei & Nannini coffee which Hélène had commissioned us to bring back as soon as she heard we were Lucca-bound. I don't know how she knows about it, but it happens to be made in Lucca, so of course it is a perfect souvenir for us (well Iona actually, as I prefer instant) and a present for those back home. That means one for our son, one for Gardiner who phoned the hotel for me, and one for the neighbour who lives down the lane because she looks after the cats. Just as well they are vacuum-packed and don't weigh very much.

But which to pick? *Forte, delicato, macinato moka* or even *decaffeinato*, which seems to me to be as pointless as alcohol-free whisky, (as good an example of oxymoron as you are likely to come across) which, as far as I know, has not been "invented" yet, thank God, though they have done that to the wine and the beer. Yet, in this secular age, where nothing is held sacred, it would not surprise me one of these days, to find on my supermarket shelf, a whisky boasting 0% alcohol – proof that the lunatics have finally taken over the asylum.

If I had thought there were a bewildering amount of coffees, that is nothing compared to the aisle of pastas. Even Iona is impressed and hadn't noticed it at first until we got to about two-thirds down the aisle when she suddenly remarked, in a tone of awe, "Do you realise this aisle is full of pasta?" As I was marching on smartly to get to the wine and spirits aisle, I hadn't paid it much attention, especially as I am not a pasta lover, by and large, especially the big thick tubes which look like the arteries of some poor slaughtered beast. She's right. It's incredible the number of things that the Italians have thought up to do with pasta; there must be as many types of pasta as brands of whisky. Each unto their own.

It's when I am standing in front of the bottled water, funnily enough, that it happens. My stomach rebels and turns to water, only that doesn't convey the pain of it. Imagine a fist of iron clenching your guts in a vice-like grip and squeezing, then letting go again, then a few minutes later, grabbing your entrails again. It is not the sight of the water that is doing it. After all, I am accustomed to putting some in my whisky and I do my teeth with it, so I am not totally unfamiliar with the substance. No, I know what the problem is: it's the peanuts. I am paying again, not only for my recent transgressions, but last night.

"Dov'è toiletten?"

I have no idea if the last is an Italian word or not, but the girl at the till seems to understand me well enough, or at least the desperate look on my face, for she points to her left and in which direction I head right away just as fast as a clenched sphincter will let me. Which is not very fast, considering that it includes a forced stop as the cramps come again and I find I am powerless to move until they go off again.

But when I get to the exit/entrance, no sign of the pabby can be seen, nor are there any signs to them. There is, however, a flight of steps down to the car park. Perhaps they are down there. Have you ever tried going down steps with your buttocks pressed as tightly together as an Aberdonian's grip on a £5 note? Probably not and I don't recommend it, if you don't want people to fall about laughing at your eccentric method of locomotion. At the bottom, (no pun intended) still no sign of any toilets, but just then the doors of a lift slide apart and a young woman emerges pushing a trolley train in front of her.

"Toiletten?" I am so desperate now I am down to the bare essentials of speech.

She says something and points up the stairs. Slowly I came down and even more slowly I go back up, but it is a masterpiece of good timing because my arrival happily coincides with the lift, disgorging the same young lady, who, finding me looking about helplessly, and without the need for me to say anything, once more repeats her directions and points to the back of the shop. As I hobble off, out of the tail of my eye, I notice that Iona is coming along with the purchases. But this is not the time to stop and have a chat.

If a fairy princess were to turn up now, or godmother, or whoever it is in such far-fetched tales who has the power to grant three wishes that your heart most desires, I would have blown them on: a pabby, making it on time, and plenty of paper. You've got to treat fairies or those who grant your wishes very carefully and with suspicion. You have got to think things through. Look at what happened to Midas.

But once more, at the back of the shop, there are still no signs to what, at this time, I desire most in all the world. From the trolley lady's gesture, I had expected to see the toilets in the back left-hand corner, but to my utter dismay, there is still no sign of them. In a bizarre parody of John Wayne's rolling gait,

I mince along the back of the supermarket, still seeking them more desperately than ever. Then, when the cramps bring me to an enforced stop yet again, I stop an employee, a man this time – whom, from the way he is dressed rather than from his personal appearance, I take to be a butcher. In actual fact, he turns out to be an angel. He shows me the way and I trust and believe and he becomes my saviour.

The toilets are where the trolley lady indicated after all, but you have to go through the plastic doors into the warehouse and there they are, just in front of you – one for women and one for men. Fortunately, the latter is not occupied. Even if it had been and the other had been vacant, I couldn't have cared less what law or laws of social propriety I might have been transgressing, I would have gone there and willingly faced the consequences afterwards, for the consequences of not doing that would have been a lot more dire. A severe case of dire rear in fact.

On my exit, I check to make sure, than in my *extremis* I had not somehow missed the signs – as if it were likely a drowning man would not notice a bit of timber floating by. Just as I thought. At the other side of the plastic doors, on the shop side, there are definitely no signs to let customers know where the throne room is. I suspect I have been a privileged visitor to the employees' toilet. Thank God that they did not tell me, as some other institutions might well have done, that it was for them alone.

So that is how I ended up visiting a place that few, if any tourists to Lucca have ever been before, never mind the Lucchese themselves. However glad (and grateful) I was to visit it, I shouldn't bother to put it in your top fifty things to do in Lucca though, if I were you.

When I meet Iona by the multi-coloured flower stall, her look says it all: "Well did you make it in time?" and it also says: "I told you not to eat so many peanuts."

Yes, indeed. But as Burns had observed more than a couple of centuries earlier:

> *Ah, gentle dames! it gars me greet,*
> *To think how mony counsels sweet,*
> *How mony lengthen'd, sage advices,*
> *The husband frae the wife despises!*

CHAPTER THIRTY-THREE: A CHAPTER OF DISAPPOINTMENTS

It is almost as pleasant a walk along the avenue of pollarded lindens, crunching through the ankle-high leaves, as to walk along the walls, but best of all is to be able to walk naturally again.

Our route takes us past the cemetery again, but now in daylight, I can see that what I had taken for monumental tombs are chapels, one on the left and one on the right, but through the huge entrance gates, I can see in the distance, some edifices that *are* tombs and which are not a great deal smaller. If we really run out of things to do, I can think of worse things than to explore this place, even if it does not have any famous residents, which is my primary reason for visiting such places. And, I reflect, it is another place that the majority of visitors to Lucca probably never dream of visiting. All the more reason to pay a visit, therefore.

The gin and the Limoncello di Capri (there is not a brand from Lucca, unfortunately) goes straight into the fridge. Hopefully, by the time we get back from the Baralla, the latter will be at the required temperature. For we have unanimously decided that that is where we will go tonight. For a start we know where it is; we know the food is excellent; we know the atmosphere is ambient and after the privations of last night, we can afford the extra expense. Besides, apart from all that, there are other attractions: the food is presented very attractively too.

Thus a few hours and a few apéritifs later (but not too many as the drinks police was out in force) and bearing in mind it is a Saturday night, we present ourselves before mine host at an hour earlier than we might ordinarily have, anticipating that it would be not just busy, but very busy. And so it is.

"Have you a reservation?" says he, and I have to confess that I have not.

A certain look suffuses his countenance. Was that resignation, regret, ridicule or any other of the three Rs? Actually, I think it was a look of: "Wait here and I'll see if I can perform a miracle." But never mind what he communicates nonverbally, what he actually voices is: "Momento" and whilst we wait in anxious suspense, for we have no plan B, he returns, true to his word, a moment later and bids us to follow him. Which we do, relieved and happy to find there is room in the inn after all.

We find ourselves at the back, not far from where we were the last time, in front of the huge mirrors that make the place seem bigger and even more full of patrons. At the table to our right, with rather more distance separating us than the couple of inches that divided us from the American ladies the last time, we have a man and a woman, not quite as mature as us, talking in muted tones like any respectable married couple. I presume they are Italian, but even if they were speaking English, there isn't the remotest possibility that I could make out a single word they are saying. No fascinating family secrets to be divulged then, no skeletons crawling out of cupboards this evening. Disappointment number one.

Disappointment number two. We have a different waitress, not the sultry one I am half in love with. And I know she *is* here, because I have caught a glimpse of her (not that I was especially looking out for her). Whoever coined the aphorism *enough is as good as a feast* should have had his head examined, although it would be an appropriate turn of phrase in the present circumstance. I have an aphorism of my own, and maybe I need my head examined too, as you may have already concluded by now, but after these two setbacks, it confirms me in my belief, motto number two, that you should *never go back* because whatever it is never lives up to your expectations. Having said that, however, the wine is as good as before, and it is a litre as before, and the same colour as before. We are getting into staid old ways, like an old married couple, right enough.

And yet, maybe not. I have used the time back at the hotel profitably and have caught up with my notes. I am bang up to date and can devote my attention to indulging in a real conversation, for once, with the one to whom I am most devoted.

"Have you noticed," says she, in hushed tones, as if she were ashamed of the fact, "that everyone else has only a half-litre carafe of wine?"

That is certainly true of the couple next to us. And looking about me, aided and abetted by the mirrors, as far as I can see, she is absolutely right, as usual.

"Do you not think," she pursues, "that a half-litre carafe would be enough in future?'

That is a rhetorical question if ever I heard one. Considering that I had helped the American ladies polish off their half-carafe on our previous visit, it seems totally inadequate to me, especially when they insist on selling it off at such a ridiculously low price. In fact, it seems to me that buying the litre carafe represents a saving. The more you spend, the more you save. That sounds like good economics to me.

She sees the scepticism in my face, for she adds, a trifle too hastily: "I would let you have the bigger part…"

"Well, maybe…"

I am far from convinced, but I can see that a discussion on a matter of such vital importance is not conducive to the general ambience and tone of the evening. And arguments are best conducted in private, not a foot away from your nearest neighbours, who, even if they can't understand a word you are saying, will nevertheless get the drift that not all is well between us.

"So next time we go out, we'll just have a half-carafe, OK?"

"Hmm."

Disappointment number three.

But it is not all gloom and doom. Our food is delivered by you know who. Unfortunately it doesn't take long to place it before us. Not half as long as it would have taken had I asked her advice on what I should eat. I am indecisive at the best of times but I find choosing from an extensive menu particularly troublesome. I am therefore, always open to suggestions from comely waitresses. Without the benefit of her advice, I had eventually decided on the pheasant since I have only had it once before and that was forty years ago.

One of my landed cousins had shot it and presented the poor bird in all its feathered glory as an act of kindness to my poor, widowed mother. She said at the time and I agreed with her: "I wish it had been walking about the fields still." It was a cock pheasant, which must rank as one of the finest of indigenous British birds. Had it been a hen, I confess I probably would have felt less regret, because as is so common in nature, until you get to the human species, the female is much plainer than the male. Yet, sparing our sentiments, my mother did what needed to be done (I could never have done it) and we dined right royally.

Iona, more timidly, has chosen ravioli. I suppose, when in Italy...

The Italians at the next table appear to be vegetarians and not like me, hypocrites. Furthermore, they seem to be addicted to mushrooms. Mushroom soup for a starter followed by some sort of mushroom quiche. Not to my taste. The most delectable waitress in the world could never have persuaded me to choose this, for I have a problem with mushrooms. I can never, somehow, get it out of my head how poor, misguided Claudius, (at least as far as his choice of wives was concerned) was fed poisoned mushrooms by his last wife, Agrippina. I have a feeling he ate them, knowing she poisoned them, just to get away from her for good.

Disappointment number four. I could have predicted it. The pheasant is not as nice as the boar was. Not that it is not tasty. By no means. But it is a bit picky to eat. Too many small bones. Too much like hard work. But it does slow down the eating process and makes the wine last longer. I suppose I could regard it as practice for the leaner times ahead, but for the time being at least, I have enough to drown my sorrows.

Mine host is hard at work too, hovering over one table to exchange a joke or pleasantry, moving on to the next where he might spend a longer or lesser time, spreading his bonhomie like a bee pollinating flowers. That *is* the career I should have had. I could have done that, but whether I would have thought of installing mirrors in the place to make the place look busier or checking to see if a table is available every time a customer appears without a reservation, even although I know perfectly well there is, I don't know.

But what I *do* know is when he gets to us, I want to ask him a question. Our bill looks like a heart monitor screen. The only thing I can make out is the total at the bottom.

"Can you explain this to me, please?"

He can and does without hesitating or stumbling once. I still can't read it even when he goes through it line by line, but it is what we had ordered and he has either a prodigious memory or those squiggly lines really do mean something to him. And having explained, he has flitted onto the next table.

"This is for you," says the lovely waitress handing me the Visa receipt.

"And this is for you," I reply, giving her a bigger tip than usual.

If I thought that was going to impress her, I was in for a disappointment. And if I thought that was the last disappointment of the night, then I was wrong about that too. If I had had any thoughts that a nice chilled *limoncello* was going to act as some sort of aphrodisiac, then I would have been severely disappointed, as despite all this time in the fridge, it is still not nearly cold enough to enjoy it at its best.

So it's just as well that I wasn't counting on that wasn't it?

CHAPTER THIRTY-FOUR:
ON THE TRAIN FROM HELL

Railway stations, I always think, are amongst the saddest places on the planet, as if all those goodbyes and farewells had somehow imprinted themselves on the atmosphere. Somehow, I don't think of them as places of arrival and reunion which they must also be, but for every arrival there must be a departure, sooner or later, and that is what, it seems to me, gives railway stations their air of melancholy.

This station, at this time of the morning, seems particularly so, with no hustle and bustle to drive the ghosts away. It might be different if the sun had come up, but after so many days of getting up early, it has decided to have a long lie this morning. No such luxury for me however. There was nothing else for it but for me to make the supreme sacrifice and get up early. With so much to see, so much to do in Florence, I had booked tickets for a train at a time I would normally be in bed: not asleep, just too tired after a sleepless night, to drag myself out of it.

When I go for the Big Sleep, they should bury me in my bed because I never slept in it much when I was alive. Besides, with the strike looming, an early return is imperative. A taxi back from Florence would certainly not be good for my heart and could even possibly be fatal.

That is why, at 9.35 in the morning, I am sitting at the railway station scanning the tickets to see if they have a time of departure printed on them. If so, it will be written in stone, not just in ink, as this is Italy and famously, since Mussolini's time, the trains have been running on time. I regret each minute I sit on this bench with the cold permeating my buttocks when I could have been tucked up in a nice warm bed. And we hadn't needed to break the four-minute mile barrier to get here either but Iona has a terror of missing trains and planes and such things and although we had got up in plenty of time, she had nevertheless set off at such a pace that you would be forgiven for thinking that our train was due the very next minute and with a bit of luck, we might just catch it.

Perhaps it was the sight of the tickets in my hand that made Iona think of asking the rhetorical question.

"Have you validated those tickets?"

I don't waste time in making a reply. Now the interminable-seeming minutes until the train is due seem painfully all too short. I shoot down the underpass and on to the platform on the other side where I know, for a fact, I have seen a validating machine outside the ticket office. They may, or may not have one on our platform, but I can't afford the time to look, only to discover there isn't. Hastily, I feed the first ticket in. What's wrong with the damned thing? Why won't it take it? I take it out again and feed the other ticket into the slot. Same result. I'm sweating again now, despite the chill of the morning air. What am I to do?

Then I remember having seen another machine at the far end of the platform. Regardless of how far away it is, it seems a better option than beating up this machine until it decides to work. Panting, I arrive at it, only to discover that it is not working either. At which point, hard on the heels of panic, the voice of reason speaks in my ear: "Just a minute. They can't both be broken. Perhaps it is you who is at fault."

Perhaps I *am* doing something wrong. I take the ticket out, turn it over and words can't describe my relief as the machine makes some intestinal digestive noises and regurgitates the ticket with a date and time stamped on it. It *was* only me after all. With no pressure driving me on, I would have worked this out calmly and logically but blind panic had taken over and driven out my wits.

And panic again is what I do as I see, off to my left, a locomotive lumbering into view. By the time I dive into the underpass and pop up again on the platform, it has come to a halt. Iona has been able to follow my antics all this time and to judge by the strangulated look on her face, her knickers must be twisted into a tight knot.

"That's what I call timing!" I manage to gasp, though if the truth be told, it was just a bit of bravado. It was too close for comfort, even for me.

Yet in the event, there was plenty of time, for we must have sat in the station for a whole minute or more before we pulled smoothly out at 9.37 precisely, just as it was scheduled to. I should have been feeling relaxed at having made it, at the thought of having nothing to do (apart from my notes) for the next ninety minutes or so but let the train whisk me to Florence. But for some reason, I have a sense of foreboding that the journey is not going to be as smooth as the way we pulled out of the station without the slightest jerk to announce we were on our way.

It was a disappointment to find that it wasn't a double-decker train after all. It is however, the next best thing: some carriages are more elevated than others. When we boarded, we were faced with a choice of turning left to the lower carriage or right, to the more elevated one. Naturally, we chose the latter as it would give us a better view of the countryside. Apart from that, the lower carriage was pretty much fully occupied, whereas there was no-one in the upper carriage, I happened to notice, apart from a couple of young men.

Though I could understand that a better view of the countryside might not be one of the highest priorities after their thousandth trip along this line, I nevertheless mused on the eccentricities of those railway passengers who seem to prefer a more crowded carriage to an empty one. Perhaps it is love of their fellow man that makes them all want to crowd in there like sardines, or maybe they were just too lazy to climb the few steps to the upper compartment.

We have barely had time to sit down, get our jackets off and make ourselves comfortable when the real reason makes itself known, and hence my sense of foreboding. From behind us comes a voice, not just loud, but very loud. It has to come from one of the two young men, yet not from him either, but something he has with him like a radio or something. I resist the urge to turn round, for to do so would be to signal that I had heard it and that it had irritated me. Instead, I try to remember what they look like. Would I dare tackle them or were they just so scary and intimidating that I would meekly creep out of the carriage, pretending that the lower one was far preferable to sitting here after all. Young, black, smartly dressed. Uh huh! I should have guessed right away.

"You are BLESSÈD in your body. You are BLESSÈD in your mind. You are BLESSÈD in your family. You are BLESSÈD in your life. You are BLESSÈD in your saviour, Loord Jeeeeesuz Christ!" At which point the mechanical voice stops and a calmer, less manic voice pronounces, in a normal speaking voice: "Amen! Amen!"

That is the short version. There were actually more "BLESSÈDS" than saints-awaiting in the Catholic church, and I won't try your patience by mentioning them all, but suffice it to say my patience and good temper did not feature among the list.

It is clear now why this carriage is so empty. I have just been subjected to their antipersonnel device. For so great is their love for their fellow man, they must sit above the unsaved in an elevated carriage, as if having a foretaste of what it will be like in heaven, the few lording it over the many down below, in hell, and gloating.

I hope that as the train picks up speed and goes clickety-clack over the rails, that it will drown out the sound should it be repeated, and I will be able to ignore it. But I doubt it.

One thing is for sure: I'll never be able to endure it all the way to Florence.

I am the world's biggest wimp as I have already confessed elsewhere when I couldn't even stand up to three barely teenage girls whose "music" from their stereo player had irritated me almost to the point of insanity. Now, if I had been asked which out of these two pestilences, would I prefer to spend an eternity in hell with, there is no doubt about it – I would have chosen the girls a hundred times over. That is why I am desperately hoping that it won't end in a confrontation. Grimly, I am holding onto the faint hope that maybe it was an accident; maybe it won't happen again.

But it does. And funnily enough I don't even have to screw my courage up to the sticking place. I find it so intensely irritating I don't wait for the message to stop. I just snap. With one swift movement, like a spring uncoiling, I stand up and turn to face the noise polluters. Even now, I can't tell from whom or what the noise is coming from although they have spread themselves out – each sitting at either side of the carriage. Perhaps it was even worse than I realised. Perhaps it is in stereo.

"For God's sake, will you turn that BLESSÈD noise down!"

I must have been yelling to be heard over the din. To them I must have looked apoplectic with rage, something that my naturally florid complexion would have done nothing to dispel.

"Sorry!" says the one on the left, looking somewhat astonished. The noise stops instantly and I can only think it must have been emanating from the phone which he appears to be holding.

"Thank you."

And before he can think of anything else to say, before he has time to notice that I am just a wee, middle-aged runt having a rant, and not nearly half as intimidating as I sound, like the Wizard of Oz, I turn my back on him and collapse into my seat. I notice I have broken out into a profuse sweat again. The third sweat of the day and it's not even quarter to ten yet.

I would never have expected it to be that easy and am on tenterhooks that it will happen again. Then what will I do? That's the moment I have a *déjà vu*. It takes me back, years ago, to a campsite in the Black Forest. In the middle of the night, we were awoken by ribald laughing and shouting. The farting didn't bother me: it was too far away, even if there had been any smell, drifting invisibly in our direction, and likely to paralyse us. No, what annoyed me most was the swearing – swearing of the most foul-mouthed kind. Had it been in German or a language with which I was unfamiliar, that would not have bothered me half so much, though I probably would have been able to tell it was obscene. But it was in English and that did upset me and not just because I had two young children (even although one was deaf).

I don't remember how long I lay there, trying to ignore it, hoping it would stop, but instead it got progressively worse until I could stand it no longer, struggled out of my sleeping bag and tent and marched towards the offending orifice. It was easy to find: all I had to do was follow the noise. The flaps were not tied and I flung them apart. Inside were three youths lying on their sleeping bags and drinking beer by the light of a torch. I just had time to notice the startled look on their faces at this sudden intrusion, the next curse or bout of laughter, dead in their throats.

"Do you realise the disturbance you are creating? The whole campsite can hear you! And what's more, your language is disgusting. You are a disgrace to your country! Now shut up and go to bed and go to sleep and let everyone else get some sleep too!"

And with that, I marched smartly back to my tent. Part of it was anger; part of it was a desire to return to anonymity for the purposes of cowardly self-preservation. Anyway, it worked, for not a word was heard for the rest of the night. I know because I didn't sleep, worrying that they might start up again.

Next morning, as I saw them come down the path, they were clearly scanning the campers for the most likely suspect. As I crouched over my cornflakes, I heard one say: "I think he came from that direction." He was right. I did. It was a close call, but I got away with it.

There was the next night to worry about too of course, like I am worried now. We are rattling along, (well not really; it really is incredibly smooth, like walking on silk) but being an express, stops are few and far between, which means that the zealots and I are in enforced companionship, probably all the way to Florence. So far there have been no more "BLESSÈDS" thank God, and while a part of me is relieved that that is the case, I can't help but feel that the silence is like an ever-expanding piece of elastic and it is only a question of time before it snaps...

For the moment, they seem, or at least the one directly behind me, seems to be occupied on his phone. Normally that would be irritating, but it is far preferable to the other thing that phone can do. I had really been looking forward to this journey and now I am spending it in an agony of anxiety. Time and time again I have been disappointed by the reality of an anticipated pleasure and yet I never seem to learn that I should pretend I couldn't give a fart about anything that is important to me.

Take the scenery for instance. If I had hoped that we would be threading our way through narrow mountain passes, I would have been severely disappointed, so it's just as well I hadn't expected that, but having said that, from a scenic point of view, there hasn't really been that much to write home about, or even record in my notebook. People would have been more interesting, but unfortunately I am marooned here with only a couple of zealots and my wife for company.

And here's another point and which perhaps explains why I regard stations as such melancholy places. You should never, if you can avoid it, approach any city by rail if you want to retain an image of it as a place of refinement, beauty and culture. Cities always present their most ugly face to the railway tracks. You should, if possible, approach them from the sea – like Naples for instance.

There is, however, an exception to every rule, and this might just be it – our first stop, Pescia. Before we drew in to the station, I had noticed acres upon acres of allotments, gardening gone crazy or growing on an industrial scale. And indeed, Pescia is not at the heart of the fishing industry as its name might suggest, and which you would not be surprised to learn, given its distance from the sea. Nor is it at the heart of the peach industry, though that is a bit nearer the mark. It is in fact, the centre of vegetable and flower production. To come by train into Pescia, at the height of the blooming season, now that would be a sight to behold – as long as the flowers had not already been cut down for market.

Life is full of disappointments as the last chapter illustrated, and this one seems to be set on the same tracks. The zealots do not get off and our compartment is only augmented by one. He sits at the very front, while we are two seats from the rear. He doesn't look the sort of person who would be very useful in the event of another confrontation with the enemy. I wouldn't care to pinpoint his origin exactly, but certainly from somewhere in South America. Before long, he delves into his pocket and produces a book.

Even from this distance, I can see it is the sort of book that is intended for children. Pictures with writing underneath: for example, a butcher or a baker, with the Italian for the trade inscribed beneath. It's just as well as he is not sitting where I am. Obviously he is just getting to grips with the language, but having said that, I bet his Italian is better than mine because, in all likelihood, he did not come up the river Pescia on a banana boat yesterday. And if I can understand what had been inscribed on the back of my seat in black felt-tipped pen, I am sure he would be able to, better than me. In all likelihood, he already has been exposed to the sentiment: *Via tutti qu' immigranti* or as the zealots in our compartment might have put it: "Get out of here, scum."

It is not until Prato, the last stop on the line before Florence, that our religious friends get out, as does the language scholar. The platform is heaving with immigrants and now our compartment is full. It goes some way to explaining the reason for the graffito, even if it does not excuse it.

I should have been more aware that Florence was drawing nigh. I suppose there had been so long between stations up till now, I did not expect it to appear quite so soon after Prato. Lots of tracks, lots of unlovely buildings, the glimpse of a distant dome and suddenly a platform appears and the train slows down to a crawl.

I don't know the reason for the rush, but everyone, including Iona, is on their feet immediately, gathering their belongings together, and stepping down from the train even before it has come to a complete stop. Plainly, Iona does not regard me as one of her belongings, or else she has carelessly forgotten me, because no-one is left in the compartment by the time I have struggled into my jacket and shoved my feet, but not my heels, into my shoes.

As quickly as my partly-shod condition will allow, I hobble after them.

CHAPTER THIRTY-FIVE:
ON A HIDING TO NOTHING

Firenze Santa Maria Novella railway station is as vast as it is busy and echoes with din. It is a sad-looking place for all its hustle. Ticket machines by the score; a queue out the door of the ticket office; a huge departure board over our heads and a confusion of timetables at ground level surrounded by puzzled passengers. Like us, they know where they want to go, but not exactly how to get there.

Last night we had decided that the first port of call would be the Cappelle Medicee in the Basilica di San Lorenzo. The only problem is we have no idea where, exactly, we are in Florence, nor how to get to it. The first priority therefore, is to find a Tourist Information Office, and get a map.

As we leave the station by the exit to our left, we have to pass through some barriers, and I happen to catch sight of a hardcover book placed on top of one of them. Someone must have dropped it and some kind, thoughtful soul, instead of pocketing it, must have picked it up and put it in this prominent place in case the owner should come back in the hope of finding it again. Some hope, I think, as I stop long enough just to see what the title is. *The Book of Mormon*, in English. My faith in human nature is restored. I put it back. I bet it is still there when we come back. Even if it had been an Italian translation, I bet it would have no takers.

There is an Information Office just across the street from the station in an abandoned church. No doubt it is busier now than in its previous existence, although it is not very busy at this precise moment, and we can walk straight up to one of the assistants in his booth.

"Have you a map please…? Thank you. Now can you show us how to get to San Lorenzo and the Medici Chapels?"

"That is very easy."

And he shows us on the map. I can hardly believe my luck. No buses required. It is very near, within easy walking distance, and what's more, it is on the way to the Baptistery which happens to be next on our hit list. Perfect.

"But I am sorry to tell you that it is open on the first, third and fifth Sunday of the month. This is the second Sunday of the month – unfortunately." And he smiles and spreads his hands as if to say that is just the way things are in Italy, and there is nothing he can do about it.

This is a blow. What did I say about not looking forward too much to something?

"But the Church. It will be open, won't it?" I ask hopefully, even if I have a feeling that I know what the answer is going to be, even if it is a Sunday.

This was the Medici's local and because they had a bit of cash to splash about, the inside is supposed to be quite spectacular. It wouldn't hold the same fascination for everyone of course, but for a grave man like me, a point of interest is the grave of Cosomo I, the founder of the ruling dynasty that was to last for two hundred years. Ironically, he has nothing more to mark the spot than an unostentatious slab on the floor, unlike Michelangelo's tombs to Lorenzo the Magnificent's son and grandson in the Medici chapel. As a matter of fact, he never finished Lorenzo's tomb, becoming somewhat disenchanted with his employers and fled the city in the 1530s. Which is a bit of a shame really, because out of the entire dynasty, Lorenzo was the one probably most deserving of the greatest tomb by the greatest master, since he was an enthusiastic patron of the arts and considered an all round general good egg which is why his fellow Florentines, not he himself, named him "the Magnificent."

And although not part of the Church, the Biblioteca Laurenziana, the library that Pope Clement VII, (another Medici) commissioned Michelangelo to design, is entered through one of the aisles. It's not so much the library I want to see however, but Michelangelo's staircase, having been immediately impressed by a photograph I had seen of it. Occupying almost entirely the room in which it is situated, it is divided into two by a banister that runs down the middle. While one side is composed of an "ordinary" flight of steps, the other seems to ripple downwards with the viscosity of melted chocolate until it ends in three large, solidified, hemispherical pools at the bottom.

Apart from all that, amidst other sights, are the cloisters, a couple of bronze pulpits by Donatello, (his last works) and, it just so happens, his last resting place is here also.

"Alas, no. I am sorry. Not today."

"But this is a Sunday!"

"They will both be open tomorrow," he adds helpfully.

"But I am going back to Lucca tonight and there is a public transport strike tomorrow," I point out, more in sorrow than irritation.

All our sympathetic informant can do is spread his hands and look apologetic, as before.

"Well, thanks anyway."

My disappointment is only surpassed by my incapacity, and not for the first time either, to understand the reasoning behind Italian logic. It seems perverse to lock you out of a church. There is no telling when you might feel the need to have a bit of a pray, especially on a Sunday, and along you trot, eager to get down on your knees, only to find you can't get in. But at least we have the map and we may as well go past the Church and see it from the outside, especially as it is on our route anyway.

We take the crowded Via Panzani, then striking off to the left, the Via del Giglio and before we know it, we have arrived at the unprepossessing entrance to the Cappelle Medicee. In fact, if you did not happen to notice "Cappelle Medicee" carved above the door, you might well walk past the place, unaware, distracted as you might well be, by the stalls of the leather sellers lying in wait to sell you their wares.

Taped to the inside of the glass door I can read, in Italian and English, the days and hours of opening: "Closed Sunday before the first, third and fifth Monday of any month with an R in it. Other months open the second and fourth Sundays before the Monday, unless there is not a fifth Monday in the month, in which case the fourth Monday should be read as being the fifth Monday." All right, I admit that is a bit of a liberal translation from the Italian, but basically what it amounts to is that they make it as hard for you to get into this place as a medieval knight on crusade did when he left his wife at home in a chastity belt and took the key with him.

However, should you look up, as we tend not to do, as I have earlier pointed out, you will be rewarded with a wonderful sight. From a distance, it is the second most impressive sight on the skyline of Florence. The first of course, is Brunelleschi's dome on the Duomo, the second is this: Buontalenti's dome on the Cappella dei Principi. But second only in height and mass – for my money, first on artistic merit. While it may not have the lantern and prominent white ribs of the Duomo, (which I find particularly appealing) what I like about Buontalenti's dome, which copies the same shape, is not so much the cupola itself, but the bell-shaped windows beneath it like a set of fairy lanterns on a Christmas tree.

If the entrance to the Medici Chapels is unprepossessing, then it is an absolute shock to come round to the front and see the façade of the church. Never, in the history of architecture, can there be such a plain façade to belie the magnificence within. It would be wrong to say that it is unfinished: more accurate to say that it was never begun. It is composed of bare brown brick - and not very nice brick either. Michelangelo was commissioned to design the façade by Pope Leo X, who just happened to be Lorenzo the Magnificent's second son, and although Michelangelo worked long and hard on the project, the money was not forthcoming and obviously never has been since. The interior of the façade was, however, completed to Michelangelo's design and of course, bags of money were subsequently made available for the tombs and if that doesn't tell you a thing or two about the Medici, then I don't know what does.

At the bottom of the steps, at the right, on a massive plinth, is a statue of a mean-looking hombre whom, we are told, is Giovanni dalle Bande Nere. Who you may ask? I will tell you. Real name, Giovanni de' Medici, he was a mercenary and father of Cosomo I, the black stripes sobriquet a result of the same being added to his insignia after the death of Pope Leo X (well he was a relation after all). I only mention him in the passing because the statue is so big and so prominent on that massive plinth, that you can't fail to spot it and might wonder who the Nora he was, the name itself telling you nothing unless you have an encyclopaedic knowledge of the Medici family history and which gets a bit complicated to say the least, as many of them shared the same name.

Actually, if it weren't for the height of the plinth, you wouldn't notice him at all unless you manage to break through the massed ranks of the leather goods stalls that lay siege to the Basilica, and stand on the steps. The city fathers, in their wisdom, banned the traders, but the people, in their folly, demanded their return, so now the unhappy tourist has to run the gauntlet of this Jainist nightmare of wallets and purses, boots and shoes, coats and jackets, handbags and hats. So many stalls selling the same things, you wonder how they can compete with each other – unless they don't, and it's all one massive cartel.

Whatever the truth of that, it is one massive menace to the tourist who can't see anything of the Basilica because of them.

So it's just as well that the sides are just about as unexciting as the façade, or they would have annoyed me even more than they do already. For to make your way down the narrow Borgo San Lorenzo, through that mêlée, is like a seriously myopic person with Parkinson's trying to thread a number 10 needle.

CHAPTER THIRTY-SIX:
BUMS AND OTHER BODY PARTS

Coming eventually to the Via Cerretani and turning to our right, it is an astonishing sight that suddenly presents itself before our eyes. From here we can see the Baptistery and part of the Duomo with Brunelleschi's magnificent dome looming over it on the left and the tip of the campanile towering over it on the right. It is astonishing to come upon the Piazza di San Giovanni so soon, for we have come hardly any distance since the Basilica San Lorenzo and I know that from the Duomo it is not much more than a stone's throw to the Arno and before that are the Piazza della Signoria, the Palazzo Vecchio and the Uffizi. It is amazing just how compact the main sights in Florence are and indeed, how many of them there are.

But that is not the primary reason for my reaction to the sight before me. I felt astonished, though a more apt word would be shocked, the first time I saw it and I experience the same feeling again as the sheer ornateness of the Duomo and the hideousness of the Baptistery literally take my breath away. The Duomo may have its fans I suppose: the sort of people who like Thomas Kinkade paintings or Daniel O'Donnell concerts. Each unto their own, as I said before. There's nowt so queer as fowk.

The Duomo, the most celebrated tourist attraction in Florence, and arguably the most visited in the whole of Italy, is closed naturally, this being a Sunday. But it matters not really, as we are here to see the interior of the Baptistery, which by the grace of God *is* open and what's more, we could just walk right in if we wanted to. In fact, by standing on my tiptoes and tilting my neck at an angle of 45°, I can see so much of its celebrated ceiling through the open door, I begin to wonder if it is worth paying the €3 entrance fee.

But first I want to have a closer look at the famous gilded bronze doors on the east side, the so-called *Gates of Paradise* depicting Old Testament scenes, famous for their realism, dramatic groupings and use of perspective. Last time I had only been able to catch a glimpse of them from behind a human barrier of tourists five-deep, as it was the height of the season.

No such problem this time. I can get right up to the railings and poke my camera between the bars and what's more, spend as long as I like as the only other people showing any interest, apart from me, are a couple of nuns. It is rude of me to eavesdrop I know, but I couldn't help but prick up my ears when I hear they are less interested in the panels and more concerned with finding a man.

I am a man, albeit an old and wrinkly one, and I am sure I can help them there. Nuns hold a fascination for me, though I have to admit I find them a bit on the scary side. But these two, not being dressed in black, look much less severe and seem friendly enough, though it has to be admitted, they will not be winning any beauty contests. I confess I am hardly an expert on nuns, but I've never seen a good-looking one yet, apart from Audrey Hepburn – and she was only pretending.

Actually, not to dissemble any further, I am looking for the same man myself – the self-portrait of the artist himself, Ghiberti, who had already designed the doors on the north side of the Baptistery and who defeated some pretty stiff competition, including Donatello and Brunelleschi, to get the contract. There are a few heads to choose from, but that's him, so my guidebook says, the fourth head from the top, on the right-hand border which runs round the panels of the left-hand door. No wonder the nuns are confused. And so was I.

Having found him however, he looks nothing like my idea of an artist, more like Chaucer's miller, bald and middle-aged, though maybe not quite as rough. What he does not look at all like is the trail-blazing artist of the Renaissance that he actually was, inspiring the great Michelangelo, no less. As a matter of fact, the doors took a quarter of a century to complete – you can't just create a masterpiece overnight (or you couldn't in the days of the early Renaissance) and the artist has chosen to represent himself from his earlier years, (when he would have been pushing fifty) rather than how he was when the doors were completed.

That's fair enough; it's natural to want to be remembered as you were when you were at the peak of your powers rather than in your dotage. He only lived another five years after the doors were completed. But he still doesn't look like a revolutionary to me, more like a bishop. Still, the nuns seem very satisfied with him. They thank me for my help and I tell them they are welcome and we say goodbye.

"Where have you been all this time?" Iona asks. I might well have asked her the same question and if I didn't know her any better, I might have detected a slight crispness in her tone.

"Just chatting up a couple of nuns," I reply truthfully, for I have never had such a long conversation with a nun before. Never *had* a conversation with a nun before in fact, such is the deprived life I have led.

Iona makes a sort of growling noise in her throat. "Just look at the queue to get in now!"

She's right. Where there had been no people before, there are a great many now, not queueing in the British sense of the word, but in the sort of loose, ragged formation that passes for that on the continent. We join in at what we deem to be the end and slowly we shuffle forward and slowly we get nearer to Andrea Pisano's south doors featuring no less than twenty scenes from the life of St John the Baptist on the upper part, and the eight Virtues at the bottom, one of which is Temperance and that is all I need to know to make me want to look away. I don't want any lessons on that, thank you very much. Not that you can get a good look at the panels anyway because of the line of people filing past them into the Baptistery.

I feel a bit sorry for Andrea, and not just because they gave him a girl's name. Despite that curse, he still fathered two sons and was obviously considered good enough, once, to design doors for the Baptistery. After all, his teacher was Giotto, who didn't just do frescoes. They call the campanile Giotto's tower because he designed it, though unfortunately, he only lived long enough to see the ground floor completed. His star pupil, Andrea, took up the task, to be succeeded in his turn by Francesco Talenti.

From this list of talented artists, you might be forgiven for concluding that the campanile had a curse upon it and the wisest thing to do would be not to touch it with a bargepole, but actually Giotto was 67 when he began the project in 1334 and then work stopped when the Black Death came along in 1348, the same year Pisano died.

That's not why I feel sorry for Andrea though. He knocked his pan in, taking six years to create these panels, yet who spares them half a glance these days? Even if you wanted to, you couldn't very easily, because it is obscured by all the visitors. He was born just a tad too early for the flowering of the Renaissance, a mere rung on the evolutionary, revolutionary ladder stepping up from the Byzantine, begun by Giotto, and it just so happens that Ghiberti, coming nearly a century later, was a rung or two higher up. So, when it comes down to having to choose between which doors are going to be the entrance to the Baptistery and which are going to be displayed as works of art, I'm sorry Andrea, but it had to be yours. You happened to be in the right place but at the wrong time. That is why I feel sorry for you.

Actually, I am feeling a bit sorry for myself and Iona is quite right to be annoyed with me. While it is annoying enough to find ourselves at the back of the queue, (and if you cast your mind back to the beginning of this narrative, you may remember how much I detest queueing) it surely must also mean that it must be pretty crowded in there by now.

But there is yet worse to come, for as we funnel nearer to the entrance, people are trying to muscle in from the sides. You might have thought it was the queue for the last lifeboat on the *Titanic* the way they are so desperate to get into the Baptistery before everyone else. Iona, more annoyed than ever by this development, is determined not to give way. She is standing so close to me that you might have thought we were inseparable, joined at the hip. In fact, I can't remember the last time when we were so close together in the physical sense, at least with all our clothes on. In fact, come to think of it, I can't remember the other time either.

Despite Iona's iron will, (and mine) not to let anyone push in front of us, an even more determined woman has shoved her way in ahead of us, not because she has more will necessarily, but because she has more cheek, two of them actually, two enormous gluteus maxima with which she bulldozes us aside; a matter of mass over mind, you might say. And we mind a lot, Iona muttering under her breath that she would like to kill her and me looking at her big fat backside in such a way as to provide the daggers by which she might perform the deed.

It's funny how religion can bring out the worst in people, be such a source of hate. I wonder if I had been able to see that panel of Temperance whether it would have had any effect, reminded me to moderate my temper, but I doubt it. Why couldn't we all queue up like nice, sensible people? After all, the Baptistery, as we see it today, has been here since the eleventh century, one of the oldest, if not *the* oldest building in Florence, and it doesn't look as if it is in any danger of not being around in the next five minutes.

Which is just as well, as it turns out it takes about that long before it is our turn as The Bulldozer appears to be buying tickets for her extended family which must extend some distance behind us if the length of the strip of tickets she is passing over our heads is anything to go by. Our managing to separate her from her uncles, aunts, cousins, and second cousins once removed, (it is inconceivable that she is married or has children) has turned out to be only a Pyrrhic victory.

But at last we are inside. And for the second time today, and not long either since I saw the Piazza di San Giovanni and the Duomo in all its Hansel and Gretel sugariness, I have the stuffing knocked out of me – for I am overwhelmed by the vastness of the Baptistery. We need not have worried about it being crowded, which it is, but there is plenty of room for all, even with Fatbum and Family.

After all that standing, it would be nice to sit down and take the weight off our feet, so we make our way through the throng where there are rows of pews and manage to squeeze onto the end of one, the first time my bum has warmed a pew, I think, since the talk on Giotto's frescoes in the Basilica of St Francis in Assisi. But it is mosaics not frescoes that we have come to admire now.

It is a bit dark, but the mosaics gleam with an awesome luminosity, particularly the massive gold image of Christ on high, sitting in judgement over the dead at His feet. A cheery subject for a baptism. There you are, a babe in arms, just begun on life's journey and they are already thinking of your end. Or perhaps, as an adult, you have just been accepted into the church and then you look up and what do you see, but a message that you had better be good or you will end up suffering throughout eternity. I wouldn't like to belong to a club like that because I find it impossible to be good some of the time, let alone a lifetime, and it amazes me how they manage to get so many members. Masses of them in fact.

As usual, it is the group of mosaics on Christ's left, the damned suffering punishment in hell that has more of a resonance with me. Poor devils. I don't know if they are allowed to choose their punishment or whether it is commensurate with the severity of the sin, but on the menu are: being burnt alive; roasted on a spit; crushed with stones; eaten by monsters or swallowed by serpents. It's not much of a choice. Maybe I'll just try harder to lead a better life.

If the *Last Judgement*, occupying three of the eight sides of the building, is the focus of the ceiling as you face forward, there is so much more to see behind us on the other five sides. And I don't need Iona to remind me, if only if I hadn't lost the binoculars, we would have been able to see them so much better. From the top down we have: Choirs of Angels; Stories from Genesis; Stories of Joseph; Stories of Mary and Christ and lastly, Stories of St John the Baptist. While I haven't read the Book in which these characters appear from cover to cover, I have dipped into it and although I generally prefer the book to the film adaptation, (the exceptions being the novels of Dickens and Hardy) it is entertaining, if not more than a little painful on the neck, to gaze upwards and try and spot the illustrated stories which, to even a heathen like me, need no introduction.

While the magnificent ceiling is undoubtedly the main attraction in the Baptistery, and everyone, without exception, does naturally look up here, the visitor should not, on this occasion, forget to look *down* and admire the geometric patterns on the floor which, if it weren't so hard, you might mistake for a Persian carpet. The same could not be said of the walls however, which, with their bold black-and-white design, are as shocking as the exterior, if not worse. No, that's not true. *Nothing* is as bad as the exterior of the Baptistery.

But here is something much more to my taste: a tomb between two massive Corinthian pillars. How fitting to bury someone inside a baptistery! But, as a matter of fact, it is not so strange as it seems. The original Baptistery was actually in the middle of a cemetery and in any case, the sacrament of baptism is closely related to death. After that life-altering experience, it represents the start of a new life in heaven for those who have been accepted into the Church – and have been good, of course. And that is why the Baptistery is the shape it is. For medieval Catholics, the octagonal shape symbolised resurrection and rebirth, echoed in the baptismal fonts and the pulpits too, like the elder Pisano's, as I described earlier. Hence also, why the *Last Judgement* is such a prominent feature.

Anyway, whoever he was, he must have been a pretty important chap to be buried here and in such an impressive tomb. Beneath the kind of canopy you might expect to see over a four-poster, a gilt effigy of the deceased lies on a bed, supported by a lion at each end. This is vaguely interesting in itself, but what is especially interesting is that unlike any other recumbent figure on any tomb I have ever seen, instead of imitating sleep, silently snoring through eternity on your back, this person's face is slightly turned to face the viewer, which is just a little disconcerting, but which might just have made some difference to his snoring.

Beneath the bed and above statues of the three Virtues of Faith, Charity, and Hope, (in that order) the Latin inscription on the plinth tells us who this Very Important (Dead) Person is: "John, the former Pope XXIII. Died in Florence A.D. 1419."

Just a minute! Pope John XXIII! There must be some mistake. I remember him well. I watched his funeral on TV, never ever imagining for the moment that I would ever meet him in real death, almost as close to him as Iona and I were before we came in here, separated only by the thickness of a pane of crystal glass, his aquiline hooter practically touching the glass canopy above his head.

The reason for this strange encounter is that when they opened up the pope's coffin, just to see how he was getting on, (as you do) they found his body uncorrupted. Sounds familiar? So they hoiked him out, dressed him up as Santa Claus and put him in this glass coffin while the Powers that Be decide if he is a saint or not.

As for the other, the alternative Pope John XXIII, who died nearly five centuries earlier, they opened his coffin too, in the 16th century, (the tradition of peeking into pope's coffins goes back a long way, apparently) and found he was dressed just as represented on the tomb. And that's the point. On his head, a bishop's mitre, mark you, not the tiara a pope would wear.

In short, this turns out to be the tomb of the Antipope, going back to the time of the Great Schism, when there was a pope in Rome and another in Avignon. I'll spare you the details, but the decision of the 20th century pope to call himself John XXIII was a clear statement that the bones before me, but hidden from view, unfortunately, never formed the frame of a pope.

So how come a pope that never was, comes to be buried in this prodigious place? Well, the answer is, that like Julius Caesar, he had a will, and when you have a will, as Fatbum will tell you, you have a way to get in here. So what was in this will?

Well, for a start, there was a bit of money, but better than that, he had a greater legacy than that to bestow upon the Florentines, a precious relic – nothing less than the forefinger of St John the Baptist, the very one which he used to point at Christ and said in perfect Latin, (as he might well have done, if he had happened to pick up a bit of the language of the invaders) *Ecce, Agnus Dei.* For those of you who have let your Latin slip a bit, or never were exposed to it at all, since regrettably, (though I hated it at the time) they stopped teaching it in schools some time ago, it means: *Behold, the Lamb of God.* John XXIII himself had inherited this grisly emblem from a long legacy of (real) popes, but now he had bequeathed it to Florence, his favourite city. And what more fitting tribute could the Florentines possibly offer in return, than to plant the cardinal here, in the Baptistery?

Actually, John XXIII's association with Florence went back a bit further than that. In 1405, he was instrumental in the Florentines' defeat of Pisa, and call me cynical if you like, but I can't help wondering if it might possibly have had anything to do with his making the Medici the Vatican's bankers.

And what became of the finger? Now, it just so happens, I am in a position to answer that question. Years and years ago, in Brittany, on the worst holiday ever, (especially for our children) and by way of a change from comparing the stone crucifixion scenes or calvaries outside the churches and for which Brittany is famous, as a special treat, we went to the village of St Jean Le Doigt on a mission to see the famous forefinger. Imagine that! They named a whole village after the relic. Only, when we got to the church, it was to discover we had been conned: *le doigt* was so precious that it was banged up in a wall.

On the other hand, (so to speak) if you were to go to the Nelson-Atkins museum in Kansas City, Missouri, they will proudly show you the finger in a transparent reliquary. I am all for transparency, just as our Government also purports to be. And to be fair, I suppose that is fair enough; it would be normal to have two forefingers, wouldn't it? So, one there; one in France. But with which one did he point at Christ? That is the question. Anyway, his mum should have told him it was rude to point.

And on the subject of relics, everyone has heard of people being two-faced, but no-one has ever been six-headed. Yet that is what we are being asked to believe about John the Baptist. Six different places claim to have his head, the whole head, and nothing but the head. But why stop there? There are bits of the skull, not to mention *whole* hands and other bits, scattered about the globe.

That's what I love about the Catholic Church: you keep stumbling over relics all over the place. One of the best I ever came across was in the convent of Santa Catalina near Marine de Sisco in Corsica which boasts the following: not the finger of John the Baptist, but that of Enoch (nearly as good); an almond from the Garden of Eden; and get this – the best of all – a bit of the clay that was left over when Adam was made!

It's no good going to see these wonders however. As in St Jean Le Doigt, they are locked away and nobody is allowed to see them. I think it is really mean of them to keep these wonders to themselves. I mean, if you don't actually get to see these treasures, you might actually begin to think they aren't there at all, and your faith might go a bit wobbly.

Sadly, hardly anything remains now of the font (in which no less a person than Dante was baptised) except the remains of the base, but despite this, as we make our way out of the Baptistery through Ghiberti's north door, (well it is his lesser work and it is kept closed except to let people out) I am well satisfied with my visit. As I have so often discovered, as far as Italian architecture is concerned, the interior and exterior can be complete contrasts, aesthetically speaking, and that is particularly true in this case.

The mosaics were every bit as wonderful as I expected them to be, while for a grave man like me, the serendipitous discovery of the tomb of the antipope was a close second. That's what I love about travelling – the unexpected discoveries you make. Of course, as I know better than most, they are not always of the most felicitous kind...

CHAPTER THIRTY-SEVEN:
ON BEING AS POOR
AS CHURCH MICE

That was good, a pleasure even better than expected, but now for the highlight of the trip, indeed the main purpose of the visit – the Uffizi. I hope it will not be a disappointment, and I know that the best way to avoid that is not to look forward to it too much as once the gods get a whiff of how keen you are, they make damned sure you won't enjoy it. You have to act casually therefore, look as if you are not too eager, give the impression that since you are in Florence and since you just happen to be passing the Uffizi and it doesn't appear to be too busy and there's nothing much else you can think of to do in Florence, you may as well poke your head in and see if there is anything worth having a look at.

A horse, on his lunch hour, having a break from hauling tourists about, is happily munching hay from a nosebag. It provides me with the inspiration for the perfect delaying tactic. Or, I suppose, another way you could look at it might be to say that it reminds Iona it is lunchtime. But then Iona, having been brought up in this newfangled Christian tradition, doesn't understand the mysterious ways the gods move in order to thwart mere mortals' aspirations, but it suits my purpose on this occasion and we set off therefore, in the search of a pre-Galleria meal.

We find it on the Via dei Calzaiuoli. In fair exchange for the equivalent of one of our tenners, we are now the less-than-happy possessors of two sandwiches (mine at least providing a couple of mouthfuls) and a can of a fizzy drink, which in the interests of remaining solvent, we are going to share. That is the price you have to pay for being in a place like this, I reflect unhappily.

And being in reflective vein, I think this on life's missed opportunities and how to get through it with the least effort and at the same time amass a reasonable amount of bucks: why go to all the trouble of being a restaurateur, making delicious food, when all you need to do is slap a bit of cheese or salad or cold meat between two slices of bread, then put some drinks (that you can get from the wholesaler for a song) in the chiller cabinet and sell them on at 1000% profit? The hardest thing would be to try not to let your customers see you laughing all the way to the bank. It wouldn't work everywhere of course. As ever, location is paramount and no doubt the rates here are as high as Giotto's Tower.

It doesn't make me feel any better though as I can't dismiss the thought from my mind that I have been ripped off and I certainly don't feel in the mood to contribute any more to the profits by buying an ice cream from the inevitable wide range on offer. But should I be suddenly smitten by a sudden bout of insanity and change my mind, I would certainly not have chosen *Zuppe Inglese* or English Soup. The name itself is enough to put you off. Would oxtail count as a typical English soup? If not, what would? Heinz Cream of Tomato? Had it been *Zuppe Scozia,* Scotch broth or cock-a-leekie would immediately have sprung to mind, though the thought of that, or any of the others as an ice cream, is enough to make the gorge rise. Past experience of Italian ice cream however, tells me that such an outrageous concoction is not only possible, but just the sort of thing the Italian masters would seek to create in the everlasting quest to advance their art. The Renaissance is alive and well in Italy – at least as far as ice cream is concerned.

Actually, it is not as disgusting as it sounds because it's what we know as "trifle." And if it had been *Zuppe Scozia* I might just have been tempted because the difference between the English and Scottish variety is that the traditional Scottish version contains raspberries and is laced with a double dash (if you are lucky) of sherry, or preferably brandy.

But Scottish soup this ice cream is not, and if tastes anything like its English cousin I would be very much surprised. For a start, they have put the sponge on the top, and you really couldn't trust an ice cream that gets that so fundamentally wrong could you? It would be nice to test my theory but I just can't afford the investment to be proved right. Interestingly, no-one else has been tempted by it either and the scoop lies on the top, unused.

We're not going to eat our sustaining meal just yet though – we'll do that when we get down to the Arno. The sound of jazz music seduces us from our route however, and we arrive in the Piazza della Repubblica to find it alive with a festival-like atmosphere. In addition to the jazz band, there is a merry-go-round and an excellent marionette show which further diverts us – a white hillbilly vocalist singing to his own guitar accompanied by a Creole female who is dancing along to the rhythm.

Nearby, a sign warns us in five languages that it is an offence to buy replica goods, punishable by fines ranging from €500 to €10,000. Nevertheless, the blacks are there in force, with their Jimmy Choo handbags, although they do not appear to be getting much in the way of trade, or even anything much in the way of interest. Still, if I were to hang around here for long enough, who knows what might happen? Would a plain-clothes policeman suddenly arrive and arrest a potential purchaser, while the vendor looks on, bemoaning his luck that yet another customer has been nicked? That sounds as if it might be the Italian way right enough, for the blacks look as calm and unconcerned as if they had never seen any such warning, for they do not appear in the least on the qui vive for the police, in or out of uniform. Alas no-one is obliging enough to make a purchase and we move on, I at least, feeling rather disappointed.

That was just a minor diversion, a short step up a side street and back on the Via Calzaiuoli, we come upon an unusual sight: one of the most unusual churches in Florence (or anywhere for that matter) and whose unusual appearance stems from its unusual history. It is the Orsanmichele and it originally began life as a place where the grain merchants plied their trade. The building, as we see it today, was begun in 1337 and replaced an earlier arcaded building which was damaged by fire and had a particularly interesting feature: one of the pillars was decorated with an image of the Madonna and before very long, people began attributing miracles to her.

Because of these miraculous powers, the building was shared with a confraternity who raked in the cash that the Madonna generated in gratitude for favours and miracles granted. Especially the latter. A mere eleven years later, the Black Death struck in Florence and did not merely decimate the population as it did elsewhere, but actually *halved* it. Imagine that! Not the sort of odds you'd like to hear unless it is your chances of winning the lottery. Having said that, out of a population of 100,000, there were still a lot of people grateful to the Madonna.

During the course of the next quarter of a century, the importance of the religious confraternity superseded that of the grain merchants and the Orsanmichele was transformed into a church by the blocking-in of the arcades. The faded Madonna was replaced with a new, better, brighter painting by Bernado Daddi but the same miraculous (and earning) powers were apparently also miraculously transferred. And why not? It was a copy of the original after all, only better and maybe the miracles were even more miraculous too.

Meanwhile, the guilds (the Trading Standards Agency and Trades Union of their day) were charged with decorating the exterior of the new building. They began by building Gothic niches to house the patron saints of their particular trade, but an early reluctance to fulfil their obligations by producing the statues to occupy the niches turned out to be time well misspent, coinciding as it did, with the first flowering of the Renaissance. With each guild vying with the other to produce the most elaborate and costly statue of their patron saint in order to demonstrate their richness and therefore their superiority, this competition explains why, as you go round this three-storey edifice that doesn't look like remotely like a church at all, on each side you will find statues executed by such masters, (to name but a few) as Nanni di Banco, Giambologna, Donatello and Ghiberti whose statues for the cloth, wool and bankers' guilds were made of bronze which at the time, was much more expensive than marble. In fact, all the statues are deemed to be of such merit that these are copies and the originals are safely stored in the museum upstairs, apart from the two Donatellos, which are in the Bargello and Santa Croce Museum.

Stained glass windows, appropriately showing miracles performed by the Virgin, were also added. Unfortunately they are boarded up at the moment but thankfully we can still see the tracery at the top. As far as I am concerned, however marvellous the statues are, not to mention the niches themselves, the windows are the best feature. And if I thought the mullions in the Campo Santo were magnificent, then these are something beyond even that. Being bowled over by works of art is quite a common experience in Florence.

Our luck is in. The Orsanmichele is actually open and we enter by what must be the finest door in all of Italy. Well, there is nothing special about the door itself, just a plain wooden affair, a pair of them actually, but the beautiful and intricate stonework of the doorway echoes the mullioned windows and it is hard to imagine that any doorway on Earth could be more fair than this. So fair indeed, it could well serve as the doorway for the gates of Paradise. Ghiberti's doors presumably, would be the actual doors through which one passed to gain admittance.

So to pass through these portals should presage some transcendental experience, right? In that undiscovered country, from whose bourn no travellers return, some *have* in fact, returned since Hamlet's time, and report seeing a bright white light to which they say they were irresistibly drawn. That is certainly not the case here. On the contrary, it is as dark as Hades in here. It might be different if the stained glass windows were not boarded up, not only for the light it would let in but for the light it would shed for me on all those miracles the Virgin performed, for I have to confess in my ignorance, I can't think of a single one.

The darkness apart, there is another obstacle to our not being able to see what splendours might be in here. Most inconveniently, a service is in progress, but I suppose it is a Sunday, and at least we did get in, and it was free.

What we *can* see, however, glowing faintly at the far end of the church, is Daddi's *Madonna delle Grazie* in a tabernacle so ornate it looks like the façade of some cathedral that has been constructed out of lace. Andrea Orcagna's intricate sculpture took eleven years to complete but in my opinion, he shouldn't have bothered, regardless of what artistic merit it may be deemed to have. Surely a less ornate "frame" would have been less distracting and focussed the attention more on where it should be directed - on the painting itself. It must have cost a pretty penny too - money which would have been better spent on the poor, though to be fair, the money that the Virgin brought in was redistributed amongst the poor – part of the confraternity's duties.

I could do with a sub myself after buying that lunch, but though this may be the right place to ask, this is alas, not the time. We creep out quietly, not as silently as nuns might, but like two mice in a time warp who have dropped in for lunch at the grain store, only to find they have arrived just a few centuries too late and hope to sneak out, undetected, before they have to suffer the opprobrium of being mistaken for the church mouse in the simile.

An association of ideas makes me think of Lady Macbeth when she was inciting her husband to murder, comparing him to *the cat i' the adage.* It baffles modern audiences but Elizabethans would have immediately understood the reference. Lady Macbeth was referring to the cat that wants the fish but doesn't want to get its paws wet.

That's like me. I'd like to go to heaven, but I don't want to have to do all that religious stuff first. I'd rather lie in bed listening to the omnibus edition of *The Archers* than go to church on a Sunday.

It could be a costly mistake and one I'll regret all my death.

CHAPTER THIRTY-EIGHT:
STORIES IN STONES

The Via dei Calzaiuoli disgorges us into the top left-hand corner of the Piazza della Signoria where we can see the entire square spread before us. It is dominated by the Palazzo Vecchio, or Old Palace, old now, and became old in 1549 when Cosimo I de' Medici moved across the river to his rival's former residence - the Pitti Palace. It's funny how I never noticed it before as it seems so obvious now, but looking straight on at the façade of the Palazzo Vecchio, the tower that rises above the crenellated battlements like a stubby pencil, is not placed at the centre of the building. That's because it is built upon the foundations of an earlier tower belonging to an earlier palace.

If the Orsanmichele is an open-air sculpture gallery, such a description is even more true of the Piazza della Signoria. In front of the Palace is Donatello's heraldic lion known as the *Marzocco* and Bandinelli's *Hercules and Cacus*. Cacus was a charming chap who foolishly, and fatally, aroused the ire of Hercules by stealing some of his cattle although his preference was to dine on human flesh. And if that were not gruesome enough, he nailed the heads of his victims to the door of his cave.

Donatello's lion seems unremarkable to me, but I think Bandinelli's sculpture is magnificent, full of rippling muscles, though Cellini described Hercules' six-pack as a "sackful of melons." Cacus, conquered, is at Hercules' feet but instead of dramatically depicting Hercules about to bash his captor's brains out, he is merely restraining him by the hair with his left hand, while in his right, his iconic club is held by his side, innocently enough, but only a foot away from Cacus' nose who is looking at it in rather a worried sort of way.

The tableau is meant to convey the merciful character of the Medici and if anyone believed this bit of propaganda, then they should have boned up on their Roman mythology to find out what happened next. As for Cacus, he needn't have looked so speculatively at Hercules' skull-splitter either, for what Hercules really did was to strangle Cacus so tightly with his bare hands that his eyes popped out and he kept on squeezing his throat like a lemon until he had squeezed out every last drop of blood from his head. Personally I think I would have preferred the club. We needn't waste too much sympathy on Cacus though as he was such a nasty piece of work, but any Florentine sufficiently clued up on his mythology might well have taken it as a metaphor for being bled dry by taxes.

The most famous statue in the Piazza of course is the aforementioned *David*. Only not today. Last time I saw him, he was boxed up in a crate as if about to be dispatched somewhere but it was still possible to see him clearly enough. Now you can't. So it's just as well that I hadn't come here specially to see it, though of course, this is only a copy. All the visitor can see now is a photograph on gauze. It looks like he has finally been sent off for a bath, something he was in dire need of thanks to the pigeons who mistook him for a public lavatory. Philistines.

No such problems however, with Cellini's bronze *Perseus*, in the Loggia dei Lanzi, adjacent to the Palazzo Vecchio. In a grizzly little scenario, Perseus is seen standing on the corpse of Medusa with his weapon of bloody execution in his left hand while his right is holding aloft the head, dripping with blood. *Perseus* is wired in such a way that any pigeon daring to land gets a bit of a shock. It is carefully calibrated apparently. Not strong enough to scare it so much that it loses control of its bowels, but just enough to scare it off before it makes a deposit.

Cellini himself, in his autobiography, recounts a shocking little scene between him and Bandinelli. As you might expect, there was no love lost between these two and Cellini candidly relates how, in a heated argument near the end of his life, Bandinelli shouted at him, "Shut up you filthy sodomite!" I don't know why Cellini should have been so shocked by this, considering he had been convicted of it twice and charged with it on another two occasions, but anyway, he was totally mortified. What he seems to have failed to realise is that is just the sort of personal remark that, in the heat of the moment, you could expect to be cast up against you, especially by someone who was losing the argument.

When Bandinelli himself died, he was working on a statue of Neptune to be the centrepiece of a fountain in the Piazza whose subtext was to demonstrate the upwardly-rising Florentines' ambition to be a naval power, but actually commissioned to celebrate the marriage of Cosimo's son, Francesco, to Johanna, youngest daughter of the Holy Roman Emperor, Ferdinand I. The unfortunate Bandinelli, being unable to fulfil his contract, being in either heaven or hell at the time, the commission was awarded to Ammannati who sycophantically modelled the head on Cosimo I. That might be one way to make sure you got the job but Michelangelo, who was his teacher, was not impressed. "What a beautiful piece of marble you have destroyed!" he told the artist, though he was referring to the sculpture as a whole, not just the face.

What must it have been like, being an artist, especially a sculptor, during the early part of the 16th century? All the rivalry, the competition for commissions, the jealousy amongst fellow artists whom you regarded as your friends, and your masters, for the most part, the Medici family. It's a wonder anything was done at with all that adverse criticism flying about and having to look over your shoulder half the time in case you were offending the Medici.

Apart from the statues aforesaid, the most arresting statue in the Piazza is the equestrian statue of Cosimo I, which I only mention in the passing as it is by Giambologna, and for my money (which you don't need here at all) he is the greatest of all the sculptors represented here, even if that does include the great Michelangelo and *David.* As I said earlier, I don't know much about art and I night be betraying my ignorance here, but I would never ever include the *Mona Lisa,* for example, in a list of my top ten favourite paintings, though I know enough to know that it was not painted by Michelangelo. And I would certainly never hang it over my mantelpiece. It wouldn't be good for my paranoia, her looking at me like that and smirking at me as if she knew some sort of salacious secret about me.

Similarly, I have seen many sculptures more impressive than *David.* And one of them happens to be here, by Giambologna, in the Loggia dei Lanzi. In fact, he has two very fine exhibits here: *Hercules beating the centaur Nessus* and an earlier one, the one I really, really admire: *The Rape of the Sabine Women.*

The scene depicts how to pick up a woman, Roman style. You don't bother with small talk, just hoist the lady into the air as if she were a ballerina. But if the anguished look on her face is anything to go by, she is not in the mood for dancing. Meanwhile, between the rude intruder's legs, is the crouched figure of a terrified man, who in a hopeless, helpless gesture is pleading with him to put his wife down. They have apparently been in bed as neither of them are wearing any clothes, which must be a trifle embarrassing, especially for the lady.

She mightn't have been so worried if the unexpected visitor too, had not been in the nuddy when he came to call. Maybe his intention was to show that he came unarmed and wasn't concealing any hidden weapons. For her part, naturally, she fears a fate worse than death and doesn't know (how could she?) that she is not going to be raped at all; she's merely going to be made an offer which she was quite at liberty to refuse – the Romulus plan: full Roman citizenship with all its rights and privileges in return for giving up her husband and remarrying and making lots of little Romans. What would *you* do? A bit of a dilemma really for there was no way of knowing then that the infant Rome was going to become one of the greatest civilizations ever. I suppose, if it were me, and putting myself into the position of a prospective wife, it would all depend if you were allowed to choose the new husband or had one thrust upon you.

Apart from the movement and drama in this sculpture, what appeals to me most is the way you can walk round it and see the action from different angles. There is no one particular point of view or position from which it should be viewed, no front and no backside, which is what you would see if you were to walk round *David*. Whichever way you look at it: from Romulus' point of view, or mine, or even from hers, had the lady not averted her eyes, it can be seen that the abductor does not pose an immediate threat, for the angle of his supposed weapon of mass reproduction is at a respectful dangle. That should have been a reassuring sign for her, had she happened to notice it. And if I had been her, I might just have chosen to be a Roman matriarch after all, just as long as I didn't get the blame if there was no patter of tiny Roman feet just as soon as conceivably possible.

There are many more sculptures of merit here and I will spare you the details, as no doubt you've had quite enough by now already. Iona certainly has, because she has disappeared, just like she did the last time we were here. Then, she had gone off to admire *David* again, as if she didn't have one of her own already whom she could see any time she wanted, if not admire exactly. But since he isn't here, God knows where she could be, as from my elevated position on the Loggia I can see no sign of her, which is not too surprising, as even at this time of year, the Piazza, bathed in brilliant sunshine, is pretty crowded. But you don't get rid of a wife as easily as that and I know if I just stay here she will come back to reclaim me, like a piece of lost luggage. Damn! Why did I think of that? I've been so entranced by (nearly) everything since we got to Florence that I had completely forgotten about the source of all my troubles.

To take my mind off them, I turn my attention to the sculptures again, this time to one of those near the back, *Menelaus supporting the body of Patroclus,* a Roman sculpture from the first century A.D. itself a copy from third century B.C. Greece. Absolutely magnificent, amazing, incredible, the drama, the muscle tone, the weight of that limp body, the curve of that lifeless head that leads the eye down the entire body to the buckled knees. A reminder, if ever there were one, that in the 16th century, we were just beginning to catch up again with Classical Greece.

A sudden shout makes me start. I look down from where I had been studying Menelaus' winged helmet to where a young woman, looking highly embarrassed, is straightening herself up. There are stone steps, doubling as benches, running round the back and right-hand side of the Loggia where art students are copying the works of the maestros into thick sketchbooks. This young woman is no artist, just a weary tourist who has thankfully found a seat where she can take the weight of her feet without having to cash in her pension for a cup of coffee. She has, apparently, in her weariness, been leaning against the pedestal of one of the statues. The source of the shout comes from a young man with bulging biceps and enough muscles visible beneath his T-shirt to guarantee him a job as a model as Hercules himself. He is pacing about the Loggia like a caged beast. I for one, certainly wouldn't mess with him but it seems he is not just a bear with the toothache looking for someone on whom to vent his anger – he is dressed in a little brief authority, for on the back of the chest-hugging T-shirt is written "Tourist Police."

What the young lady did seems a small offence. Her leaning against the pedestal is hardly going to harm it after all, so what she did must be regarded as a mark of disrespect. I suppose you wouldn't do that in a proper art gallery and perhaps they are right to be vigilant, for the statue of Neptune has been frequently vandalised, especially in the past twenty years or so. It seems to be as much a magnet for vandals as *David* is for the pigeons.

On the other hand, it seems to me the police would be better employed protecting the tourists rather than coming down on them like a ton of bricks or an over-toppled statue for that matter. After all, it was the security cameras that really were responsible for tracking down the most recent vandals on *Neptune.* So why don't they stick a camera in here to look after the statues and let cops like Muscleman loose, free to roam the streets to protect tourists from pickpockets and conmen? I'm sure he'd be a lot happier with this roving commission and so would I.

One day, along by the Arno, I had been approached by three self-styled plain-clothes police officers who demanded to see my passport and had I produced it, I am sure that would have been the last I would have seen of it and would have embarked me on a whole sea of troubles to which my past and present predicament would seem as the merest ripples in a puddle.

Ah, here comes Iona to collect the baggage. Where has she been I wonder?

She's been back to *Neptune,* not so much to see him, but the figures around the octagonal fountain. And if I had witnessed something she hadn't, she in her turn, has seen something I am sorry to have missed. She has stood on the actual spot where Savonarola and two of his acolytes were burned during the infamous episode known as the "Bonfire of the Vanities."

In 1494, during one of their periodic exiles from power, the Medici were replaced as rulers of Florence by the priest, Girolamo Savonarola, a zealot of the first water, whose first act was to make sodomy punishable by death. Naturally, this led to a mass exodus of artistic talent from Florence, but Savonarola had barely begun. On Shrove Tuesday, 1497, he lit a mighty bonfire of all the things he disapproved of: gambling tables, mirrors, fine dresses, women's hats, musical instruments and chess pieces, to name but a few and of course books, poems and paintings which he, in his wisdom, deemed immoral. Botticelli, it is said, under the influence, personally chucked his own classically-inspired paintings onto the flames.

With regard to the gambling tables, you might just about be able to see where the arch vandal was coming from, but as for the rest, you can see right away he was a proper misery-guts. Furthermore, he was always prophesying doom and gloom and the apocalypse, if not now, then quite soon, with many gullible people expecting something significant to happen in 1500, if not before. He had gone just too far this time however. Protests turned to restlessness and restlessness turned to rebellion and rebellion turned to riots. The taverns reopened and there was cake and ale once more. Savonarola and his cronies were arrested, put on the rack and duly signed confessions. Savonarola was kept in a cell in the tower of the Palazzo Vecchio and in what may seem by some to be rather a fitting irony, he and his two fellow zealots were burnt on the very spot where the Bonfire of the Vanities took place. A circular plaque marks the spot and Iona has stood on it, the hotspot.

Like Cacus, I don't have a great deal of sympathy for him either, but he wasn't all bad. Over-zealous he may have been, but for Savonarola, public enemy number one was the incumbent pope, Alexander VI, otherwise known as Rodrigo Borgia, regarded at the time as an improvement on his predecessor, Innocent (sic) VIII, supporter of the Spanish Inquisition, instrument of regime change in Naples, institutor of simony (not sodomy, note) at the papal court, father of two acknowledged children and with more "nephews" than even he could keep track of, just to mention a few of his venial sins.

Rodrigo, by contrast, a well-known sufferer of syphilis, only produced four children, the youngest of whom, if you haven't already guessed, was named Lucrezia. Need I say any more?

Damn! I would have liked to have stood on that spot too, but Iona is desperate to devour her meagre rations and it being in the opposite direction from the intended picnic spot, we leave the Piazza della Signoria and head towards the Uffizi and the river. I might have suggested having our sandwiches in the Loggia, but since no-one else seems to be eating there, I don't. You wouldn't would you, have your lunch in the middle of an art gallery? In any case, I am too scared of getting a bollocking from Muscleman on the one hand and from my wife on the other, and from one of them in particular.

After all, it is only a plaque, I console myself, as we head towards the Uffizi. Probably not the real site at all, just an educated guess where the cross where the three hung in chains above the bonfire was situated. It's not as if it is a real relic. There's nothing to see.

Actually, now I come to think of it, that *does* make it like a relic. In fact they made damn sure there was nothing left of Savonarola and his companions at all, poking the fire until there were no hard bits left and then sweeping up the ashes and scattering them into the Arno for good measure. By removing all traces of this pestilent priest, the intention was to leave nothing around which a cult might be formed by those who might have regarded him as a martyr, or a saint even.

And the Renaissance, after this brief blip, could begin the process of getting back to the future.

CHAPTER THIRTY-NINE:
A HORRENDOUS DISCOVERY

What I like about Florence, if you haven't already noticed, is that you don't need to pay to see great works of art, especially if your preference is for sculpture, and for me sculptors are the greatest of all the artists. Like musicians and painters, they transcend language barriers and can speak to people in all countries and cultures, something that writers can only do through translation with questionable success, especially in the case of poetry. But the task of the sculptor, it seems to me, is infinitely more difficult than that of the painter. Imagine, there you are, confronted with a massive block of marble, which, just to make things a little more difficult, might have a flaw in it and out of that you create something flawless like the *Rape of the Sabine Women* if your name is Giambologna. If, on the other hand, you are a painter and your name is Leonardo and you feel that that smile is not quite enigmatic enough, just give it a wee touch of the brush, and there it is, hey presto! Now imagine doing that with a chisel!

If, like me, then, you are an admirer of sculpture, you don't have to wait very long or go very far to see some more, if when you leave the Piazza della Signoria, you go down to the Arno via the U-shaped Piazzale degli Uffizi. There you have the chance to see 28 more statues of the great and the good - and the not so good too, if you count Machiavelli. Scientists, inventors, sculptors, architects, painters, poets and writers: famous Tuscans all, a glittering array of talent, especially when you consider how small Tuscany is. They are set in niches in the twin façades of the Uffizi, which, in his wisdom, Vasari, the architect, designed in this way so that the immense Galleria degli Uffizi did not look too forbidding.

At the entrance, very few people are queueing to get in, just as Dorothy said, as this is November. In the summer, the queue had run down the entire length of one side, along the bottom of the U and beyond. The distance between each pair of columns, we were told, represents thirty minutes, yet people were prepared to stand there for hours, in the shade of the colonnade, squandering the sunshine, such was their dedication and determination to get into the Uffizi. Now, there is space to spare between the first two columns while in front of them stands a living Dante, the copy of the statue in the niche, but not standing anything like as still. He is having a break apparently, or perhaps with so few people about, he finds it hardly worthwhile to begin work by doing absolutely nothing.

We can hardly believe our luck that the queue is so short, and not only that, but once inside, it means we will get really close to the paintings without having to view them over the heads of hundreds of others. But just in case the shortness of the queue has also something to do with it being lunchtime, we hasten our steps down to the river. It won't take us long, but the sooner we eat ours the better.

From here we can see the mid-fourteenth century Ponte Vecchio, its shops and arches reflected in the still waters below, while running along the top is the Corridoio Vasariano which links the Palazzo Pitti with the Palazzo Vecchio so the Medici could get from one to the other; from the not-so-humble home to a day at the office without bumping into any riffraff on the way, or being bumped off by one of their enemies. It is the oldest bridge on the Arno and only survived the Second World War it is said, thanks to Hitler, who forbade its destruction when the Nazis retreated in 1944, blowing up every bridge behind them. If true, it just goes to show you, that like Savonarola, who was not all wrong (and whose ashes were scattered near the bridge by the way) Hitler had another saving grace to the one already mentioned. Probably the only other one, though it was said, he was kind to animals.

There are no benches or anything to sit on and for a moment I consider sitting in a pool of sunshine on the pavement but at the last moment, Iona spies an empty stone bench, the very last under the arcade and although it is in the shade, it looks like it will have to be there or nowhere. In fact, the bench is not quite unoccupied, for someone has left half a *panino* on my part of the bench. I say "my part of the bench" because in fact, a tiny segment of it is lit up by a sliver of sunshine, and we both know that is mine and therefore the *panino* is mine too. And I might well be in the need of it, I think hungrily, as I look in dismay at the miserable apology for a sandwich that Iona hands me with about as much ceremony as it deserves. The line between shade and sunshine marks the demarcation line and the fizzy drink is put between us on the shady side of the bench because there is no room for it for a start and also to keep cool – not that it will make much difference.

Our repast is interrupted by a sudden clamour of klaxons. Alarmed, the blacks are beginning to bundle up their handbags and other items into the sheets on which they have been laid out for display, ready to make a sharp exit. In an instant, they could be off, albeit hampered with their wares. But already they are beginning to relax as they realise it is a false alarm. Motorcycle outriders first, then a police car, then the main event – could it be the President on his way to an important summit meeting or to a party? No, it is only the Fiorentina bus transporting those modern-day gladiators to entertain the crowds in the Stadio Artemio Franchi from which they will return victorious, hopefully, and likely to do so unless they are facing their fiercest rivals: Milan (AC and Inter); Turin (Juventus) and Genoa (Sampadoria). Intercity rivalries are still alive and well in Italy – only not so many people get killed nowadays.

As well as the drink, we share the sandwiches, swapping when we have eaten them halfway through. A couple of bites in other words. It's not enough for me. I look at the abandoned *panino* speculatively. Why did the person who forked out at least an hour's minimum wage for it just leave it there I wonder? Did he or she just not like the taste of it? Looks like pastrami and I don't know what else besides. It's a bit hard to see without picking it up to have a look, but I have a particular partiality for pastrami. Can't see any sign of teeth marks; looks like the part that has been eaten was torn off rather than bitten. That means no-one's gob has been near it…

"No. Don't even think about it."

"What?"

"You know perfectly well."

She's probably right. It looks untouched but who's to know that a pigeon hasn't been pecking at it first? I know my place in the pecking order and don't argue the point. I haven't read *Macbeth* without learning a thing or two from Lady Macbeth about the dangers of protesting too much.

"Right! Let's go!"

It's probably taken us not much longer than a couple of minutes. The queue, if anything, is even smaller now, but before we go in, we are faced with a barrage of notices and just so there is no room for any doubt, illustrations, of the things we are not allowed to bring into the museum. It's as bad as boarding a plane. We're not even allowed to take in any water. At least, not in a bottle. It doesn't say anything about taking it in inside you. It is the day for sharing apparently. We make short work of the water we have left as we want to keep the handy little bottle into which we have decanted it from the big bottle we bought in Esselunga. And just in time too, for we are now in the foyer of the Uffizi. I should think we have been queueing for less than a couple of minutes.

It doesn't come cheap. But now we've paid, we are free to enter. But first, just like boarding a plane, we must put our coats and hats through the x-ray machine before we step through the metal detector ourselves. Off with the lid; off with the jacket. Now for my pouch which I keep slung round my neck and which has my credit cards, money and the all-important documents relating to the luggage – the proof of postage of Carla's bag and proof of ownership of ours. Which is when, in a heart-stopping moment, I realise I have been robbed.

In a futile gesture, I slap my chest to make sure I haven't, in an act of supreme caution, placed the pouch next to my skin. This pouch was Iona's idea. Rather than carrying a wallet, which might get lost, it should also ensure, by being placed under my jacket and out of sight, I am safe from the predations of pickpockets. Now, however unlikely it may seem, it looks as if my precautions have been in vain.

"Someone must have slashed the cord!" I exclaim aghast to Iona and to the man operating the x-ray machine, and to anyone within hearing range for that matter, who might be wondering what the hold up is, why we are not following our possessions and going into the gallery.

And then a sudden realisation leaps into my head and cold horror grips my heart. Almost as soon as those words have left my mouth, I realise the appalling truth. I haven't been robbed. I wouldn't have minded that half so much as I could hardly be blamed for that. But I *can* be blamed for this, and I will be. I need have no fears of that. I feel like a condemned man as I realise there is no-one to blame but myself. I know where my pouch is. Or at least I know where it was when I saw it last.

I can see it now, where I had tucked it into the space between my seat and the window. I'd taken it off so I could relax and enjoy the journey, before the "BLESSÈDS" began, without feeling the weight of it round my neck. Of course, if Iona hadn't been in such a mad rush to get off the train, I might have noticed it, instead of madly rushing off after her.

So it's partly her fault. But she is not going to accept any culpability for that. I am in deep, deep trouble.

Iona knows from the look of horror on my face that something has happened.

"What is it?"

"I know where my pouch is…I've left it on the train."

For a moment there is silence while the enormity of what I have just said has time to percolate in Iona's brain and for her to realise yes, I really could be that stupid.

"For God's sake!" She looks to heaven in silent prayer, probably for the strength not to murder me right there and then. Then the inquisition starts. "How? How could you possibly lose it? Unless…You did, didn't you? You took it off didn't you? What on earth possessed you to do that?"

I squirm like a worm on a hook under that gimlet gaze, knowing that to tell her will be like throwing petrol on a bonfire.

"So you could feel more comfortable! More *comfortable*, indeed!"

Words fail her, or the presence of witnesses restrains her from saying any more – for the present. The security guard lifts the nylon band that forms a barrier, and sheepishly I pass through and collect my hat and jacket while Iona gets our money back.

"Police station. Outside. To the right," the man says, turning his back on me and indicating with his hand the right direction to take, as if I were some sort of moron. I thank him for his solicitude.

We find ourselves in a corridor with no-one else about. The coast being clear, we may as well take this chance to explore the Uffizi. We may not see any paintings, just bare walls – but then we didn't pay anything either. And so we find ourselves at large in the basement of the Uffizi with no-one to say boo to us. And if anyone had stopped us and asked us what we were doing we would have said that we were merely looking for the toilets.

Which is no less than the truth, for Iona had spotted a sign and bearing in mind the water we had just drunk, not to mention the fizzy drink and no doubt a lengthy interview at the police station to follow, she wants to go and go now when she can. Very wise. And very wise of me to agree with her, even if I say so myself. I am not going to disagree with anything she says, at least not for the foreseeable future, and I have to remember that although I may give Iona the hump, we are not all built like the proverbial camel, which, as everyone knows, can retain water for long periods of time, and so can I.

Having said that, I resent the delay: the sooner we report the loss, the better the chances of recovering the pouch. Or so I would have thought, although it is probably already too late. And yet, though I dare not give voice to it, at the back of my mind I retain a scintilla of hope that I might yet be reunited with it. After all, have I not lost it three times before and always got it back intact? Unlucky to have lost it in the first place, but in other ways I have the luck of the devil. My mother always said I had that. She put it down to a pact I must have made when her back was turned. This is the first time, however, that I have lost it while Iona is with me – and that could be an omen that things are going to turn out differently this time.

On and on we walk unchallenged in these wide and blank corridors. Not a labyrinth exactly because it doesn't wind about, just goes on for what seems like miles. Theseus, even without a thread, could quite easily find his way out of here in a matter of moments, especially if there was nothing to distract him. But imagine Theseus stopping to look at paintings on just one side of this corridor, never mind the other. If he, or you, were to devote only a couple of minutes to each painting, you could be here for hours – and that is only one corridor.

These blank walls seem such a waste of space to me, and this, you might have thought, would have been precisely the location to brighten up the place up with a few reproductions. Except I suppose, they don't look too favourably on reproductions here – except in the gift shop which, I suppose, they must have here. And if this is the case, it might have occurred to them to have used these blank walls to advertise copies of the masters available for sale as well as giving the punters something to look at during their long trek to the toilets.

You wouldn't have had to have been desperate though, that's for sure, I reflect, as I hang about waiting for Iona. What's more, had this bare corridor been covered with wall-to-wall reproductions, it would have made up for the disappointment of not getting into the Uffizi proper and might have assuaged Iona's wrath somewhat. But more than that, personally speaking, that would be just about as much of the Uffizi as I would have wanted to see – especially if they had cherry-picked the best from all periods in the gallery. And although only copies, it would have represented very good value for money indeed for our admission price.

Except they haven't and I couldn't have afforded the time to look at them anyway. I have to begin looking for something much more important.

CHAPTER FORTY:
A VIEW FROM THE OTHER SIDE
OF THE BRIDGE

Following the instructions, we come finally to the police station, though a fortress would be a more apt description. It is enclosed by tall, iron railings and the gate, it comes as no surprise, is locked. An intercom is attached to the pillar. I press the button and it crackles into life. So what happens now? Do I speak first or the policeman at the other end? Since nothing seems to be happening at his end, I take the initiative.

"Hello? Hello?"

Crackle. Crackle.

"I've lost my wallet." No point in complicating matters by calling it a pouch, a word that the invisible policeman might be unfamiliar with at best, or at worst, would put him on his guard against some witty prankster who, on further questioning, would describe the lost article as being brown and furry, last seen just below his waist and belonging to a certain Mr Bee, known to his friends as Wally. In other words, none other than the famous Mr Wally Bee, all the way from Australia.

There is the faintest of clicks and I realise that the gate has now been unlocked and we can go in. Our deaf son would never have heard it. In fact, what would he have done when faced with the intercom, assuming he had got as far as that in the first place? Not for the first time I reflect that for the deaf, life is full of challenges and foreign travel, I suspect, would have been a step too far for me, had I been deaf.

The invisible policeman makes himself visible. He has come to the top of the steps to meet us.

When I explain what has happened, he tells me in Italian that I have come to the wrong place, that I must go to the International Police, which I will find on the Borgo Ognissanti. It is easy to find: just go down to the Arno, pass the Ponte Vecchio, then after two more bridges, we will see the Excelsior Hotel. We are to pass that and we will see the police station on the street to the left. It's amazing how few words you actually need for directions, augmented by a bit of sign language. Being deaf abroad may not be so daunting as it seems.

Sounds easy, but how far is it? Once outside the fortress again, Iona consults the map in the guidebook. It looks like miles. She snaps the book shut. It makes me think of a guillotine on its last few inches of terrible travel.

"Right. Let's go!" And with this she stomps off.

I couldn't agree more. I follow meekly behind, making no attempt to fall into step with her. There is no point in saying sorry. Better to let the pavement take a pounding, let her work off steam. She'll feel better for that. In this heat and at this pace, the sweat should be appearing as fast as the steam should be disappearing.

Passing by the Ponte Vecchio, I stop and look back at it. I've never seen it from this side before and I wonder just how many have. I wouldn't mind betting not all that many. Most, I bet, approach it from the direction we did, then cross it to where the Pitti Palace, like a big fat toad, and the Boboli Gardens, lie in wait. Been there, done that.

On this side of the river and further up, the International Police Station hardly seems to offer much competition as an attraction, yet I suppose quite a few tourists visit it annually, though hopefully only a small minority out of the hundreds of thousands who visit Florence every year. That is a mildly comforting thought – that I am visiting a part of Florence that not so many people see. Nearly everyone goes to the Uffizi, but how many only prowl about the basement without seeing a single painting? How many bother to look at the Ponte Vecchio from the upstream side? (If my instinct is right, for you can't tell from the water as it is as still as a mill pond.)

The questions are of course, rhetorical, but for your information, at this side of the bridge it scarcely seems any different, while the river shimmers placidly towards the horizon. Further upstream, on the other side of the river, where the sun is shining with as much strength as it does on a Scottish summer afternoon, I can see a new sight – the enormous dome of a church. It's certainly not St David's but I wonder what could it be?

"What do you think you are doing?"

It's another rhetorical question of course, but anyone who could be so stupid as to leave all their valuables on a train could easily mistake it for a proper question and at least she is talking *at* me again, if not *to*. (And if that is not a perfect example of how you *can* finish a sentence with a preposition, something up with which Winston Churchill would not put, I don't know what is.) At any rate, I pretend it is a real question and explain that just because we have a crisis on our hands, (completely my fault of course and we will probably never again have the chance just to stroll into the Uffizi again just like that) we should, nevertheless, not forget that we are still tourists and should make the most of this unexpected turn of events and make the most of this alternative Florence.

Certainly not the trip we had envisaged, but none the less interesting for all that, as we wait to see what the ensuing events might have in store for us – a bit of an adventure in fact. Actually, that is how foreign travel should be: it's best not to be too rigid in your plans. It is the unexpected events, the misadventures that lend spice to a trip. I want to tell Iona that this is a trip she will remember all her life. She will be able to dine out on it; she will be able to laugh at it later.

Only, at this precise moment, as we resume our journey, present laughter is very far from our minds. This trip is turning out to be just a tad too spicy for my taste and not so much a trip but more like a full-length-falling-flat on your face sort of humiliating accident.

Mixed metaphors apart, although it may be unseen Florence, I am not looking forward much to visiting the International Police station. Like hospitals, they are best avoided on all accounts if you possibly can.

CHAPTER FORTY-ONE:
COOLING MY HEELS IN THE JUG

You can't miss the Excelsior, or the Grand Hotel, at the other side of the square. At the far end is the church known as Ognissanti. And there, to the left of the church, is what I am looking for – the red, white and blue sign that says *Carabinieri*.

There is an office in an arched gateway that leads into a courtyard. Two women have arrived just a moment before me and are being interviewed by a young policeman half their age, and mine. I don't know what he is saying, but I don't much like his tone. Far from being sympathetic, his questions seem almost inquisitorial. Eventually, the women are dismissed and instructed to pass through the arch and I step into the firing line.

"Passport," he says, the word snapping out of his mouth like a bullet.

"I don't have it with me."

"I need to see your passport."

Oh dear. I see trouble ahead. I take a deep breath.

"I don't have it with me. You see, I've lost my wallet. And if I had had my passport with me, it would have been in my wallet and I wouldn't have been able to show it to you anyway."

He looks distinctly irritated. He leans forward and in a bit of pantomime, puts his left ear closer to the glass.

"I can't listen to you," he says in precisely the sort of tone you would use if someone had interrupted your viewing of your favourite TV programme and you had missed a vital moment.

320

Now it is my turn to feel annoyed. In a voice strictly louder than necessary, I try to reach his brain through that orifice as if by mere volume alone, I may stimulate into life the organ in his head that has long since been dead.

"I was saying that I don't have my passport. I have lost my wallet." It would have sounded better I think, if I had been able to say it had been stolen, but if he wants to assume that that is what happened to my passport along with my pouch, so be it.

He looks at me for a long moment as if I were dog poo on his shoe. If this is how they treat law-abiding members of the public, I wouldn't like to be a criminal or a suspected criminal. His thumb jerks to the right, by which I understand we are to get out of his sight. Thank God I don't have a bushy black beard or am dressed like a Muslim.

"Room third on the right."

"Thank you."

It is a Spartan little room, with a telephone attached to the wall and hard wooden benches on two sides, but at least it is cool. Apart from us and the two women who had been processed before us, a man is also waiting. From his air of complete and utter boredom, it looks as if he has been here for some time. It looks as if it could be a long afternoon.

Iona is studying the map again. "It's not very far to the station," she pronounces. "While you are waiting here, I'll go and see if it has been handed in."

"Good idea."

My spirits begin to rise. I have great confidence in Iona being able to find things I have lost. She does it all the time, finding things in the very same place I have looked myself moments before. That luck of the devil I am purported to have may not yet have run out.

"Switch your phone on."

And with that, she is gone, leaving me to kick my heels. That's my stocking heels because I have slipped my feet out of my shoes. Just look at that! My feet have made a clear sweaty imprint on the red-tiled floor. I'm not surprised. They feel as if they have swollen to twice their size. I watch, fascinated, as the imprint gradually dries off before my very eyes. I make another, watch it slowly evaporate, make another, and another, side by side. Which of these two will be the first to disappear?

None of the other occupants of the room appear to notice this, what they might regard as bizarre behaviour and if they had, they might well be glad that they are at the other side of the room. But you have to pass the time somehow when you are waiting to be interviewed by the cops. I suppose this is what they must mean when they refer to throwing you in the jug to cool your heels.

In the fullness of time, my phone vibrates. With some amount of trepidation, I fish it out of my pocket, scarcely hoping for good news as that is an open invitation to the gods to make sure the reverse happens. I confess to my heart beating faster as I unlock the keypad. One message received. I can hardly bear the suspense. If bad, I reckon my feet will have cooled down so much that they will not be able to leave the slightest trace of a stain before I get out of this hellhole. If good, this nightmare will be over and I will be out of here quicker than the time it takes for my last footprint to dry on the tiles. And if that should be the case, Iona may be even more forgiving than she already is and it may not, even after this setback, be too late to visit the Uffizi. It could put an entirely different complexion on the rest of the afternoon. It all depends on the press of a button. I press it.

It is not as I hoped. I am going to have to cool my feet, never mind my heels, for quite a lot longer. Everyone's luck has to run out sometime, and after three times, it looks as if mine has.

I am still waiting to be admitted to the inner sanctum when Iona comes back to report that she had been to the

Information Office and had been told that we were in the right place. There is nothing else we can do now but wait. I notice that my feet make scarcely any imprint now, though I do so in a much more surreptitious manner as some instinct tells me somehow Iona wouldn't approve.

It's her lucky day. Well not exactly. But even I must admit, when we finally get into the interview room, the policeman is incredibly handsome and she can drool over him like she did that chap with the wet shirt in *Pride and Prejudice* while I answer his questions. I am not in the habit of admiring men, as it happens, but I had happened to notice that the first policeman, in Stalag 47, and even the grumpy one who directed us in here, could all have made it in Hollywood. It's all due to the uniform of course, and in Darcy's case, the shirt, as well as other clothes. No doubt that's why they joined the *Carabinieri*. Women are said to be attracted to men in uniform.

It should just be a matter of routine: name, address, hotel name and address, description and contents of lost item, where lost and so on while the Handsome One enters the details on a computer screen that is positioned in such a way I can't see what he is writing.

It gets off to a bad start. It is all rather time-consuming, especially my address in Scotland which defeats even the English, let alone non-native speakers. I have to write it down for him in block capitals. Then there is another glitch.

He is a bit puzzled by the debit card, wants to know what it is, what the difference is between a debit card and a credit card. So far his attitude has been very professional, officious even, his words coming from clipped lips. Now he is beginning to sound a little more human. Iona explains, while he maintains the formality by avoiding eye contact, dividing his attention between the computer screen and the keyboard. He must have done this countless times before, but it doesn't seem to have made him any more familiar with where the letters are, as he stabs each one painfully slowly with his rigid forefinger.

"We don't have in Italy."

"Oh, really?" I butt in.

"How much money in your wallet?" he responds, brushing aside my overture to put the interview on a more friendly, less formal footing.

Ah, he has me there. I look at Iona. How much did she entrust me with?

"About sixty euros?" I say, looking at Iona for confirmation.

She shrugs.

"Sixty euros. Definitely…Yes, sixty euros."

Handsome One pauses from his keyboard punching just long enough to give me a look. I know what it means. He thinks I'm making it up, that in the likely eventuality of my pouch not being returned, I've added enough to cover the excess on the insurance. Now that would have been an idea. But it's too late now.

It doesn't take long to realise that if anything is an exercise in futility, then this seems to be it. Both his tone and body language convey the Handsome One knows it, and thus it is transmitted to me. More than that, I also get the feeling that he is a bit irritated with the length of time it is taking, especially with these bizarre Scots words. He keeps glancing at his watch, which seems to provoke him into striking the poor, innocent letters on the keyboard with redoubled vigour.

For insurance purposes at least, I realise that these formalities have to be made, but it is doing nothing constructive to reunite me with my pouch. The assumption has already been made that it has been found and kept by some dishonest person, while I am ever optimistic that it might have been handed in by some honest soul. I would like to suggest that he tried phoning round a few cop shops but by the time he has finished typing in all the information, it is patently obvious that he has an urgent date elsewhere (probably with No 1 mistress) and I consider mentioning it only long enough to dismiss it before he, peremptorily, dismisses us.

He prints out two copies, one for me, one for him, stands up, puts his hat on, ushers us towards the door, and in the waiting room, points to the phone which we can use to report the loss of the card. It's all over quicker than I can say in a stone-cold sober state, "The Leith police dismisses us" and if you find that ties up your tongue a trifle, you should try it after one or two libations.

The waiting room is empty apart from us – making it look even more forlorn than ever. Were we the very last nuisances to be admitted before siesta time, I wonder? How, or with whom, you choose to spend your siesta, is of course, entirely up to you. The main thing is to shut up the shop so you can get on with it. The reporting of crime can take a break, even if crime itself does not.

The one good thing about the telephone here is that all the numbers you need are printed right there in front of you, next to it. Quite handy really, if you think about it, because the number you need to cancel your card is printed on the back of it and of course you no longer have that to hand. Another bonus is that it is free. The trouble is I can't get it to work. When I pick the phone up, it sounds as dead as the dodo, nevertheless I speculatively punch in the numbers. Just as I expected, nothing happens.

"Bloody phone doesn't work!" I slam the handset back in its cradle in disgust. This is a fine way to spend an afternoon in the cradle of the Renaissance.

"Maybe you should dial a nine or a zero first," Iona suggests helpfully.

She's right. I remember I had to do that once in one of my schools to get an outside line. But why did His Handsomeness not tell us that before he disappeared, I mutter to myself ruefully – for all the time it would have taken.

An automated voice invites me to choose from the menu, which only gets me as far as the next menu, which in turn gets me to yet another, until finally, I am put through to a real person. She appears to be Chinese. She is very polite and helpful. I like the sound of her voice. I can just see her: long black hair, the slit in her cheongsam displaying long, slender thighs. You could easily fall in love with someone with a voice like that, but unfortunately, we have a problem. She only understands Received Pronunciation and my Scottish brogue is just too strong for her, though others have told me I have a very attractive accent. Not that it did me much good. I don't remember having to fight off droves of women driven into a state of mad desire by my dulcet tones. But then of course, they could see me as well as hear me.

I can empathise with my Chinese lady, having experienced the same problem in reverse when my Internet connection fails and I find myself talking to someone in India. It's either a problem with the equipment or something in the ether. Ether, either, the real problem is the person-to-person communication and at moments like that I feel like calling the whole thing off, getting rid of the thing for good and regaining my sanity.

It takes an eternity, having to spell everything out syllable by syllable until the last syllable of recorded time – for our conversation is being recorded for "training purposes." Finally, I am assured all is well and my Visa card has now been cancelled.

This is unknown territory for me. On those previous occasions when I had lost my cards, I was on my own and so faced with a dilemma. If I cancelled my card, I would have no access to money, even if my card turned up safe and well, which it would be quite likely to do, the moment I had cancelled it. On the other hand, if I didn't cancel it, I may be left with no money in the world at all. That's why I take two cards with me – in case one gets lost or stolen.

It's not much help if you keep them together though. But if you separate them, so my thinking goes, you double the risk of losing one of them. I wonder sometimes, if this train of logical thought might be the result of a Roman soldier having had his wicked way with one of my Pictish forebears on one of their rape and pillage expeditions, as it has something of the Italian about it.

It seems, sadly, it is time to part from my Chinese lady's mellifluous tones. She wants to know if there is anything else she can do for me. At this distance and without a video link, I regret that is unlikely. But then, suddenly, it occurs to me there *is* something I can ask her to do for me.

"Can you cancel my Bank of Scotland Card also?"

"Yes, sir. I can do that for you."

And so our faltering conversation staggers on for a few more minutes until she assures me that that too is null and void. I am now penniless and reliant on Iona for funds. I can imagine where the cuts are going to come from, but as for the present, it is time to sever my relationship with the cheongsam forever. She knows my name and some of my most personal details and yet I know nothing at all about her: not her name, nor her age, nor indeed where she is on the planet. It's my fifteen minutes of fame, to her at least, but to me, our relationship seemed to have lasted twice as long as that at least.

But if it had not been for that, I would not have seen what happened next, for into this austere little room enters a little man. He knocks loudly on the door of the interview room, smites it a second time, repeats "Is anybody there?" in Italian and only the Listeners being present, instead of doing the wise thing and just leaving, he foolishly decides to enter instead.

That's where he is discovered when the Handsome One unexpectedly returns the next moment. Perhaps she had not waited. That's my fault, delaying him with my strange-sounding names. Or perhaps they have had a row. Anyway, he is not in the best of moods. Mercifully, we can't see it, only hear his rage and it sounds very unpleasant indeed. As unpleasant as my Chinese lady was pleasant. And she, in all probability, is nothing at all like the fantasy – could be as uncomely as he is handsome.

The unfortunate is ejected precipitately and a finger directs his attention to a notice on the door. If it is not a quotation from Dante, the one that says *Abandon hope all ye who enter here,* then it should be. Much more likely, what it actually says is *Pests and Nuisances Keep Out!*

Whatever it says, the intruder has certainly got the message – for the pointing finger now indicates the bench next to the phone and obediently, he sits. If he had been a dog, I know exactly where his tail would have been.

I am glad that we are at the point of leaving anyway and don't need to be shown the door. The Handsome One marches out again without a glance at us as if he had never seen us in his life before.

I have a feeling that that poor man will be left to cool his heels here for quite some time, long after his footprints have evaporated from those blood-red tiles. He should consider himself lucky that it's not his blood on them.

CHAPTER FORTY-TWO: A CRUEL AND UNNATURAL PUNISHMENT

Although the sun is still shining brightly, it fails to raise our spirits. Neither of us is much in the mood now for the Uffizi and so we have decided that we will just write Firenze off and catch the next train back to Lucca, whenever that is and before anything else disastrous happens. The worst scenario would be being stranded here and having to find a room for the night or paying an extortionate taxi fare to get back to Lucca.

Iona has gone charging on ahead, eager to get to the station as soon as possible on the off chance that a train is about to leave and thus avoid the tedium of having to hang around for another hour or so waiting for the next one. I, however, have been distracted by a plaque on the wall of the Ognissanti, which informs me that this is where Botticelli is buried. What a stroke of luck! I would never have stumbled upon this gravesite but for my present misfortunes. What's more, I think the church may be open too, because although the main doors are shut, there is a passage at the side and people are going down there, heading for a side entrance presumably.

I hasten after Iona to report this serendipitous discovery but in her present mood, predictably, she gives the proposed visit short shrift. Not only is the lady not for turning, she doesn't even break step as she tells me in no uncertain terms that when she says she is finished with Florence, she means she is finished with Florence. And in any case, she adds witheringly, the last thing she would want to do is poke around yet another church, just to visit the grave of one dead painter. Not even for a whole cryptful of corpses would she contemplate visiting the All Saints and that's final.

Well, that's telling me. It is a disappointment, a grave disappointment in fact, but it's only fair after all, since I have ruined the day for her. Still, it would have been nice to have added him to my collection of famous dead artists, as his paintings do have a certain resonance with me. When I think of Botticelli, I think of fat little cherubs first of all, and then I think of his *Birth of Venus,* the eponymous goddess being blown ashore on a seashell with the help of a couple of friendly zephyrs. There must have been a welcoming committee and ironically for the goddess of love, whom you might have expected to flaunt rather than cover up her wares, she is covering herself up as best as she can, being fortunate enough to have been born with extremely long red tresses. But rescue is on hand in the form of a woman waiting for her, already holding out a cloak with which she can cover up her embarrassment.

Fortunately for us, this was not one of Botticelli's paintings that was consumed in Savonarola's bonfire. It is safe in the Uffizi (where else?) and the model for Venus, Simonetta Vespucci, is also buried in the Ognissanti. And if that name sounds familiar, yes, her husband was related to the man whose name was given, somewhat fortuitously, to the American continent.

We are not to imagine however, Simonetta standing motionless for ages in a shell while Botticelli painted what he saw. She had been dead for the best part of a decade when the painting was completed. Botticelli had a thing about her, as had the rest of Florence, apparently, and whose early decease at only twenty-two provoked such a state of grief and mourning throughout the whole of Florence that it brings to mind the hysterical reaction to death of Lady Diana in our own times.

Botticelli's last wish was to be buried at her feet, which he was. Now there is someone who knew his place – and she wasn't even his mistress. Very likely that honour went to Giuliano de' Medici, Lorenzo's brother, and if only we had been able to get into the Medici Chapel, I would have visited his grave too. And his would have been a really good one too because he has a special claim to fame. He was murdered in the Duomo of all places, by the rival Pazzi family in a bid to supplant the mighty Medici as rulers of Florence. Such a preposterous idea, one of such incredible folly, that today Italians use the word *pazzo* to describe someone whom they consider to be not quite right in the head, or as we say, not the full shilling.

Retracing our steps as far as the Piazza Carlo Goldoni, named in honour of the prolific 18th century playwright, we strike up to the left along the Via dei Fossi and presently find ourselves in what at first sight appears to be a construction site but which the map confirms as the Piazza di Santa Maria Novella. What the plan may be, what will finally emerge from all this chaos it is impossible to say, but at the end furthest from us, the façade of the church looks on serenely, secure in the knowledge that despite its name of New St Mary's, as an ancient monument, (the oldest part dates from the 13th century) regardless of whatever else happens in the piazza, it is safe from the wrecking ball and bulldozer's blade.

Change in the Piazza is nothing new. In times gone by, beginning in the time of Cosimo I in the mid 16th century and continuing for more than three hundred years, the façade witnessed annual chariot races, in the Roman style. You can still see the obelisks which mark the beginning and end of the course, each obelisk curiously supported on the backs of tortoises, like the rockets at Cape Canaveral on those specially designed Caterpillars which crawl their way to the launch pad, inch by careful inch.

The Via degli Avelli leads us out of the Piazza and towards the railway station. We are flanked on our left by a long, high wall. It marks the boundary of the cemetery of Santa Maria Novella. Just above head height, for those who are not as vertically challenged as me, and a little higher in my case,

I can see a row of tombs, all looking remarkably similar and symmetrical. This is burial on a very organised and formal scale. I imagine it must have cost a fortune for your remains to be put in one of these and yet no-one passing by today has the remotest clue who you were should they stop to ponder such matters – and no-one does. I wouldn't call that degree of anonymity value for money, yet those who paid to be there no doubt died happy in the knowledge that the money they gave towards the construction of the church and which assured them this coveted resting place, would also guarantee them a more illustrious place in heaven.

That would be reward enough in their eyes no doubt, yet for the curious, there is a clue to the occupants of the tombs. You would have to be clued up on your medieval Florentine heraldry, a bit of an esoteric subject, admittedly, but for those who are, it's as easy as reading the back of a cereal packet at breakfast time, for on each tomb are carved not one, but two heraldic coats of arms with the Florentine cross in the middle, forming a sort of triptych. Why would you need more than one set of arms? Look more closely however, and you will see that although each cross is different in some way, the coat of arms on either side is either the same or a mirror image.

Above the tombs, black-and-white striped Gothic arches point the way to heaven, and behind them are deep alcoves, which, once upon a time, featured illustrations of a religious and improving nature. But now not even the faintest trace of pigment remains to show that they once existed and if anything at all remains of the former occupants of the tombs, it will merely be some dusty bones, their souls long since departed, taking inspiration, they would hope, from the arches and soaring heavenward.

Our destination, or the first stage of it, lies in sight now. But first, like the children of Israel faced with the apparently uncrossable Red Sea, we must cross the obstacle known as the Piazza della Stazione where buses, taxis, cars, mopeds,

Vespas and even bicycles sweep past in a seemingly endless and unstoppable flow, totally ignoring the zebra crossings. I have been in Italy long enough to know that they are for road decoration only and if we were to wait for the traffic to stop to let us across, we could have walked back to Lucca by then.

Fortune favours the brave; a gap in the lane nearest the kerb appears for a moment and trusting to Italian drivers' well-honed skills in driving around pedestrians, we step into the stream, where sure enough, the tide of traffic does not stop but steers itself around us and we arrive safely at the other side.

If I were right about the prowess of Italian drivers, I was completely wrong about *The Book of Mormon* at the barriers which I had confidently predicted would still be there on our return. There is no sign of it anywhere. My first thought is that it must have been knocked onto the floor, but since that is not the case, I conclude that a succession of feet stumbling across it must have kicked it yards away over the smooth marble surface like a puck in an ice rink.

My eyes sweep the concourse, albeit seen through a forest of feet, but they search in vain. However unlikely it seems, someone must have actually removed it. Perhaps it was by someone who had picked it up to see what the puck was that had nearly caused them to break their necks. Or perhaps it was by someone too late for their train to buy a newspaper, someone desperate for anything to read, foreign language or not. Or perhaps the likeliest explanation of all simply is that some people will take anything, no matter what, just as long as it is free. And if they would take a thing like *The Book of Mormon,* then my pouch has no chance of being handed in.

But wait a moment. What's this? Just to the right after the barriers, a sign projecting at right angles above a doorway says *POLFER*. I can hazard a pretty good guess at what it means. Railway police. And to give substance to my theory, two men in uniform are standing beneath it. One is speaking to a member of the public; the other is just looking on.

"Is this where you came?" I ask Iona, hope starting to rekindle that I might yet be reunited with my pouch. But even before she answers, I know in my bones this is where she *should* have been sent if the girl in the Information Office had had a brain bigger than a walnut. And I also know this is precisely the sort of joke that the gods love to play, using the disappearance of *The Book of Mormon* to reinforce the certainty that my pouch was gone for good, just so they could pull their rabbit out of the hat to much greater effect. And yet it is dangerous to raise one's hopes too much because they take great delight in dashing them to smithereens.

"No, I didn't see this place. I came in at the other end."

Another entrance? Where was that? I never saw it but if I had, it is certainly the one I would have used since it would have been the first we would have come to and I need no encouragement to take any short cuts. Thank God that Iona hadn't pointed it out to me or we would certainly not be here now. And if there is one place that any honest person is likely to hand in valuables found on a train, then this is it, provided they also know this place exists of course.

"Excuse me, do you speak English?" If I'd had a euro for every time I had said that or wished I spoke Italian, I would be rich enough not to need to bother about being reunited with my money.

"Him." The idle cop indicates his colleague with a slight sideways movement of the head.

As I wait for "him" to finish his conversation, I can feel my pulse racing as I try to suppress the feeling of excitement that is rising in my breast. When at last his conversation is over, I try to initiate my own, but when I open my mouth, nothing comes out as my throat has gone completely dry.

"Has a wallet been handed in?" I finally manage to croak.

For a moment he says nothing, just looks me up and down in a calculating sort of way as if he is not quite sure what to make of me.

"What is your name?"

I tell him.

"Describe it." I assume he means the lost article and not the article in front of him, though I can't be too sure of that as the tone he is using makes me feel as if I were the chief suspect in a murder enquiry.

Again I tell him.

"What is in it?"

"Well, there's some money –"

"How much money?" he cuts in as if it were the $64,000 question.

"About sixty euros," I answer confidently but plunge right on to tell him about the receipt for Carla's luggage. No-one could have invented that. That surely is enough to satisfy the most sceptical of cops, which he seems to be. Meanwhile, I am becoming increasingly more and more hopeful, otherwise why all these questions?

He looks at me once more as if I were some sort of chancer, but on the other hand, can't work out how I could come up with details like these unless I really was the rightful owner.

"Yes, we have it," he admits at last.

Relief, like a hot bath washes over me, leaving me feeling weak and giddy. For her part, Iona's relief is practically palpable, then almost instantly, her eyes harden and the old anger comes back to think that I have needlessly put her through all this torture, that we have wasted practically a whole day in Florence, just for it to end like this. I would call that a happy ending, but she is like a mother who has prayed for the return of a missing child then upon its return, beats it to within an inch of its life for all the worry it has caused. No doubt I have that to look forward to once I am outwith the sight of the long arm of the law, for even in Italy, I bet husband-bashing is a crime.

"Follow me."

I do, into the office, and keep following him as he goes behind a glass screen, whereupon he, surprised and not a little annoyed to find that I am still tagging onto his heels, commands me to stop and go back to the waiting room. And just in case I don't understand his English, he accompanies it with an imperious gesture of the hand, like a traffic policeman, which is what he is after all, I suppose. Just because I left all my money on the train doesn't mean I am as stupid as he thinks I look. I get both messages perfectly clearly. One would have been quite enough.

But what I don't get is why Iona was not directed here in the first place, nor why the Handsome One did not immediately contact his colleagues here. It seems the logical thing to do and it would have saved us all a great deal of time and trouble if one of them at least, had had the presence of mind to think of that. But that's Italy for you: just another example of how Aristotle's teachings were Greek to them. Which doesn't surprise me in the slightest, as they have never heard of half of the EU's directives either.

And yet, for all my moaning, that's what I like about Italy. I wish we were a bit more like that, a bit more selectively deaf, a lot less obsequiously servile to the letter of the European law. Having said that, I would prefer the policemen made some allowances for the feeble-minded like me and I also wish the drivers would pay a little more attention to road demarcations. Our son, George, who is deaf, nearly had his life cut prematurely short, aged eleven, when we snatched him from beneath the wheels of boy racers in the main piazza of Turin, which they treat more like Silverstone than a pedestrian precinct.

But we have to make allowances too: we have to remember, according to EU statistics, Italian men have the smallest penises in the Union and it seems to bother them a lot. How they came to hear of this is in the first place is a matter of mystery and why they should believe it is another thing altogether, but that is the way it is and that is why they drive so fast and give their policemen the nicest uniforms. And yet many men seem perfectly happy to be seen on a Vespa. You'll have to make your own deductions about what that tells you.

"Is it correct?"

The policeman has returned with what I instantly recognise as my pouch. He stands over me as I rifle through it, take out the notes, count them, (it *is* about €60) check my bank cards are there and pronounce everything as present and correct.

"Sign here."

He places three flimsy sheets of paper in Italian, in small writing, on the desk and marks three crosses where I should sign, or make my mark, as he no doubt expects my capabilities to run to.

"Who found it?" I enquire civilly as I dutifully append my signature to what I hope are receipts and not a contract to star in a triple X movie or even to appear in a small bit part.

"A cleaner."

"Is it customary to give a reward?"

"Not necessary. Arrivederci," and with that, he snatches up the signed papers in triplicate with one dexterous sweep of the hand and marches off with them where I know I must not follow. We are dismissed and free to go wherever we want – which is back to Lucca.

"You really are the giddy limit!" Iona says when we get outside. But the tone is a lot more light-hearted than I have any right to expect. Could there possibly even be a tinge of admiration in it, at my incredible, amazing luck, as if I am somehow anointed?

"I know." I am inwardly hugging myself, congratulating myself on my infernal luck. My record remains intact: I have never yet not had a temporarily missing Visa card returned to me. But maybe, like Faust, there will be a price to pay later. In the meantime, I regret my hasty action in cancelling my cards.

In fact, there *is* a price to pay and it comes immediately after what we had originally come here to do – ascertain when the next train leaves for Lucca. We have more than an hour to wait. While we had been engaged with the return of the pouch, we had apparently just missed one. But better a pouch in the hand than a train at a platform as the newly-coined proverb has it.

"That's plenty time for a coffee," says Iona, leading the way out of the station by the only entrance I know.

But just outside the entrance, where it is less busy, there is an unexpected development. Like the train at Adelstrop, she stops *unwontedly*. It must be really important to delay her from her drug like this: it can only be, at best, to give me a tongue-lashing for my carelessness or more likely a bit of GBH out of sight of the cops.

"Just a moment," she says, delving into the depths of her bag and producing a mysterious little woollen bundle. "You've got to wear it," she adds as she hands it over. "It's your penance."

Suspiciously, and fearing the worst, I take it from her and open it out rather than unwrap it as it is not gift-wrapped. It is a woollen garment all right, but not a pair of socks. To my horror, it turns out to be something intended for the other extreme – one of those appalling knitted hats with ears like an Afghan Hound's that she knows I detest above all other forms of headgear, like that worn by the Mad Hatter in Lucca.

"I found it in a euro shop, on the way back from the station," she explains, with ill-concealed delight.

The fact that she has not made a massive investment for her little joke scarcely diminishes the horror. Some jokes are just not worth the money, however little.

"You've got to wear it," she repeats, "for making me suffer today." And with that, she whips off my hat and hugs it to her bosom. "Go on. Put it on!"

Possession is nine-tenths of the law. Burning with embarrassment and shame, I do as I am told. It seems a punishment out of all proportion to the crime. The medieval stocks seem kinder. With my head held low and my eyes cast down to avoid the curious looks of passers-by or the sight of my reflection in shop windows, we set off in search of coffee, the tassels at the ends of the lugs swinging in a jaunty rhythm that seems to mock my abject shame.

But it's what will happen when we get to the café that is really preoccupying my thoughts. No doubt heads are turning now at the sight of me as we walk down the street, but at the café, people lingering over their coffee or beer will be able to get a much longer look. And pedestrians too, as they pass by, might even be halted in their tracks.

Doesn't she realise that it is one thing to be thought an idiot, but to draw the world's attention to the fact by wearing the dunce's cap is another matter entirely? And surely she can see that it will also draw attention not just to me, but her too, my fellow mortal, and poor, earthborn companion? And just how long does she intend to make us suffer this indignity?

If I were more of a man and less of a mouse, I would refuse to let us be humiliated in this way, but the plain truth is, I am just too timorous, even for her sake.

CHAPTER FORTY-THREE: AN INCREDIBLY STRANGE TOILET

It is some compensation to find that the train now standing at *Binario* 8 departing in thirteen minutes for Viareggio, stopping at Lucca (and various places in between) is a double-decker. It was not Iona's intention to leave it as close to departure as this, and it turns out it would have been better not to have lingered so long over the beer, for the train is extremely crowded, the numbers swollen perhaps by people like us who, through fear of being stranded, have taken an earlier train than they might otherwise have done.

It's not as if the café had been full of the sort of ambience that encouraged us to linger either, but we weren't exactly spoiled for choice. Isn't life strange? When you are looking for something, such as a café, there never seems to be one anywhere, yet when nothing is further from your mind, you keep tripping over them all over the place. And so it was with us: we didn't find one until we came to the Medici Chapels just at the point where the Via del Canto de' Nelli funnels innocent tourists and consenting Florentines into the narrow gap where the leather sellers ply their trade. It was just a trifle too public for me.

We sat outside under a canopy where a football match was in noisy progress on TV. The ceremonial chariot that we had seen earlier had delivered the gladiators to the stadium where they had donned their traditional purple outfit before engaging with the enemy. Across the street, at one of the stalls, a radio commentary was competing in volume and covering what I imagine was the same match.

It was an irritating distraction to say the least and if I couldn't give a toss whether Fiorentina won or lost, Iona was

340

doubly of the same opinion, as she hasn't the slightest interest in football of any sort. But she was the one who chose to come here, not me, so at least I couldn't get the blame for that. Actually, one of my greatest fears is that one of these days, when I am even more feeble minded than I am now, when Iona has power of attorney over me, she makes me accompany her to the sort of things that being married to me has prevented her from attending less frequently than she would have liked, such as ballets and even worse, operas, such as Puccini's *Gianni Schicchi,* which as far as I know, has only one good tune in it, and even that is spoiled by having a soprano screech it out as if she were being sawn in half.

A chalkboard on the wall had promised, for the princely sum of €4.50, (and that is meant to be a bargain) a *birra grande* of a certain brand of well-known beer which is not my favourite. I'm not saying that it is not very nice, but if you were to submit a sample for analysis to your doctor, you would be admitted to hospital immediately for further tests and your close family advised not to have any travel plans further than the end of your bed.

Bad enough, but when the bill came, another euro had been added on top. When I challenged the patron, he told me the price on the board applied to customers who stood inside at the bar. No wonder there was only one other solitary customer sitting outside with us, but whether his long face was due to the price of the beer or Fiorentina's performance or a combination of both, I couldn't possibly say.

It wasn't all bad though. I am not, it turns out, the stupidest-looking person in Florence. That honour belongs to the patron who had a sticking plaster on his nose, well his left nostril to be precise, in a futile attempt to cover up an angry red boil. The other end had come loose however and stuck up above the bridge like the antennae of a praying mantis. If wearing a Peruvian hat is eccentric, how eccentric is that? Why doesn't he stick a pin in it and squeeze it like everybody else?

And Iona's coffee, when it came, was hot and black and steaming which pleased her, but even better was the cup. In blue and white, like Delft, it depicted a 360° panoramic view of Florence's skyline. Now that is what I call a souvenir and if only I had had a handbag, I'd have been sorely tempted to slip it in there and possibly even become addicted to coffee like Iona, just so that I could look at it several times a day and bring back happy memories of Florence.

At the station, like an excited schoolboy, I clamber to the upper deck of the nearest carriage to be faced with a sea of faces and the back of heads. Just by the stairs, there are a couple of seats beside a man with a load of shopping that he has placed on the floor between his legs. It doesn't look the most inviting of berths, but with passengers still piling on, it is better than nothing and we squeeze in beside him. He makes no effort to make way for us – is determined not to budge an inch in fact, and even if he had no shopping, there still would not be a lot of room.

Imagine you were sitting on an aircraft, on one of those no-frills airlines, but the back of the seat in front has been turned round so that your knees are brushing the knees of the person in front: that is what it is like. Admittedly, such an arrangement could have its advantages. If the person opposite happens to be a long leggy blonde, depending on her legginess, she might be practically in your lap. But he's not a she and he's not a blonde either. He only has long legs. And, what's more, he is facing the engine, the way I like to be.

I wouldn't say I dislike him exactly, since I have only just met him, but I can feel his resentment towards *us* for invading what he sees as his and his shopping's personal space. And it is the shopping that I object to more than anything. I thought only women did that. Food shopping you can't help, but these are big carrier bags with the names of shops on them that mean nothing to me but amongst those in the know, are designed to tell the world how rich you are. My shops give me recycled carrier bags from a variety of supermarkets so that I may take my "new" garments home under a cloak of anonymity and they hardly take up any room at all.

Across the aisle, a couple of fat women, dressed in black, are talking animatedly in Spanish. I am sure it is Spanish, not Italian. Iona and I exchange glances and wordlessly, we slip across the passage. They interrupt their conversation just long enough to give us a nod of acknowledgement and shift their feet accommodatingly before going at it full tilt again. Meanwhile, our former companion is as motionless as a statue and if he had shown any signs that he was pleased at our departure, his features have resumed their habitual marble-like qualities and it is impossible to tell.

Precisely on time, at 5.08, we glide smoothly out of the station. We still have our backs to the engine but it does have the benefit of letting me study our fellow passengers. Not a particularly interesting lot, apart from a young Japanese, who has not found a seat but is standing in the aisle, talking to a couple of his friends. He could be a pop star, or at least imagines he is modelling himself on one, with his jet-black hair, backcombed and bouffant and as wild as a haystack in a gale. His black shirt is open at the neck, displaying a hairless chest where two seemingly identical silver pentangles dangle from a silver chain round his neck. A broad black belt with silver studs, like an abacus of would-be conquests, is not doing a very good job of holding up his jeans, also black, which are slung low beneath his slim hips. A pair of dark glasses, some more silverware round his wrists and a pair of trainers (not in black) complete the outfit. Mr Cool Cat himself. His friends, on the other hand, appear to be quite ordinary, but that adds to effect and no doubt has chosen them carefully for their mediocrity.

If he thinks he is the best-dressed person on the train, as for me, the worst-dressed, Iona tells me to my immense relief, that because we are inside, I may doff my headgear, but she still retains custody of my precious hat, which I hope, will resume its shape after it is liberated from the bag into which she has crammed it. My pouch, lightened by having paid for the refreshments which one of us had just enjoyed at the café, is round my neck beneath my jacket and however uncomfortable it becomes on the journey, however burdensome, that is where it is going to stay.

A lot of people get off at Prato, just as they did on the outward journey, including our two fat ladies who have kept up their conversation throughout, the man with the shopping and the young Japanese with his two friends. Smartly, we occupy the seats vacated by the two Spanish ladies, though there is no need for haste it turns out, as no-one joins our compartment.

Now we can face forward as nature intended and see the countryside as it rushes towards us rather than as it recedes. But more interesting than the countryside, I can now see that my comparison of the seating to that on an aircraft was not inappropriate, for above the stairs is a LED display that tells anyone who has a mind to look, (and who can resist it?) the current speed; the time of departure; the estimated time of arrival at the next station, and the external temperature, just like you get on some flights, except this goes one better and tells you the internal temperature as well (23° ext, 21° int). In addition to that, it tells you the date and time, in hours, minutes and seconds; the number of the train you are in; and the carriage number. But perhaps most useful of all, especially for incontinent passengers, or those who have overdosed on peanuts, a green light informs us that the toilet is *libera*.

Because I don't understand the cleverness of such technological marvels, this holds a childlike fascination for me. I can't take my eyes off the endlessly changing screen. One thing doesn't change however and it is another thing that the airlines don't tell you – how many minutes we are running late. At the moment it stands at one minute, which I think is scandalous. Why can't our trains be like that?

And if it were not for the blur of the countryside sweeping past at 133...135...137 km/h, you might well imagine yourself to be flying, for it is as silent and as smooth as riding on a cushion of air.

"You should go to the toilet," Iona reports on her return from that place, with a smile on her face.

"Why? I don't want to go," I point out.

"Nevertheless you should go," she advises.

"Why?"

"Just go," she replies enigmatically.

That does it. Not so much because I am a mouse accustomed to obeying orders, but because I can't resist a mystery. The LED says green, so I go.

Down the stairs and there are the toilets to the left. I press a button on the wall and a pair of curved doors obediently swings apart to reveal a cavernous space inside. I enter and the doors close behind me automatically, like a trap. Impressive enough so far, but there must be more than this I reason, for Iona's strange advice.

The throne is at the other end. Oh well, since I am here I may as well make use of it. A padded seat I see. Yes, that is quite impressive too, but surely it can't just be that either. I raise it and because I have been domesticated, put it down again afterwards. Right then, how do I do flush it? Where is it? I can't see any anything like a handle or a button to press. That's the trouble with this newfangled technology – it is often smarter than me. Thank God I didn't do a number two.

I wave my hands in front of it. I am not so technologically challenged not to realise that there is probably some infrared device that makes it work. And maybe there is or maybe there isn't, perhaps there is some sensor in the bowl or in the seat, but at any rate, without me having apparently done anything, the most amazing thing happens next. There is the sound of a fierce suction like you get in aeroplane toilets – but that's not the amazing bit. To my complete astonishment there is a whirring sound and the toilet seat begins revolving, while at the same time a spray at the back douses it with what I presume is some sort of disinfectant. I watch, fascinated, to see what will happen next, half-expecting a cloth to come out of somewhere and dry it, but nothing more happens. Is it self-drying? Will it evaporate before the next user or will they get a wet bum?

I see now why Iona was so insistent that I paid a visit. I have seen some public toilets where you can put a paper ring down on the seat before you plonk your bum down, but never anything like this. It all seems a bit germ-phobic to me. I had a girlfriend once who never actually sat down, just hovered, so I dare say there are a lot of paranoid people like that about who wouldn't object to having a wet bum if they thought that prevented them from catching some vile and nasty infection, or even getting pregnant.

But now I have a problem. I have managed to wash my hands, or at least soap them, but I just can't get the taps to deliver a drop of water. We've all seen those where you just waft your hands beneath the taps and as if by magic, the water appears and I expect no less than that in this high-tech loo, but that just doesn't seem to work however often I try it. Nor does pressing the taps or pulling them up and they certainly don't turn. What was wrong with the good old-fashioned kind like that? Even those with the single tap that you turn to the left or the right to get hot or cold, I usually know how to work, (though Iona can never get the hang of which way to get the water she wants the first time). In vain, I search for some button on the wall, some infrared sensor.

There are no towels, just one of those hand dryers that can't outsmart me. I have met them before and know they are activated when you place your hands beneath them. Well, they seem to work for most people but I often have trouble getting them to start. Furthermore, I never find them very efficient and often give up, going away with wet hands unless they are those extra powerful types that lift the skin off your bones and make it ripple it like a piece of corrugated cardboard – a repulsive but at the same time fascinating sight. I often keep my hands under them long after they are dry, just to watch my skin creep.

This is the less powerful type but at least it dries the soap, leaving my hands, ironically, feeling rather unclean and sticky. I turn towards the door and press the button to release me, which is when I am struck by a sudden thought. When the doors closed behind me, did they also lock automatically? What was to prevent someone on the outside, coming in? I am glad that I had dismissed the notion I had had to whip down my trousers just to test the dampness of the seat for I know that is just the moment when the gods would have struck and the doors would have parted as wide as the Red Sea.

"Well?" asks Iona.

"Amazing!" I tell her. "The only thing is I couldn't get any water out of the taps."

"There's a button on the floor."

Was there indeed? But why should anyone be expected to think of that? Yet she divulges this information in the sort of tone as if it were not only perfectly obvious, but a perfectly reasonable place to look. Surely I can't be the only one who was bamboozled by that? Can I?

And it beats me why would anyone go to all the trouble of thinking up these weird contraptions such as a self-cleaning rotating toilet seat or a more complicated way to do something that has been working pretty well for centuries, such as turning on a tap. Some people are just far too clever for our own good and I bet before their "improved" invention is released onto an unsuspecting general public, it has to pass the bamboozlement test first.

As far as I am concerned, interesting though it was, that toilet was more like a mantrap than a public convenience.

CHAPTER FORTY-FOUR:
CHILE, CHILLY AUTUMN TIME

We stop at Montecatini for a much longer time than that allowed for on the schedules. The LED now says that we are fifteen minutes late but offers no explanation, which I think is a bit rude, as I am sure it could if it wanted to as it can do practically everything else. By the time we arrive in Lucca, that has been reduced to seven and who is to say that by the time the train arrives in Viareggio it will not be bang on time? I, for one, would not be surprised if it were.

In what seems a miracle of choreographed Italian train management, we arrive just as another of exactly the same kind stops at the other side of the platform and there is barely time to get off before both depart at precisely the same time. It is 6.40 and already dark. No point in heading for the hotel – we go straight in search of a restaurant. Not the Baralla, though, regardless of how good the food, or how comely the waitresses. We like to spread our largesse and that is why, by accident, we come across the Osteria Via San Giorgio.

In a spacious portico, a dozen or so tables are laid out with checked tablecloths upon which candles in coloured jars are flickering so hard it looks as if they might blow themselves out at any moment. It all looks very charming and inviting and without saying anything, we step inside, knowing we have found what we were looking for. In fact I wouldn't be surprised if we have stumbled across the place where our friends from Linlithgow were the first evening.

The restaurant proper lies up a flight of stairs. Like downstairs, it is just as colourful with the same checked tablecloths in red, green and yellow and even some of the chairs are painted to match. It's like walking into a fairytale world where you wouldn't be surprised to see Snow White or

Goldilocks come to tea. There are no customers, but the tables here, unlike those in the portico, have been set with polished glasses and gleaming cutlery in expectation. Regrettably there are no candles. And if there is one thing I like, because I am such an incurable romantic, it is a candle on the table when I am taking the love of my life out to dinner, whoever that happened to be at the time.

We come to a halt in front of the bar, wondering what to do next. A waitress, somehow alerted by our arrival, materialises, probably from the kitchen.

"Have you a table for two?" I ask, all too conscious of how stupid that sounds since it is patently obvious that there are tables available for two-score people, never mind two.

"Certainly. Where would you like to sit?"

"Somewhere outside."

"You want to sit outside?"

She can't prevent the astonishment in her voice, but like a moth, I am drawn to the coloured flickering candles. Besides, when on the continent, it is our custom to eat alfresco whenever possible since we get so little opportunity at home and never in November.

"Well, yes…"

"But it's freezing out there!"

"Is it?"

The guttering candles might have suggested that to me, but my padded jacket and the march from the station have made me impervious to the cold, to the biting wind that has descended upon Lucca this evening. But above all, my new hat has to bear the greatest responsibility. It is as hot as Hades under that lid and the brain must have become poached, otherwise I would have realised that they never expected anyone to sit outside as this time of the season as the tables had not been laid and the gaily-lit candles served only as beacons to attract our attention and draw us into the restaurant.

She makes no reply and although it is anything but cold in here, the silence between us reminds me of Joseph Addison and his far-fetched but amusing tale, *Frozen Voices,* where it was so cold conversations froze in the air and to the speakers' consternation, when the air warmed up again, their voices appeared out of the ether – with some embarrassing results. I am in no doubt that if our waitress were to say anything, it would be that she would prefer not to wait at that table down all those stairs in what she regards as the frozen Arctic and serve us food that will be stone cold by the time it reaches us.

Actually, now she has brought it to my attention, it doesn't seem such a good an idea to sit outside after all. We will sit inside, in the windproof warmth and I will be able to take off my hat.

"We're from Scotland," I explain. "We don't feel the cold!"

"I'm from Chile," she reciprocates.

"No wonder you feel the cold!" I say in jest and she has the grace to smile. "We'll have this table," I tell her, already sitting down at the nearest one and respectfully doffing the millinery.

No cutlery or wine glass at my place, nor a place mat either, but that doesn't matter. It is an easy matter to move them to my present location from which I can have an overview of the restaurant in the likely event that we will not be the only diners in this place tonight. After all, it is still early in dining out terms, even for Britain, but especially for the Italians. They are probably only at the stage of phoning their mistresses; she has still to have a shower and slip into the silky underwear, put on her face. It's going to be ages yet before anyone appears.

It's no great surprise that the first people to arrive are a foursome of Anglophones. Fortunately, they are despatched to the naughty table in the corner where, hopefully, we will not be able to overhear their conversation which will deceive us into thinking we are somewhere in southern England rather than in Tuscany. But that is the price you pay for coming to centres of cultural interest – half the world comes with you, even when you travel off-peak as we are.

Having said that, Lucca, apart from its own attractions, is a lot less frenetic than Pisa and Florence, not to mention the slight matter of being a lot less expensive. More than that, it has the advantage of being within easy striking distance of its more popular neighbours, public transport strikes not withstanding. Yes, I congratulate myself, it was a masterstroke of mine to decide to stay in Lucca. If only I had been half as clever by the time we landed in Pisa...

In addition to the house wine (red) we order a bottle of water, in the Italian way. That means *frizzante* for us. The waitress, ever solicitous, and without a hint of irony, wants to know if we would like ice in it.

"I like your hat," she observes as she pours the wine, nodding in the direction of the discarded garment now occupying the place at the table that was meant for me.

It is my turn to be astounded. She cannot be serious! I suspect sycophancy in search of a greater tip or like at the hairdresser's, idle chatter to cover up an awkward silence.

"Well, thank you," I reply, pretending to take her at her word. "Since you like it so much, you can have it. Would you like it? It's very warm," I add.

But she only laughs, not realising I am perfectly serious. It is more of a woman's garment anyway, halfway to a Heidi hairstyle. But what if she was being serious too? Maybe she really does like it. Maybe they wear them in Chile and it reminds her of home, she's just too embarrassed to take gifts from a customer. What if I were to accidentally leave it behind? To think is to act. I remove it from the table and place it on the chair.

"Make sure you don't forget to pick it up when you leave," Iona says eyeing this manoeuvre over the rim of her glass of water.

And that's another thing I reflect gloomily, looking at the half-litre carafe of wine we have ordered, already looking depressingly half-empty and our glasses only half-filled, just the way the waitress poured them, not a sip having been taken yet. This is the start of the new regime according to the edict issued last night at the Baralla.

Never mind, the food is good: a starter of baked cheese and vegetables then a pizza marinara for me – chillies, tomatoes, oregano and garlic – and pink tagliatelle, artichoke and tomato for Iona. That looks like food unbecoming for a man. Mine looks much more the part. It comes on a wooden plate that is not so much a plate, more like the cross-section of a tree that someone like Robin Hood stood his sword up in when he wasn't using it to smite the ungodly – for it has a massive split in it, and scratches by the score where the murderous-looking knife that accompanies it, more of a dagger than a knife actually, has carved up countless pizzas before.

It is now nearly eight and some more diners have arrived, thank goodness, for it is always entertaining when dining out with one's wife, to have something else to look at, however delectable she may look. Now my attention has been drawn to the table nearest us that has just been occupied.

They are both very smartly dressed, he in a blazer and a pink bow tie, she, of Oriental extraction, in a black cocktail dress. They are wearing wedding rings but that does not necessarily mean that they are married to each other, except in this case, I would lay my bottom dollar that they are as they look so sober and serious, especially him. It's his hair that does it, parted down the middle and plastered to his skull, looking as hard and bright and shiny as the carapace of a beetle. From his head to his highly polished shoes, he is the very image of someone caught in a 1920s time warp. He does not have a pince-nez, but he should have in place of the gold-rimmed spectacles he is wearing.

I never met him, only saw a photograph of him, but Iona agrees that he reminds her very strongly of her deceased grandfather, Percival. I am sure this specimen must be called the Italian equivalent of that and he must be a lawyer by profession. Or he might be an undertaker. Something that requires a great deal of gravitas anyway, but not a judge: he is far too young for that. He does look a fine, upstanding and moral member of the community though, just as Percy MBE was. In his private life, I am sure the latter would never have raised his fists to anyone, but professionally, he produced weapons of mass destruction. That's why he got his MBE: he was the superintendent of a munitions factory during WWII.

Our new neighbour's first action upon sitting down is to instruct the waitress to remove the wine glasses. That's exactly what Percy would have done too. He also was a teetotaller but in his defence I have to say there was Methodism in his madness. He couldn't help it: it was just the way he had the misfortune to be brought up and that is how he, in his turn, brought up his daughter, my mother-in-law. Fortunately the contagion stopped there, for I came along and broke this unnatural cycle. But why this latter-day Percival does not have wine with his meal, I have no way of knowing, but to be an Italian and not avail yourself of the local wine and at these prices, now that, it seems to me, is a terrible waste of one of life's pleasures. Maybe that *is* the reason. He doesn't look as if he indulges in pleasure much.

To accompany their tap water, Percival's wife chooses ravioli, while Mr Serious himself has spaghetti with mussels, neither of which I can imagine our Percy touching with a bargepole. I may be doing him a disservice here but I bet he would have regarded it with suspicion as Johnny Foreigner food. Besides, these Eyetie blighters were on the side of the Ungodly during the War.

They don't converse much during the meal – a sure sign that they are married to each other. There's nothing wrong with that – Iona and I don't talk much either during a meal as you know. One has one's notes to write up after all. And it doesn't necessarily mean their marriage is as unexciting as his stiff and formal dress and demeanour seem to suggest, but I wouldn't place any bets against it.

Whatever the truth may be, they certainly have provided a welcome diversion for us – Iona from her absent husband (though physically present) and me from the absence of wine. Half a carafe is better than no wine at all but not nearly enough. I'd like to stick with the litre but I don't see Iona agreeing to that. A bottle would be a happy compromise. I'll propose we have that the next time. Maybe that's why a bottle of wine is the size it is; just the right size for two people, as long your wife lets you have the greater part. That's what a successful marriage is about – compromise.

She's not yet prepared to compromise about the hat however, reminding me, as we take our leave, that in addition to everything else I had lost on this holiday, I may as well add my memory, because is that not my new hat on the chair beside me?

Yet, as we wend our way back to the hotel, melting into the darkness of the ill-lit and moonless and meandering back streets of Lucca, I have to confess (though I would never admit it to Iona as it would compromise my negotiating position) that at this precise moment I don't mind it at all.

According to her, it is not just chilly, but bitterly cold and she can't wait to get back to the hotel to thaw out. When I opine that, on the contrary, it is quite warm, she bids me remember it is November and I must be mad if I think that it is anything remotely like tropical. That's a bit removed from what I actually said but my cranium with its in-built solar panel, is as snug as a bug under this woolly helmet, as are my ears, and what's more, I don't have to worry about it suddenly flying off and making a spectacle of myself by running after it.

This is not the right time, but when the time does seem right, I'll propose another compromise: that during the hours of darkness I will wear the €1 hat if I am allowed the one from Montana during the hours of daylight. And like the words in Joseph's *Voices*, when she thaws out, by which I mean from her present physical state as well as her entrenched position on the dunce's hat, I hope she will agree to this revised modus vivendi.

CHAPTER FORTY-FIVE:
THESE FOOLISH THINGS

Usually no-one is manning the desk when we come back to the hotel, but because we are earlier tonight, there is someone on duty tonight. Not Gisele though. We haven't seen her since we gave her the plant. There it still is, on the desk, in the same state as it was before, only more dehydrated. Iona suggests she is probably leaving it there so people could see she was appreciated. I tell her *it* would appreciate a drink, but I don't add, "like me."

Having eaten so early, the long evening ahead of us in the rather Spartan hotel room seems to offer an unappetising fare of a different sort, not counting the *digestifs* of course: the *limoncello* chilled, is absolutely delicious. I could drink a whole bottle of it – only I won't be allowed to. Nor will I be allowed to switch on the TV. Iona doesn't approve of TVs in bedrooms at any time and especially if it's in a foreign language. But even worse is when it's in a foreign language she does understand such as CNN News. I have to admit I can't disagree with her there.

I have no book other than the guidebook, but I brighten at the prospect of being able to check my e-mails, since on this occasion, I happen to have taken my laptop with me. I never normally do but the hotel had advertised free Wi-Fi Internet connection and I am expecting a rather important e-mail.

Downstairs, at reception, the young man gives me a card with a code on it. He shows me how I have to go on to the site and then type in the code. That's all there is to it. Sounds easy. But of course for me, it doesn't turn out to be. After repeated attempts, and feeling a bit sheepish at not being able to accomplish such a simple task, I decide there is nothing else for it but to ask for help.

The receptionist is poring over a book and appears to be completely lost in it. It looks like a bad time. I feel like tiptoeing away but then I tell myself not to be such a wimp. I am a man, not a mouse and there probably never *would* be a right time. Eventually he tears his gaze from the book, probably unnerved by this presence hovering over him like a foul smell, making concentration impossible.

"Er…that card you gave me doesn't seem to work…" I say hesitantly, proffering the offending card for his inspection.

"Just bring it down," he replies, meeting my eyes but completely ignoring the card as if he knows there cannot possibly be anything wrong with it.

"I'm afraid I can't do that," I tell him, feeling my face grow hotter. "You see, I have to have it plugged in all the time because the battery is finished. It only lasts a couple of minutes…"

"All right, I'll come up in a moment," he says about as enthusiastically as someone who has been told he must have a tooth pulled out but unfortunately, it will have to be without articaine.

"Thanks."

I retreat, embarrassed at being such a nuisance. At least I've proved it is not true what it said on the website about the helpfulness of the staff. I vow to write a recommendation when I get back.

As Iona stitches away, quite happy and contented with life, there is nothing I can do in the meantime but sit on the edge of the bed and wait. And the longer I wait, the more uncomfortable I feel. I have a nasty feeling that this is going to end up with me looking really stupid. Again.

A few minutes later he arrives and I give him the card. He sits on the edge of the bed as there is nowhere else to sit and begins to type…

"There you are," he says a moment later, getting up to go, problem sorted. Over his shoulder, I had watched him as his fingers moved swiftly and blindly over the keys. How did he do that? He didn't appear to do anything complicated or esoteric. Nothing I hadn't done. I just don't understand how it had worked for him, yet it wouldn't work for me. Bloody computers. Bloody technology. They have got it in for me.

It is small comfort to have my premonition confirmed. I thank him profusely and close the door behind him as if to prevent my humiliation crawling down the stairs after him. At least it hadn't taken up very much of his time but it's precisely because of that reason that I realise I must have made a very basic error, the type than even an imbecilic two-year-old wouldn't.

"I just don't get it!" I mutter, half-dejectedly and half in exasperation, half to myself and half to Iona in protest at the unfairness of the world. "I did nothing different than him."

"You can't have done. Let me see it," she says, looking up from her sewing and holding her hand out for the card with just an edge of brittleness to it so I know it is my German wife, Frau Ning who is addressing me. She is annoyed by this interruption to her sewing, to the thread of her concentration being broken.

I don't see what good it's going to do, but I let her see it anyway.

"I bet I know what you did," she pronounces a moment later.

"What do you mean?"

"Is that an O or a zero?" she replies, handing me back the card with the air of someone who is perfectly sure she has cracked the case in the light of irrefutable evidence.

"An O," I reply after scrutinising the string of letters and in the sort of tone which tells her that while she may think I am stupid, I am not actually *that* stupid, for God's sake. I am of course, unwittingly giving lie to the truth because despite her hint, I still don't get it.

"There you are!" she crows. "That's your problem!"

Eh? What's she on about? But now, when I look at it more carefully, I can indeed see that what I thought was an O is indeed a 0. Well anyone could make that mistake couldn't they? What's a zero doing masquerading amidst a string of letters like that anyway? But more than that: why hadn't I asked Iona to have a look at it first, I ask myself regretfully? Then there would have been one person less in the world who knows what an idiot I am. But she had looked so peaceful and engrossed in her stitching I didn't like to ask. Besides, I didn't expect her to come up with the answer at all, let alone as pat as that.

Oh well, no good crying over spilt milk. Right. Login details. E-mail address. Easy enough. I know that. Password. Just a minute, what *is* my password? I try all the usual suspects. But it's no use. I've forgotten it. All that for nothing.

But there is one thing I *can* do. My iPod battery is very low, showing red. Between now and the time when I put an end to this most endless of evenings by going to bed, I can charge it up. I'm sure you are ahead of me in this. A search of the computer bag turns out to be fruitless. Even Iona, who can usually find in seconds what I have been searching all day for, can't find it. I have either forgotten to pack the lead or it is in the case at the airport.

Despair has no greater depth than this. Not only am I faced with the prospect of this interminable evening, but an endless, restless night ahead as well. God knows how I'll ever make it through the night without my podcasts from Radio 4. When you are down, you are really down. That's because it's easier for the gods to kick you in the teeth.

It's enough to drive you to drink, yet I know I daren't have another *limoncello*. Although she looks relaxed and at peace with the world, underneath that calm exterior, the drinks police is vigilant and waiting to pounce. I've already had two and I know she will say that's my limit. And it's not exactly as if I had tanked up on the wine in the restaurant either. This is rapidly turning into the worst evening in Lucca since I discovered I had picked up the wrong luggage.

There's nothing else for it, desperate situations call for desperate measures. I go into the bathroom and wash out two pairs of socks. It's not as if I'm going to need a clean pair before we leave but it does give me something to do and when I wring the water out of them I imagine it is someone's neck. I don't know whose, just anybody's and then I hang them up to dry beside a pair of Iona's knickers on that radiator thing I can't get to work.

That's how bad it is and when Iona goes to the pabby to perform her ablutions before retiring, I take advantage of her absence, no not to get another *limoncello,* there's not enough time for that, but to switch on the TV, being careful to hit the mute button as I do so. As I flick through the channels, not that I am deliberately looking for it you understand, it seems that game show where ladies take their clothes off does not appear to be on tonight. Maybe it's not true, just a myth. But wait a minute! What's this? Up till then, my thumb which had been shooting down channels as if it had been firing bullets out of a machine gun, now hangs suspended over the up and down button of the remote control. This looks rather interesting.

The scene is a very luxurious room, but not a bedroom mind you, and there is a lady in it, walking about completely bare, as you do, when you don't give a brass monkey about your central heating bills. Then the door opens and a handsome young man comes in without even knocking. She is not in the least put out by this unexpected appearance, if it is unexpected. In fact, she seems rather pleased to see him. It's a bit hard to tell how pleased he is to see her at the moment, but he's not exactly pushing her away and I expect I'll find out before very much longer.

But I never did. I can only guess and that's the really frustrating part. In all the hotel rooms in all the countries I have ever been in, this is the only porno channel I have ever come across that's free to view and I have to switch it off right there and then because there is the sound of another door opening, the inner one in our toilet and by the time the second door has opened, I have switched off the TV again and am lying nonchalantly on the bed doing nothing, just as I have been all the livelong evening.

"What have you been doing?" Iona asks suspiciously, her eyes darting immediately to my empty glass.

"Nothing."

She's unbelievable. She really is. And she doesn't believe me. Even when I am sitting doing nothing she knows I have been up to no good.

As I brush my teeth vigorously in the bathroom mirror, I reflect on how it could have been a much more interesting evening than it was. I wish I had never gone behind her back and turned on the television. Like the date of your own death, there are some things it is better not to know, but anyway it did teach me one thing – that Italian TV is not as bad as some people claim it is.

A fat lot of good it did me though.

CHAPTER FORTY-SIX: SOME GOOD NEWS AND SOME BAD

Another beautiful morning for our last full day in Lucca. We've seen everything we want to see and can see in Lucca, but because of the strike we are marooned here. Like Chuck Berry, we have no particular place to go. Except he had an automobile, the lucky fellow. And if only we had, we probably would have gone down to the coast to Viareggio or up into the hills to explore some little villages.

I'd like to see Viareggio particularly because of its Art Nouveau architecture and for its beach. But not for the reason you might expect, not to ogle ladies in bikinis (on a day like today they are bound to be there in their hundreds) but because that is where Shelley's body was cremated. And if you think that is a bit weird, then you would be wrong, because Shelley was a Romantic and I admire the Romantics. Never mind the poetry: they had such interesting lives and Shelley's death and cremation was particularly interesting, but I'll not go into such ghoulish things here.

There is no point in getting up early, especially since I have had such a bad night with nothing to listen to except the sound of Iona breathing softly and peacefully. There is nothing more infuriating than someone sleeping like a baby beside you, especially when they tell you that thanks to you being so restless they haven't had a wink of sleep all night.

It seems as if it is going to be a wasted day and it's a criminal waste of sunshine not to be outside soaking it up. But I have that covered. It's a bit of a struggle since they are so warped, but eventually I succeed in pushing the shutters wide open. Down below, I can see Gisele chaining her bike to the fence. That's good. That means that I won't have to slink past the receptionist of last night.

The sunshine is a pool of light on the bed, just as I hoped it would. Off with my top, then I lie down and close my eyes, luxuriating in the delicious warmth. There is no hope of sleep but this is balm to my tired eyes and body. There is no reason in fact, why I should not take my boxers off too, but something tells me that in a reversal of the scenario of the film last night, this might be just a step too far for Iona's sensibilities when she emerges from the bathroom.

It's bad enough when she does come out a few minutes later, her hair swathed in a towel like Osama bin Laden.

"What are you doing, you lazy pig? Get up!"

"It's all right for you. You had a good sleep last night."

"I had nothing of the kind, as I already told you. Come on, get up!"

"I'm just resting my eyes."

I know from the noises she is making that she is getting her hair dryer out, plugging in the adaptor, followed by the sound of rushing air. I should be good for at least another minute's more sunbathing while she concentrates on that operation and before the command to get up comes again.

Already the sun has moved and half the bed is in shadow. I am now as far over as I can possibly get and still be in full sun. It's amazing, it really is. We know now that it's not the sun that is moving but us, yet we go about our daily business without realising that we are we are spinning through space at the dizzying speed of more than 1,000 mph. It's a wonder we are not thrown off the surface of the planet by some centrifugal force and that jet aircraft travelling at half that speed in the direction of the spin ever get anywhere. Already I can feel a difference where the shadow has started to creep up my legs. It won't be much longer before I'll be in complete shadow, then I'll get up.

But someone has other ideas. She can't bear to see me doing nothing. Even at home when there are no household chores to be done, she invents them. Anything rather than see me pursue my natural talent for idleness.

"Oh, all right," I grumble, shuffling off to the pabby, consoling myself with the thought that my face is red enough already without the need of sunshine making it redder.

"What do you think you are doing now?" Iona asks, impatient to get to breakfast and seeing me, after my ablutions, fiddling about at the window shutter.

"Just hanging these out to dry, dear," say I. My socks are still pretty damp and Iona's knickers scarcely any drier.

"Let me see…You are NOT hanging those out to dry, like a white flag of surrender," she says, snatching her knickers from me and marching back to put them on the radiator that doesn't radiate.

I shrug my shoulders in resignation. Even when I am trying to be helpful, it's the wrong thing, but at least my socks will be dry by the time we get back.

Although Iona is impatient to be off to breakfast, politeness dictates we stop to pass the time of day with Gisele and bring her up to date on the case of the troublesome case. And when we get to the Scilla there is a surprise in store – it is shut. It must be closing day. Is it the start of another day full of troubles, I ask myself?

Perhaps not, for there is another bakery just along the street which serves the same fare and we even manage to squeeze onto stools at the narrow plank that serves as a bar, to consume the croissants and coffee in relative comfort. And then, just as we approach the gate into the medieval city, I spot a strange sight that raises my spirits.

"Would you just look at that!"

"What?" replies Iona, seeing nothing out of the ordinary.

"It's a bus, isn't it?"

An empty blue vehicle is even now threading its way through the arch and is lost to sight. Iona, however, has spotted it in time and confirms it was not a mirage and we quicken our steps after it.

In the Piazzale Verdi another amazing sight meets our eyes: I have never seen it so full. It is absolutely crowded and filled with the chatter of excited youngsters. It looks as if every schoolchild in Lucca is gathered here today. My guess is they are being sent home because of the strike. Our hopes that it had been called off melts away like candy floss in the mouth, only the taste is more like sour plums, (*soor plooms* in the Scottish dialect) a confectionery that was popular in my youth and which also served as a simile to describe the physiognomy of someone who regards life as a series of severe trials to say the least. Just like mine at the moment I imagine.

Yet, just to make sure, we go into the office and elicit the information that there is a bus to Viarregio, just leaving now as a matter of fact but that is it; there will be no more until tomorrow. So, we can get there but not get back. The gods give and the gods take away and on Mount Olympus they are laughing merrily at their latest joke.

That being out, the next on today's agenda is to head to Esselunga to buy some flowers for Beate and Roberta. At this time of day, in this weather, it is a very pleasant walk between the lindens, the leaves gyrating gently down to carpet the ground even more thickly and more colourfully, where plump pigeons in a supermarket of their own are busily turning over the leaves in search of the tastiest morsels.

Beate is at her post in the tourist office but if we had any hopes of killing two birds with one stone then we are out of luck. Roberta is at the office down by the station and in fact we are lucky to catch even one bird, for by rights Beate should not be here either. Firstly, her nose is dripping like a tap and secondly, she is working overtime as someone else has been too ill to come in to work.

She's not ungrateful but doesn't want to accept the flowers at first.

"But I didn't get your case back for you," she protests.

It doesn't take long to bring her up to date with our latest activity on that matter.

"He should go to Livorno," says Beate, sniffing. "Let me see your notebook."

Personally, I think it is a bit much to expect that of signor Cremona, not too sure how long a journey that would involve, especially when it wasn't his responsibility in the first place. I hand her my notebook. And then, a moment later, it hits me: surely she is not going to chastise him for not doing that or to suggest that to him? That would be going beyond helpfulness.

I'd only dropped in to give her some flowers; hadn't expected her to do anything more for us, trusting to providence that matters would be resolved by tomorrow, but now I find myself in another potentially embarrassing situation. If she is going to phone anyone, let it be the Post Office to find out where Carla's case is now.

Maybe that is exactly what she is doing, for after dialling and saying nothing, she hangs up again. Probably got that infernal automated voice again. But now she is phoning again and it has to be Elba this time. Oh help! I grip the top of the counter for support and scarcely dare to breathe. I'll know from the tone of the conversation how it is going.

"Signor Cremona?" That much I understand and then that she goes on to introduce herself and my legs begin to buckle and my head seems filled with air as I hear her say: "Fantastico…fantastico…fantastico…grazie…ciao."

I've not been here a week yet, yet I have understood every word of that conversation. Isn't that an amazing thing!

Beate fills in the details. The case had arrived only ten minutes ago, during which time signor Cremona had checked it and had decided all was present and correct, though how he would know what was in his wife's case, let alone what was missing from it, God alone knows. Not only that, but he had phoned the airport and the hotel. He sounds a really nice man. He didn't have to be so quick off the mark in making those calls after all we had put them through; he could have made me sweat a bit. Maybe we should have made that trip to Elba after all. I don't think I would have ended up a pulpy mass on the dockside after all.

The timing of Beate's phone call had been perfect. Any sooner and signor Cremona would not have had time to go through Carla's smalls then make that vital call to the airport.

Now her conscience will allow her to freely accept those flowers. I would kiss her if I could leap over that chest-high counter, but there's another barrier besides: she has a really nasty cold.

CHAPTER FORTY-SEVEN: ANOTHER CRISIS

Lunch for us is an omelette sandwich bought from the same old place on the Via Paolino and consumed at the same old place – on the walls. And when in Lucca, what better place is there than that? I'm not a complete boring old fogey though, as the omelette sandwich is a first.

Next task is to deliver the flowers to Roberta. I'm beginning to feel just a little bit conscious of carrying them about and although they weigh nothing at all, they are starting to become a burden. I am, however, happy to report that I am suitably dressed with the hat from Montana restored as my crowning glory. No words have been exchanged, no negotiations necessary and it looks like a visit to ACAS or the Marriage Guidance Council will not be necessary. Furthermore, although it looked a bit dented at first, its natural curviness is beginning to reassert itself, which shows you what a good hat it must be.

Despite the incalculable number of the fallen, there are still plenty of leaves left on the trees and the dappled sunshine and the cooling breath of wind combine to create a kaleidoscope of colours that is a pleasure to the eye, while the crunch and rustle of their dead companions underfoot makes an equally satisfying sound.

At this time of year, this is no less than an avenue of death if you choose to regard it in this way. It seems somehow disrespectful to tramp unceremoniously over the bodies of the fallen like this, while they, who are left on the tree, are scarcely in a better position, only hanging on to life in the most fragile of fashions. They will fall to earth soon, the slightest puff of wind enough to dislodge them from their tenuous grip of life, their parent, the living tree.

It doesn't seem right for the progeny to predecease the parent like this, but that is what life is like for a tree and not for the first time I find myself pondering on the merits of such an existence: normally a very long one, depending on the species, and you don't have to do much but stand there and grow, though sometimes you have to bear the ignominy of being tattooed with slogans like: "Jade luvs Wayne" with a heart and an arrow through it. Still, that's better than being one of those trees that is sacrificed every Christmas like a turkey and better still than being a leaf. However, having said that, I think we could learn a lesson from the humble leaf and if possible, we should go out in a blaze of colour like they do, unlike so many human lives that, thanks to medical science, cling on to life pointlessly.

This may seem a digression, but actually, it is an inspiration. I now know how we should while away the rest of the afternoon: we should go to the cemetery, naturally. It had looked so intriguing by night; in strong sunshine like this it will lose some of its attractiveness, but in the absence of anywhere better and since Iona can't come up with an alternative, that's what we are going to do once we have, like Interflora, delivered the flowers to Roberta.

Incredible, but true, when we walk into her office, she is startled to be presented with a bouquet of flowers from a man whom she doesn't recognise. It must be a relief to her to see that he is accompanied by a female companion and he is not some madman who has come to propose marriage. You would have thought that she would recognise the hat at least and it's equally hard to believe that she has totally forgotten about the tourist who had picked up the wrong case. Surely there can't be that number of people whom she has helped with a problem like that? It's a bit chastening and also slightly humiliating.

Still, it doesn't take her long to remember both; you can see the recall lighting up her face like the sudden appearance of the sun from behind a cloud. She thanks us for the flowers and then listens bemused to the tale of the lost pouch which she receives courtesy of Iona, whom you might have thought, would have preferred to have kept that under her hat. But strange to tell, far from being embarrassed by these events, now that it is all over, it sounds as if she is getting a vicarious sense of pleasure from recounting this latest tale of her idiot husband's exploits.

We take our leave from Roberta for the last time and since we are so near, we may as well visit the station to see if there is any activity, not that I expect there to be any. And so it proves. It is a quiet as the grave.

The booking office is empty apart from a few desultories and hopefuls. The ticket windows are closed. To get onto the platform, we have to step over the outstretched legs of a young man with very long hair whose back is resting against his backpack, which in turn, is supported by the doorjamb. He obviously prefers this slightly inconvenient location though he could have had his pick of several benches or any amount of wall to lean his backpack against. If he is aware that he is causing a slight obstruction, he doesn't appear to be, unconcernedly concentrating on rolling a cigarette.

The platform is bathed in sunlight and we sit down on the nearest bench to soak it up and to enjoy the peace and solitude, the one place in the whole of Lucca where you can be guaranteed that today. As I did this morning, I close my eyes. The fear that I might be mistaken for an underdeveloped woman and arrested prevents me from taking off my shirt, but I do remove my jacket and roll up my shirtsleeves as far as they will go. Ah, this is heaven! And to think that this is November!

Gradually I become aware of some voices off to my left and under the brim of my hat open a lazy eye, to investigate the cause of this disturbance. A couple of police officers, a man and a woman, are bending over the young man. What sixth sense, what intelligence had sent them to this hotspot of antisocial activity? I watch with interest to see what will happen. I know if it were me, I'd remove myself from there and pretty damn quick too.

But not he. I haven't a clue what they are saying of course, even if I could hear the conversation properly, but it seems clear enough to me that they are asking him to move because he is causing an obstruction while he, for his part, is asking what obstruction? His legs hardly form an insurmountable barrier. Besides, there is another door isn't there? And the place is hardly milling with people. It is his right as an Italian citizen to sit where he wants and that is what he is going to do. It's not as if he's sitting on the rails or anything is it? And in any case, even if he were, what difference would it make today, so if they don't mind, would they mind slinging their hooks and leaving him in peace?

And that's exactly what they do and the silence comes surging softly backwards as the police officers saunter along the platform, pretending they haven't lost the argument, while the young man hasn't budged an inch, doesn't even so much glance at us, seeking approbation of his victory as I would have done had I had the courage to take on the forces of law and order.

This is the sort of trivial detail that I record in my notes, and I must record this now before I forget it. Reaching down for my jacket, I go straight for the inside pocket where my notes should be – only they are not. Nor are they in any of the other pockets. With a rising sense of panic, I get up and look under the seat, not really expecting to see them there and I am right about that at least. My notes are gone.

You can't imagine how serious a situation this is. It's only notes, you might be thinking, not the sort of loss that bank notes would represent, but to me this is a calamity worse than all the other losses put together. It is nothing less than the death of part of myself – my memory. The last time I remembered seeing them was when I gave them to Beate. But did I take them back? For the life of me, I just can't remember and neither can Iona.

The only course of action is to retrace my steps to the Tourist Office, keeping my eyes on the ground but I have no reason to suppose they should have fallen out of my pocket. Indeed it is difficult to see how they could have done so. I *must* have left them in the office and feel reasonably confident that I will be reunited with them there. I agree to meet Iona at the Porta Elisa, the one part of the town we have not really explored much.

To my disappointment, Beate has been persuaded to go home and her replacement knows nothing of any notebook. She couldn't be more helpful, phones Beate at home and when that produces no result, even invites me behind the counter to look for myself. It is clutching at straws and a bit like looking for a needle in a haystack amongst the stacks of pamphlets and paper and, as expected, produces no result. Perhaps I had left it in Roberta's office (though I don't remember taking it out) or lost it on the way there, on the only stretch of ground that I had not covered again.

I had hoped by now to be on my way to my reunion with Iona who, before very long, will be wondering what is keeping me and will no doubt assume that I am lost, never mind my notes. So it's back the way I came, for the third time, this time not enjoying the walk in the slightest.

Roberta remembers me instantly, and looks even more startled than before to see me again. By now all hope that they would be there had evaporated and so when she tells me she has not seen them, it is not as if it comes as a massive blow.

She's not likely to forget me in a hurry I reflect, as I walk out of her life for the last time. But such foolishness or eccentricity is a hard price to pay for such notoriety and even although it is fruitless, I nevertheless decide with one last desperate throw of the dice, to go back to the station since I am not completely sure of the precise route we took. Bearing in mind that my devil's luck had restored my pouch after I had given it up for good, might this not be the very moment that I will find my notebook? And if it is, I won't mind in the least the pointless miles I have walked in the hot sun and will laugh to think how ironic it would be to find it only yards from where I had discovered the loss. And I will laugh heartily with the gods at playing such a funny trick and will forgive them for what they have done, if only please, it will turn up within the next few yards.

But this time, finally, my luck really has run out. I even go back to the bench, stepping over the young man who seems to be resigned to staying there for the duration of the strike, which will be until 8 am at the very earliest. Only seventeen hours to go.

Iona too bears a look of patient resignation when I meet her at the designated place. She, however, is standing. A bench is nearby but a tramp is sitting on it and she chooses to stand rather than sit beside him, even although her back is sore and her feet are weary with all the walking she has done, not to mention all the standing while waiting for me which she avows is even more tiring. I'd agree with her on that last point but I don't share her scruples about sitting next to my fellow man. I recognise the type. He wouldn't have been like that all his life. Life has dealt him some bad cards and he's one of life's losers, that's all.

Iona delivers an ultimatum: she must go back to the hotel for a rest before we embark on the next planned entertainment of the day, the highlight, the walk round the cemetery because if not, she will have to be planted there as she will neither have the strength nor the will power to make it back to the hotel after that. She's not good in the heat and in the eventuality that she should expire there, my last act would be to find her a shady spot. But of course I don't want that to happen and readily accede to her request. There is only one problem: where we are now is about as far as from the hotel as it is possible to be.

And if a rest is a priority for her, a new notebook is one for me and I know the very place. Not only will it be cheap but we will pass it on the way – the €1 shop owned by my Canadian lady friend with the vermillion hair. And if I thought I would renew our acquaintanceship in the process, I was severely mistaken. In this Aladdin's cave, once again I fail to find what I am looking for and have to ask for her assistance. This time she doesn't need to help me look, and as she tells me she doesn't stock such a thing, it is clear that she doesn't have the slightest recollection of ever having seen me before.

Of course she must see hundreds of new faces every day but nevertheless I derive a certain amount of comfort from this non-recognition because it tells me that since neither she nor Roberta remembered me, at least to begin with, I must be neither so odd in my behaviour, or as odd-looking as I was beginning to fear.

To be perfectly honest, so many things have gone wrong on this trip, and are still continuing to go wrong, I was beginning to wonder if I were not starting to lose my marbles, that these events were the harbingers of early senility and those people with whom I had come into contact in this respect, must regard me as some kind of eccentric oddball.

It's a relief to find that that's not the case at all.

CHAPTER FORTY-EIGHT:
THE REMAINS OF THE DAY

Somewhere, on the way back to the hotel, my phone rings. It is the airport to tell me that signor Cremona has phoned and that I may now come and collect our case. Well, they certainly took their time, I must say. It is past 4 o'clock now. Even if we could have, we wouldn't have bothered going for the case, not with less than twenty hours before we must be there again anyway.

Gisele too has news for us which she delivers in a matter-of-fact of tone as if delivering stale news, though she is not to know that we already know. And if she is surprised by the lack of joy with which we receive these glad tidings, for my part I am surprised at her apparent lack of interest in the resolution of the case with which she had been involved since the start. Maybe she is feeling like you do when you come to the end of a good book – sad there are no more tales to savour, that the saga is over.

In our room, Iona shows me her feet. She has an impressive pair of blisters on her right foot – one on the ball of her big toe and another on her little toe, so big it almost doubles its size. Her feet must have been killing her after all. If she chose the Peruvian hat as my memento of Florence, this is hers. Trust her to go to the other extreme.

"I would lance them if I were you," I advise, impressed by the sight, "let the fluid out."

Before she does that however, I have to take photographic evidence of what my folly in Florence had subjected her to: the actual operation she will perform on herself. The blister on her big toe proves stubbornly resistant and in the end, she begins attacking it with her sewing scissors. I have to look away.

While she recovers by lying down with her feet up, I get my head down and make a start on my notes in a little notebook that I got in a souvenir shop for an extortionate €2.90. I don't begin at the beginning, but at the present time, intending to work my way back, relying on Iona's elephant memory to supply the details I can't remember. But there are some things I'll never forget.

At last Iona feels sufficiently recovered to discharge herself from her hotel bed and announces we may as well go to the cemetery. It's not the most ringing of endorsements I've ever heard, but she is tired of doing nothing and to spend the rest of the afternoon within these four walls, while not quite a fate worse than death, is certainly bad enough to persuade her that it would be better to spend some time with those who had already met that fate.

In a kind of aperitif, before the cemetery, we come to a war memorial and if it is an indicator of the sort of thing we are about to see, we are in for a chilling time. The memorial is a new one, only erected in 1998. The main plinth has a gigantic bronze head, several times life size, of a soldier wearing a helmet with a massive black plume. To the left are four smaller granite blocks, each decreasing in size, the tops sliced off at a 23° angle, so that the eye is led in a perfect straight slope to the main plinth. So far so good, but what gives me the shivers is that on the top of each one is a massive dead raven, one black wing drooping obscenely over the edge of the block. Or so I think to begin with, but to my relief, they actually turn out to be only smaller versions of the plumed helmet. They are big enough to give me the creeps though - and Iona agrees and she doesn't even suffer from a feather phobia like I do.

The approach to the cemetery is rather grand, dominated by what looks like a large-scale model of the Capitol in Washington DC and to the left and to the right, are two more imposing buildings in classical style. Such grand and imposing buildings are wasted here, at least as far as tourism to Lucca is concerned, for I bet very few take the trouble to come here, though it must be admitted the buildings at either side would benefit from a bit of restoration and maintenance. We choose the building on the right as the door is invitingly open, while the other looks as if it has been closed since the day Miss Havisham was jilted.

This turns out to be a memorial to the prominent citizens in Lucca. In an alcove, reminiscent of a cathedral chapel, the three walls are filled with three tiers of high relief plaster casts of those who had made a name for themselves. Here is Dottor Pietro Pfanner, for instance, who died two days after his 71st birthday and the garden of whose ancestral mansion we had been able to admire from the walls, near San Frediano. The whole thing looks like a massive coin collection, each bust being placed in a roundel, set within a square frame. Another apposite comparison, even if I do say so myself, because I wouldn't mind betting that most of these people were pretty well off, which may not necessarily of course, have prevented them from serving their community, like Dr Pfanner, for instance, described as an *apostolo di bene,* and who thus richly deserve to be honoured here. They may, or may not have paid to get in here, just as I didn't, but I have the benefit at least, of not being dead yet.

Take this family whose memorial faces the coin collection; they must have had a bob or two, to have erected a memorial like this, in this place. But how sad it is. What value money when your three daughters, Amelia, Iolande and Italia, born in 1908, 1911 and 1915 respectively, all died in the same year – 1918. But how? Was it something to do with the war? Was it a disease? An accident? There are screeds of writing beneath the names and if I had paid more attention to my Latin, I might have been able to make more sense of it even if it is written in Italian, but from words like *lacrime* and *immenso dolore di un padre* (what about the poor *madre*?) I think the inscription has less to do with explanation and more an outpouring of grief.

And what makes it even more touching, makes you feel more connected to these dead little girls, is that you can see them: their photos are displayed above their names, taken the year they died, apparently.

It is common practice on the continent of course, to have photographs of the deceased on the headstone. They have been doing it for years (as this testifies) a trend I have noticed that is beginning to catch on in Britain and a practice of which I heartily approve. It is much more interesting, when you wander round graveyards, as you do, to see what those beneath your feet looked like before the worms ate them. With the aid of this little illustration, you are much more likely to stop as you pass by a stranger and read the details of the life now ended.

I'd like my photo on my headstone, (Mrs Addison please note). But not one of me taken in the same year as my death, unless it happens to be about now. I'm not exactly improving with age and if I lived to be, say 87, I wouldn't want one taken then. Nor would something taken when, like Jean Brodie, I was in my prime, be appropriate. About now would probably be about right. Let's hope, it is not *too* near the mark. And I would like it to be in colour; that would make it stand out more, just as long as use is made of the modern technology to tone down the redness of my face. And if possible, I'd like to be shown wearing my hat because it is part of me, my image. And I'd like one where I am looking relatively cheerful too. Not to show that I am glad to be there, down below, but to show that when I was up here, I was happy to be there.

Ah, there's the rub; that could be a problem. I don't think there are any photos of me looking happy. At least, there are none when I am on holiday and that is usually when I am in front of the camera lens. If I want that for my tombstone, I'm going to have to pose for it and the conundrum is: how will I be able to look happy when I know that that is what it's for?

Some people may think that graveyards are gloomy places, but in actual fact, they are dead interesting, (no pun intended) in sculptural terms. There is a prime example adjacent to the three little girls where the standard of sculpture is the equal of anything in the Piazza della Signoria and that is saying something. One tableau shows a rather dolorous-looking maiden in a rather diaphanous gown whose extended arm is resting on a waist-high plinth. She is holding an egg timer and the folds of her sleeve, draped over the plinth, lead the eye downward to where a young man, holding his head in his hands, has obviously just received the bad news that for him, the sands of life have run out.

In another monument, the angel of death is nursing the head of a young woman while another young woman with her back to us supports her feet. Her lover, though I suppose it could be her husband, is kneeling beside her, taking one last, lingering look before she is transported to heaven. To the right of the deceased, an older woman, possibly the girl's mother, is staring straight out at the viewer but with downcast eyes containing such ineffable sorrow that you can't help but empathise with her. She is carved in such high relief that she seems to be stepping out of the scene, almost a freestanding statue in fact, while the figure with her back to us, and who is also carved in high relief, draws us back in to the drama.

Apart from these two, as you look from right to left, the other figures are carved with decreasing degrees of relief so that the figure of the dead girl stands out more prominently than her lover, while in the hollow of the upraised right wing of the angel, in the faintest relief of all, as if they are as ethereal as from whence she has come, there appear to be two more figures, so indistinct that it would be easy to miss them with a cursory glance. But if you look really, really closely, they appear to be a man and a woman, and speaking as someone who doesn't care for clothes, I would say that they appear to be in 17th century costume. The poor dead girl is about to join her ancestors. But the message is not is as simple as it looks; there is sorrow on earth certainly, but not much joy in heaven either, for the ancestors are looking on with as much pathos as those below.

And that's not all – just bear with me and let me describe two more, which I must just mention for the skill of the artist as well as the contrast they provide. The first shows an attractive young woman in the full bloom of her firm young flesh (no-one here seems to die at a mature age, let alone a ripe old age) who could, just as easily, be sleeping peacefully. This is Keats's *easeful death.* The other is an emaciated figure of Christ, his skin-and-bone arms raised above his head, displaying the vestiges of biceps. But this is no ordinary or typical crucifixion scene. For a start, there is no cross and the arms are not stretched so far apart as usual. But what I notice most is the way the hands are cupped as if drawn in by the tendons, which I believe is what *would* happen if a nail were driven through the palm of the hand. And in another expression of realism, this pose highlights his clavicles, the tendons in his neck, and his ribs in such detail that those who teach anatomy could use it as a model. It could be an illustration from Gray's *Anatomy of the Human Body.* Eat your heart out Michelangelo.

And who is the sculptor of this masterpiece? And who created these others I have described? The styles seem so different that I can't see them emerging from the same chisel, unless they represent a development in this unknown master's style, which might be a possibility. As I have already said, sculpture is, as far as I am concerned, the highest form of art – how these living figures emerge from the blank stone seems to me nothing short of a miracle and there is every possibility that he who created these masterpieces lies here somewhere in some inglorious spot. As another Gray put it much more eloquently – *Some mute inglorious Milton here may rest* and I am sure he does, the bare winds blowing over his forgotten grave. It is the fate of many geniuses to be laid to rest, undiscovered in their lifetime, far too late to collect any royalties. Shakespeare was never a rich man in his life, but he left a legacy behind, and now he is immortal.

Wandering about outside, there are many, many more examples of funerary statuary that I could describe (but don't worry, I am not going to) except perhaps, just to mention this one. What makes it interesting is not the bronze head of the deceased at the top of the monument with the gold mosaic background like some saint in some Byzantine painting, nor the realistic, life-size grieving widow kneeling at the bottom, but that they died only two months apart – he on April 2nd, she on July 3rd. That's dedication.

Apart from the sculpture, there are massive monuments that you just can't ignore: family tombs with impressive porticos consisting of groups of larger-than-life statues and classical columns and even stained glass windows and other such follies to show that no expense has been spared in the quest for immortality. There is an impressive war memorial too, like a Norwegian stave church with a huge angular pointed roof pointing to the four points of the compass.

My curiosity is aroused by a cluster of much more modest headstones, small and identical, laid out in formal serried rows like in a war cemetery but made of red sandstone rather than white marble. What can they be? We wander over to take a look.

They turn out to be the graves of stillborn babies or babies who died after only hours, or days, of life. It is a sad sight and sobering that there should be so many of them. Here banks of flowers bloom in remembrance, and taking the cemetery as a whole, despite this little pocket, it is, overall, a cheerful sort of place thanks to the splashes of colour provided by the masses of flowers everywhere. In fact, if you could disregard the tombstones, (a bit difficult I concede) you might imagine yourself in a garden centre, since so many of them now sell various kinds of statuary with which you can transform your modern, average, pocket handkerchief-sized garden into a grand estate, or so they would have you believe.

Yes, there are few better places for a stroll than a cemetery. What more could you ask for: beautiful flowers and sculpture worthy of an art gallery and what's more, there is always something interesting to read, which is the disadvantage of hill-walking or a walk round your local country park.

But this pleasant occasion comes to a sudden stop as we stand aghast in front of this monument that has loomed up unexpectedly out of the blue. If the dead ravens on the war memorial shivered my timbers, this makes my blood run cold. Whilst I may not approve of memorials featuring over-the-top expressions of grief such as distraught maidens in classical dress drooping inconsolably over the headstone, nor angels, nor cherubs, nor urns with vines entwined – they do not, at least, have the effect of filling me with dread such as this one does. This looks more like an advertisement for something out of the Hammer House of Horror than a memorial for a family tomb.

Cast in bronze that has blackened with age and which adds an appropriate sombre effect to the piece, the central figure is a woman with demonic eyes. That is, I *think* it is meant to be a woman, for although she has a woman's figure, the face is that of a man and the expression, stern and disapproving. But frightening as that may be and terrifying though the mad, evil eyes certainly are, there is something even worse that fills me with revulsion. This creature from the murky depths of hell has outspread wings, not the feathery wings of an angel but the thin, taut, transparent wings of a bat with its horrible membranes. If birds' wings are my phobia, bats' wings are the stuff of my nightmares.

Under the umbrella of these hideous membranous wings, a trio of figures is placed at either side of that hellish figure. On its left, a young couple look as if they have just kissed each other goodbye, while on the right there is an older man and a woman, who it appears, want nothing to do with each other, each facing in opposite directions. A naked child with her back to us stands at their feet, a grandchild I would have thought, rather than their child, and from her sagging posture (I think it is a girl because of the length of the hair) you can tell she is upset.

By contrast, at the feet of the young couple, a kneeling figure is seen in profile. Like the main figure, it is a bit hard to determine the sex, but judging by the well-developed muscles in the shoulders and arm, I would guess it is male. He is holding his head in despair and I would too in his place, because he looks well-stricken in years and it can't be long before that Harpy drags him off to the everlasting torture chamber with those reptilian claws that are extended towards the viewer like the absurdly disproportionate forearms of a Tyrannosaurus Rex.

At the bottom of the sculpture is an inscription which, unfortunately, I can make little sense of, but I am able to work out that at the beginning it says something about the "shadow of wings" which is enough to give me the screaming heebie-jeebies, let alone the poor bloke in the sculpture, at the thought of those monstrous membranous flaps coming to get me, and then it goes on to say something about "lugubrious silence."

Whoever chose this epitaph chose well, for the words seem to match the scene above for gloom. Considering the sort of thing that could happen to you after that creature got a hold of you, I would settle for a "lugubrious silence" and consider myself lucky as having got off so lightly.

The quotation is by Carducci, the unofficial national poet of Italy who won the Nobel Prize for Literature in 1906, the year before his death. His most famous poem, or should that be, infamous poem, is his *Hymn to Satan,* which led some people, perhaps not unsurprisingly, to assume he was a Satanist. What they had failed to realise was that they were actually looking at it through the wrong end of the telescope; it was more an attack on the interference of the Catholic Church in secular matters, than in praise of Satan.

As a matter of interest, my national bard also wrote a similar piece, and like Carducci, he too was a freemason. It was called *An Address to the Deil* but its jovial, bantering tone is at odds with Carducci's more cerebral poem, but they have this in common: it too is a satire, but this time on the Presbyterian Church, particularly its doctrine of predestination. Same point; different Churches.

Where is the comfort, where the solace, when family members come here to pay their respects to their ancestors? Talk about sermons in stones: this is precisely the sort of sermon that Burns objected to but which you can still hear, even today, amongst some extreme Scottish Presbyterian sects, particularly on the west coast, and whose ministers take a delight in reminding you of the black pit that is waiting for you unless you mend your ways.

Somehow the gloss has gone from our tour of the cemetery and in a rather sadder and more pensive mood, we decide it is time we headed back to the hotel. The sun, low in the sky, sends our long shadows before us.

CHAPTER FORTY-NINE:
A NARROW ESCAPE

Something is different about the room this morning but I am too tired to think what it is and turn over and try to get back to sleep. Gradually my ears become accustomed to an unusual sound and after a while I realise what it is. After yesterday's beautiful day, it looks as if the weather has broken. There was an autumnal feel to the evening as we walked home from the restaurant last night, our breath like puffs of steam, and before I could start my notes I had to stick the point of my biro in the flame of a candle to make the ink flow, rather like that other Addison, Joseph, had to dip his quill in ink.

By the sound of it, this is not the sort of drizzle that we had experienced up till now, but the sort of steady rain that must be inducing panic amongst the Lucchese, enough to send them scurrying down to the DIY store to buy wood and nails for the construction of an ark in their back garden.

I am in no hurry to get up. After all, there is no hurry. Our flight isn't till 5 pm, 4.50 actually. Another day with nothing much to do. And then it comes to me, the way ideas do when you are not thinking of anything in particular, but I suppose it was actually the association of ideas, the recollection of the way the day began yesterday with the search for the lost notebook. And once I have thought of it, no more sleep is possible.

I think I know where my book may be. I had not thought to go back to the bench where we had our lunch. Had I made any notes there? I can't remember, but if I did, and assuming they are still there, they are going to be in a fine sodden state by now.

"Iona?…Iona?…Iona?" I whisper, louder and still louder when it elicits no response.

"Mmm. What is it?" she murmurs sleepily.

"Do you remember, did I write any notes when we had our lunch yesterday?"

Next second, I am aware of a sharp pain in my shin.

"Ouch! What was that for?"

"You woke me up, just to ask me that!"

"Well, did I?"

"Did you what?"

"Write any notes?"

The bed heaves, the blankets migrate to the other side of the bed and I have to forcibly steal them back again.

"For God's sake leave me alone! Do you know what time it is?"

I suspect she thinks this was some last-gasp attempt at the consummation of Lucca and hasn't heard me properly. But since she has brought it up – no, I don't happen to know the time, but I assume it must be earlier than I had thought.

I lie awake, listening to the rain, thinking of my notebook getting wetter and wetter but too tired and too lazy to get up and rescue it or too experienced to know that's exactly what the gods want – for me to go out there and get soaked to the skin for nothing.

When we do get up, some time later, and Iona an hour before me since she couldn't get back to sleep, and when I finally succeed in opening the shutters, it reveals that the deluge has stopped but everything is dripping wet and miserable. That seems to put paid to the vague plan we had mulled over last night that we might spend some time in Viareggio today. There are few sights more depressing than a seaside resort in the rain and there is the added encumbrance of having to lug our hand luggage around with us. It could have been worse though – at least we don't have to worry about the big bag.

So we are all dressed and packed with nowhere to go but before we go there, wherever that turns out to be, first we must settle our bill. There is a €10 charge for our late arrival and we give Gisele a €20 tip for help above and beyond the call of duty. It's not like handing over real money, and Gisele is delighted with it because it probably represents a morning's work for her and when I ask her if there is a charge for the phone calls, I am just as delighted to hear that she has forgotten to ask the boss. So, pulling the heavy oak door shut behind us by its big brass knocker, we part with everyone feeling happy.

The Scilla is closed and so is the alternative bakers we had patronised yesterday, both businesses closed, probably due to the inclement weather, like roads in central Scotland come to a standstill whenever there is an inch of snow. We'll need to find somewhere else, and preferably before we get to the centre of town.

Again I am not sure what reminded me – perhaps it was the rumble, rumble of the wheels of Iona's hand luggage which, although compact, had been provided with this handy device, together with an extending handle so you can pull it along behind you. I had also cunningly used it to thread the straps of my own bag through it so that it rested on top of Iona's to save me the bother of having to carry it. It doesn't quite work unfortunately and I have to keep stopping to put it back on. But my patience is infinite, unlike some people I know.

Anyway, I think it might have been that – the unconscious memory of hauling Carla's case on its tour of Lucca and trying desperately to get hold of Dorothy on my phone. I now realise she never did get back in touch. Pity, as it would have been a nice way to have idled the day away yesterday, drinking wine in the sunshine in the garden of her villa. But then we probably would never have gone to the cemetery.

But just where is my phone? Now that I have thought of it, I don't remember seeing it today. I stop and pat my pockets and finding nothing, go through them, knowing as I do so that I am unlikely to find it.

Iona has stopped, wondering why I haven't kept pace, why this sudden rummaging through my pockets.

"I think I must have forgotten to pick up my phone," I have to confess.

"For God's sake! What next!"

"I'll just run back for it. You stay here," and before she can say anything, I am off.

It might have been worse: imagine if we had been rushing to catch a bus or train. We don't have our bag yet, but we have bags of time to spare. Please let Gisele be there, I pray over and over again and once more for luck as I arrive, breathless at the door, only to be confronted with another problem: how do I get in?

An intercom has been placed on the left doorjamb and it must be switched on because a red light is glowing. There is a row of buttons and I press each one in turn, then try it again only with an increasing sense of panic when nothing happens. Bloody gadgets! I give up on it and turn my attention to the good, old-fashioned brass knocker. But there is a problem with that too. Since the installation of the intercom, it is redundant as a knocker: it has been wired down and serves only as a handle to pull the door shut, just as I did less than half an hour ago, though what had possessed me to do that, heaven alone knows as usually the door is left standing open.

I can move it just a little bit. Rat-a-tat-tat. If only. It makes a feeble sort of sound that I know Gisele hasn't a hope in hell of hearing if she upstairs cleaning our room – if she is still here at all. Because I know it is making such little noise, I keep on "knocking," hoping that if Gisele is at her desk that eventually these faint scratchings will penetrate her hearing.

Apparently they have, for to my surprise, the door is flung open to reveal Gisele with a face like fizz. I thank God that

I had given her such a large tip, for when she sees it is only harmless little me, her expression relaxes into mere irritation.

"I'm sorry," I blurt out, " I couldn't get the intercom to work."

Frowning, and by way of an answer, Gisele reaches past me, presses something and the whole thing crackles into life, making me feel really, really stupid.

"Er…I think I must have left my phone in the room. Is it OK if I go upstairs to look?"

Wordlessly, Gisele opens the door wider and I am admitted. It takes only a minute. There it is on the bedside table. I snatch it up, run downstairs, let Gisele see I have found it, apologise for troubling her and make a hurried exit for what I sincerely hope is the last time.

When I get back, I am pleased Iona has found a bench unoccupied by a tramp, at least until I sit down beside her to get my breath back. Despite having more time than we know what to do with, I didn't want to keep her there with nothing to do, *nursing her wrath* like Tam O'Shanter's wife for any longer than necessary.

"Did you find it?" she had asked when I got within hearing distance. If I hadn't found it, it would have been within shouting distance, even if I had been sitting right next to her.

As we set off towards the town, Iona has a couple of questions for me. She must have been sitting there, thinking. Thinking about my recent abnormal behaviour.

"What day is it today?"

Now that *is* a good question! Just *what* day is it? When on holiday I do tend to lose track of the days. I think it must be either Monday or Tuesday, probably the latter.

"Monday."

"And what's the name of the Prime Minister?"

I know it is important to answer instantly lest I be misdiagnosed as some poor sod who has had a TIA so I snap out the answer right away: "Gordon Blair."

She can't see my face as that damned bag has fallen off its perch already. Which is a pity as I can't see hers either.

CHAPTER FIFTY:
A LAST LOOK AT LUCCA

If it had been on the bench where we had our lunch, my notebook is certainly not there now. It means another wait for Iona who sees no need for this diversion and predicts it won't be there. I am sure she is right but I have to go and check because otherwise I'll always wonder and in my dreams I'll see it there, not a pulpy mess of sodden paper but a legible document whose hard cover had largely protected the contents from harm if only I had rescued it then, when I had the chance, before someone did find it, skimmed through it and dismissed it as the ravings of a lunatic before consigning it to the nearest bin.

And then because it is so near, I may as well just go and check the Tourist Office one last time. Maybe Beate will be there, feeling a bit better and may remember what happened to my notebook. I am more convinced than ever that that is where I must have left it. And with the restoration of the lost pouch fresh in my memory, I feel I must make this one last attempt to be reunited with my memory.

Iona, however, has other ideas.

"Would you put so much time and effort into looking for me?" she objects.

"Of course I would, dearest! Especially if you had the car keys."

Well, what else could I say?

"You go if you want to, but I am not," she retorts, unmollified, then adds pointedly, "I've not had any breakfast, *may* I remind you."

I can take a hint when it is expressed as subtly this. It might well be that she will never go on holiday with me again after this fiasco, but never let it be said that I ever stopped her from getting her food.

"Right, let's get something to eat first and then I'll go back to the Tourist Office."

Creatures of habit as ever, we end up at the same place from where we have been purchasing our lunches on the Via San Paolino for the best part of the week. They at least, will be sorry to see us go.

One good thing about consuming your breakfast on the premises of a *pasticceria,* precariously balancing your coffee and your plate on the narrow ledge that they all seem to have, is that it gives you a chance to observe a little bit of day-to-day Italian life as the flotsam of passers-by is washed in through the doors. Because of our late start, the breakfast rush has long since finished. These are the retired people, the people with time on their hands, the people with no particular purpose in life and who find themselves passing the time in the *pasticceria* just because they happened to be passing it at the time and can afford to spend both the time and money.

Here for instance, is a master juggler, who, as well as his coffee, can manage a newspaper on a stick. This strikes me an essentially ancient Roman thing, a legacy from when books were scrolls and it seems to me a very civilised practice to combine caffeine with current affairs in this manner, but the only thing I have ever seen on a stick in a Scottish café is an ice lolly because we resisted all attempts to be civilised, and booted the Romans out when they tried invading us.

Having digested the news and drunk his coffee, he returns the newspaper to its place on top of the drinks cabinet and departs, mind and body refreshed. *Mens sana in corpore sano* as his ancestors used to say.

Now, for our entertainment, in comes another man accompanied by his pet, which, at first sight, appears to be a mouse on a string but on closer inspection, turns out to be a sausage dog, only it is the minutest specimen I have ever seen. No doubt it is a puppy and has time to grow yet, but even so, it is an apology for a dog. A dog, to be worthy of the name, should not be something that you could trip over, or inadvertently squash to death when you step on it. In his other hand, the owner is holding the sort of container with a wire mesh at the front that we use to transport our cats to the first name in pet care, the Alphavet. Imagine that though: where someone's idea of taking the dog for a walk means carrying it around in a basket!

And that's not all: this poor specimen of doghood is wearing a jacket – a tartan jacket of all things. Who gave it the right to do that: a German dog living in Italy? I bet it doesn't have even a drop of Scottish blood in it. The tartan is Royal Stuart of course. A bit red and vulgar for my taste, yet it seems to be the most popular choice amongst foreigners, possibly because they like to think it confers some sort of aristocratic status upon them, when in actual fact, they fail to realise that most of the Stuarts were a lot of effete wimps.

At least this owner has chosen appropriately for his pooch, so that is not really my main objection. No, what I really object to are dogs wearing clothes at all, indeed any animals wearing clothes. I think they should be naked, naked as nature intended. I know what you are thinking. You think I am some sort of perv who is about to suggest the same thing for people, since you know I have little time for clothes. But on the contrary: I think people *should* wear clothes. In fact, I would positively urge the majority of people to hide their nakedness. It might be all right for some, but most of us, apart from some former girlfriends of mine, have lost the body hair, which, in Adam's day, would have protected us from the elements. No, it's not clothes I object to, but the dedication to fashion, where the epitome of civilisation is to buy your clothes from Gucci or Armani. That is what Roman decadence has led some of us to.

It's a funny thing, but once you start noticing things, have you noticed how they keep recurring? Retracing our way to the

Tourist Office, I catch sight of a dummy in a shop window (no comment) wearing a tartan jacket. This can be yours for only €69. Once again it is Royal Stuart. Unfortunately, it is a woman's jacket otherwise there would have been no finer sight in all of Lucca than the spectacle of that little dog, liberated from his cage for a few steps, performing the evening *passeggiata* with his master in their matching jackets.

While Iona waits outside, because she thinks it is pointless, (at least that is what she says, but I have a sneaky feeling that she is too embarrassed to come in) I boldly enter the office. Straight away I can see that Beate is not at her post, but the same person that I spoke to yesterday is. Just for a moment, I consider going straight out again or pretending I have come in for something else, but I tell myself not to be so stupid. What do I care if she thinks I am making a big fuss about a stupid little notebook? She doesn't even know my name. It'll only take a minute and the less time I spend in there, the sooner I'll be gone and forgotten.

I emerge empty handed. Right, that really was the last nail in the coffin. I have to face the facts: that notebook has gone forever and with it the possibility of writing a book about this trip. That's really what my earnest endeavours to trace it have all been about. And it is the loss of the book rather than the notebook that is troubling me as we trundle our way across the square to the bus station to enquire about the times to Viareggio. We've just missed one. Had we gone straight there instead of the Tourist Office, we might just have caught it.

But I am not told that it's all my fault that we missed it. It seems rather to be put down to Fate. Speaking for myself, my heart is not in the trip anyway. I am in mourning and I suspect Iona is not that desperate to go either which is why Fate is getting the blame. In any case, there is still time to catch another one if we really want to before we start heading for the airport. We don't have to make a decision just yet. In the meantime, we can have a last look around Lucca, just in case there is a little street we have not seen before.

Here is a big church we *have* seen before – San Michele – and since it is open, I may as well see if there is anyone there who knows anything about a pair of binoculars being handed in although I know I haven't a prayer of that being the case. And I was right, there isn't: only some people who have come to have a look at the art treasures and one person who has come in to pray.

Iona, in the meantime, who did not come into the church, has found something to take home for the grandchildren – two little Pinocchio puppets on a string. What has Pinocchio got to do with Lucca? As a matter of fact, the connection is not that far-fetched. Carlo Lorenzini, Pinocchio's creator, was born in Florence, but there is an even closer link than that.

Collodi is a little village only 17 kilometres from Lucca, a medieval hillside village straggling downhill like a ribbon of molten lava and that was where Lorenzini's mother was born and that was what he chose as his pen name when he recorded the little wooden boy's adventures and that is the name by which he is, of course, better known. To honour this link, there is a Pinocchio Park in Collodi: a garden really, with statues and carvings illustrating characters and events from the story. That would have been another nice place to have visited yesterday but for the strike. But then we probably would have missed the cemetery.

We gravitate to the amphitheatre, the natural main attraction of the town, like being drawn into a black hole. Black it certainly isn't and although there is a hole there now as it was when it was the centre of the sort of bloodthirsty activities which the Romans described as "games" without the slightest hint of irony, this was not always the case. From medieval times, the arena was occupied by houses and in a shop window, a black and white photograph shows what it used to be like. Unfortunately the date is not attributed, but never mind medieval, the houses look as if they had been built in Roman times. It is a crowded little scene, not with people, but with houses – a town within a town in fact, and to which some attention has been paid to planning.

A narrow street, aligned with two of the entrance arches, runs down the centre, while the houses at the outermost edge follow the curve of the amphitheatre. The houses themselves, single storey and dwarfed by the encircling houses from which washing is strung from practically every window and with not a shutter in sight, are roofed with the sort of thick, heavy tiles that the Romans used, while the walls seem less durable, and appear to be constructed of earth and timber. At the top of the picture, after the first two houses on either side of the street, is a block of four L-shaped houses back to back, forming a back "garden" in the shape of a quadrant, although they look as dry and dusty as a novel by Sir Walter Scott. Despite their unprepossessing appearance, nevertheless, these would have been the most desirable houses in the arena.

Still, to have lived there then was maybe not as basic as it looks. If you look closely, you can see a row of telegraph poles running down the street. A few residents have gathered for a blether (they appear to be all men; the women are probably on the phone) and one or two kids are running about, just as they are now. The arena is echoing to their voices (why aren't they in school?) and apart from us and a few Lowry-like stick figures at the other side, the place is empty apart from a *spaghetteria* that has set out some tables in the forlorn hope of attracting some customers.

The photograph made the arena seem cluttered, if not squalid, and it was a good idea to clear the houses, allowing us to admire the curves of the colourful empty ellipse unhindered, but now it has a dismal look under a gunmetal sky. Like the pessimist's view of a half-filled glass, the canvas canopies in the *spaghetteria* are more like umbrellas than sunshades and even as the thought drifts into my mind, the rain starts falling again.

CHAPTER FIFTY-ONE:
A CASE OF BEING USEFUL

Viareggio was cancelled due to rain and indifference, so now at 1 pm, we are at the airport, with four hours to kill and whatever the weather may be doing in Lucca or Viareggio, it is shining brightly here. Iona, who likes to leave plenty of time for everything, is happy with that and for once, I don't mind too much either: I have some notes to write up and what's more, I can do them at a table outside in the sun. Pisa airport may have a terrifying monster canary on the lawn outside but it is one of the few airports I know where you can sit outside and not be forced to spend interminable hours cooped up in the terminal building fighting for a seat amongst hundreds of passengers, even when there is not a whole backlog of delays.

First thing on the menu is food, Iona says. We may as well avail ourselves of the free luggage locker and leave our bag until we have finished so we don't have to bother looking after it. We've not had it all week; a little longer won't hurt and I don't anticipate any difficulties. Besides, we've got two pieces of hand luggage to look after as it is, so while Iona finds a seat and looks after them, I go first in search of lunch.

I choose a *focaccia farcita del pizzailo*, a sort of *calzone* and quite a mouthful, by which I mean not only is it very filling, but a bit more Italian than I have at my disposal. And that's important, because following in the best tradition of Italian of logic, this is the system. First you have to choose what you want to eat from the selection under the Perspex display stands, then you stand in front of your choice and keep repeating it under your breath until you think you have got it right, then you close your eyes and say it until you can do it without looking. Then and only then, when you think it is imprinted on your brain, do you join the queue, muttering it to yourself all the while lest you forget it, trying not to be put off by the people next to you who are giving you some funny looks.

When you finally reach the cashier and deliver your speech (and what a relief it is when you do spit it out loud, but like Chinese whispers, you wonder how much it now differs from the original) she will then say something to you with a rising intonation at the end, from which you deduce she is checking that that's what you want. You haven't a clue what she said because she said it so quickly but because there is a long queue behind you and you don't want to have to go through all that again, you merely nod, happy to take anything you get. Next she relieves you of some money and issues a receipt which you take back to where the food is and which you then present to a server who makes a tear in it before she gives it back to you, then she goes away to get your order. Simple really, if you can speak Italian. Then if you want a drink, you have to go through the same process again. Only *Nastro Azzurro grande* is a great deal easier to say, being on the tip of my tongue much of the time in fact.

At the lost luggage office, I am attended to by a big, burly bloke with a beard and who turns out to be as surly as he is burly. There is no sign of the goddess but I thank my lucky stars that I had her rather than him the first time as, apart from anything else, he doesn't look as if he would have been anything like as helpful, had he been able to crawl through the hatch for a start. Wordlessly, he takes the proof of ownership without bothering to look at me, or so it seems, and disappears from view for a few minutes before reappearing with the case.

It has a sheet of paper attached to it, like it had before, and which he rips off and takes to the supervisor. I thought she at least, might have glanced in my direction after what had happened the last time I was here, but she merely goes to a filing cabinet where she removes a file, peruses it for a moment then hands the piece of paper back to the burly man. He chucks it in a bucket as he passes, then opens up the door and passes the case through, still without saying anything. Whilst I didn't expect any difficulties, I didn't expect it to be quite such a non-event as this either.

Thoughtfully, they did not bother locking the case again but have left the padlock hanging from its hasp. We find a quiet spot to rearrange our luggage. First the alcohol: the gin, a whole bottle, is now safer and lighter in a plastic tonic bottle, but the *limoncello* I have kept in the original bottle, carefully swaddled in clothes. It just will not taste the same otherwise.

After we have transferred that and various other sundry items from our hand luggage into the case, it feels a bit heavy but that's just too bad. If it is over the limit, I may be able to remove something and carry it on as hand luggage. That's the ridiculous thing: it's still the same gross weight, so what's the difference? And a sumo wrestler is given the same weight allowance as an anorexic ectomorph. It makes you wonder if the system was devised by an Italian.

We find a table outside and although it has grown rather chilly, I persist in sitting in the watery sunshine in my shirtsleeves. After all, I am a hardy Scot and this will be the last time I'll be able to sit outside in the sunshine this year and I am determined to make the most of it.

At the next table are some of my compatriots. Not only do I know they are Scots, but I know they are from the capital and even which district they come from. The accent is unmistakable: these are the people, who before central heating, had their coal delivered in "sex" according to their refined pronunciation. Not only that, but I know that one of them is called Mrs Harper and another must be called Jean although neither of these names has been mentioned in the conversation which we can't help but overhear.

There is no great mystery to it; in fact it is quite elementary. It is just a matter of mere observation as Sherlock Holmes never tired of pointing out to Watson and making him feel incredibly foolish when he revealed how he reached his astonishing conclusions. But even Watson, on a bad day, would have been able to work this out. The case by the side of one of the women has a rainbow-coloured belt round it on which big black letters spell the words "Mrs Harper." That is how I know she must be called Mrs Harper. Unless she borrowed it of course, which is where my deduction would have been wrong, just as Holmes' explanations are capable of alternative explanations if you stop and think about them for a while. But why choose your title rather than your initials? That *is* curious.

I admit I am on even more shaky ground on the matter of the one I have called "Jean" as her name may be Maggie, as Rod Stewart didn't quite sing. That's because she looks like Maggie Smith who played Jean Brodie with such virtuosity in the film and to whose prime and mine, I have already alluded in the course of this narrative.

Refined and cultured ladies, these. Not just because of their accents and their jewellery either: they have books with them. It never ceases to amaze me how so many people in doctors' or dentists' waiting rooms for example, never bring a book with them to make the time go faster. And here's an interesting thing: two of them, the two married ones, are reading the same author, though not the same title. Perhaps, behind their voile panels, they indulge in a bit of discreet book swapping.

One of the married ones is Mrs Harper, of course, and the one who is not, is Jean (or Maggie). I can't hazard a guess at what the other lady's name is, but I am going to call her Sophie because she is so sophisticated, smoking king-size cigarettes from a silver cigarette case. I've not seen a cigarette case for years, let alone a silver one. Her other case, the one she uses to pack her luggage, is a flamboyant, fluorescent sort of affair.

That seems a pretty unique and recognisable item of luggage and probably cost a packet. Jean, on the other hand, has a plain and simple black case with no distinguishing marks, the kind that anyone might pick up by mistake. But of course, she has no wealthy husband to support her. I bet she is a poor, retired teacher.

At the moment she is looking after her friends' bags while they have gone to do some last-minute shopping. She may not have a husband with whom she can go on holiday, she may not have the money, or be interested in shopping, but regardless of any other uses she may have as a travelling companion, she does have one as a bag-minder.

In due course, as I scribble and Iona sews, a woman comes along, leaves her case at our table and without a word to us, without so much as a *Would-you-mind-looking-after-this-for-me?* disappears. That seems a pretty good way of losing your luggage but I presume she has gone to get some food. You can't carry your food *and* your baggage. You really do need a travelling companion, even if he is a liability.

My deduction is correct as when she eventually does come back, she is indeed bearing a tray of food. Furthermore, she has been so long about it, it suggests to me that she had as much a problem as I had trying to memorise her choice. And although there are plenty of empty tables she could have chosen, she decides to sit with us and not for the conversation either, for she only opens her mouth to stuff food in it. If I had been sitting there on my own though, she probably would have moved to another table. A wife is a useful companion if you want to look normal and harmless.

The conclusion of these musings is that it would be no good me going travelling by myself: I am not safe to be let loose. As for Iona, what this should show her is that when she feels up to it, she should give me another chance as a travelling companion, even if it is just to look after the case – as long as I have got the right one of course, or haven't already lost it.

CHAPTER FIFTY-TWO:
THE END OF THE CASE

Much later, Iona suggests it is time we went to check the bag in. Reluctantly, I put a full stop at the end of my latest memory, hoping that that doesn't put a full stop to them completely. I would prefer to leave it to a bit later but our Scottish ladies at the next table had already left some time ago, while the woman at our table had departed as soon as she had finished her food. There was no need to thank us for looking after her luggage as she had never asked us to in the first place and since she had never spoken, she had left no clues as to her origins or destination. I'm sure Sherlock would have been able to tell from a host of clues, but like Watson, I couldn't even spot one.

The check-in desks are in a separate building. Iona finds a seat near the entrance opposite an unemployed young man who is paid to operate a machine that wraps your luggage in cellophane but who, in the absence of any customers, spends his time reading a magazine instead. Although it is meant to be a security device, it strikes me that this would be a pretty good way of individualising your case, as yours would the only one on the carousel that looked like something the cat had sicked up.

No point in both of us checking in the bag and so in this hall heaving with humanity, I join the snaking queue and, by strange coincidence, find myself behind the Scottish ladies. I knew we had come too soon – the check-in desk is not even open yet.

Although it is not easy to accomplish, I improve the shining hour (well that's how long it seems, but actually it took only half as long as that to reach the desk) by getting on with the notes. When, finally, it is my turn to hoist onto the scales, the bag that had caused us so much trouble, to my shock, it is nearly two kilos overweight.

Huh, I think, it's not finished causing me trouble yet. What am I going to take out to get it down to the required weight? But no: the check-in girl likes the cut of my jib, or just can't be bothered to fine me, but whichever it is, it is fine by me. Watching it progress along the conveyer belt like a coffin heading towards the bonfire in the bowels of the crematorium, is like saying goodbye to the dear departed. And it *has* cost me dear this holiday, that bag – in stress, in time, and in money. But not as much as it would have done had that nice, most beautiful girl in Pisa, (apart from the goddess) charged me extra for it being overweight.

As it disappears from sight, it's like saying goodbye to all my troubles. I can relax. Nothing else can go wrong now.

Next time, I vow, if ever there is a next time, I think I have hit upon a foolproof method of assuring Iona I will not make the same mistake again: I won't check in a bag at all if we are only going away for a week. After all, had we not managed a week without it, more or less? And next time we would pack our hand luggage with that in mind. Yes, travel light is the answer. We travel with far too many clothes as this past week has shown. And it would have saved me all this queueing too. But best of all, you wouldn't have to turn up two hours before departure either. If it weren't for all that tiresome and endless security you have to go through, you could just wheel up five minutes beforehand – in theory at least, but I know I'd never be allowed to get off with that, and to be honest, that is a just a bit on the tight side for me too, though you can usually count on there being a delay.

That's what Dorothy seems to do, though of course she may have a wardrobe full of clothes at the villa. But Leon and Tina don't and they didn't check in a bag either. They should all be about here somewhere, but it is not until we get to the departure discomfort zone, or lounge, as the airport authorities prefer to call it, that we spot them.

"I'm sorry you didn't manage to come to the villa," Dorothy says right away. "I tried several times to phone you, but I couldn't get a line out."

"Don't worry!" I tell her. "We spent a nice afternoon in the cemetery."

She takes that in her stride.

"What else did you do?"

Before I can tell her, Iona is right in there with a list of my further misdemeanours since we had last met and how the case of the missing case ended. I think it was the word "case" that did it, in fact, I am sure it did, for at the mention of that word, Dorothy's face takes on what I would describe as an ashen hue and she looks about her in panic.

"My case! Oh my God! I've lost my case!"

You can actually see the cogs of the wheels turning round as she tries to remember where she had it last. There must be only minutes left before we start the mad scramble for seats on the plane, though I recall, it didn't bother her at all on the way out and quite rightly, as the three of them did find seats together without any difficulty. Methinks, three is a handy number to go travelling together. In a plane, if two people are already occupying two of the three seats in the row, the third seat is unlikely to be occupied by another person unless it is by someone travelling alone and since most people travel in pairs, Dorothy could certainly count on a seat being available next to her relations. That does not concern her, I know, but she doesn't have much time to find her case and get aboard, especially as they have just announced we are boarding and people are beginning to funnel towards the gate.

"I must have forgotten to pick it up after security!" she blurts out and abruptly leaves us like someone desperately seeking somewhere to be sick.

Thank you, Dorothy, thank you. We never got to your villa but you have provided a valuable service all the same. It was partly your fault that I picked up the wrong case in the first place, but you have made amends now and all is forgiven. You have proved that losing your luggage is the sort of thing that could happen to anyone, so thank you for that. What's more, you and Leon and Tina, not forgetting Mrs Harper and Jean and Sophie, have just shown me the merits of a *ménage à trois*, an idea that would never have occurred to me before.

If Iona does agree to go on another holiday with me, a notion, which I suspect, is still hanging in the balance, since my sins were not all baggage-related, it might be an idea to suggest she takes along one of her friends too, for a bit of moral support and to help keep me in check. Surely she can see the wisdom of that?

Now, out of all her friends, whom would I nominate...? The crucial factor might depend on whether she snores or not. She would have to pass the sleeping test first. Hmm. Methinks there could be another tale in that, another book, perhaps a trilogy.

That future fantasy, as well as the recording of past memories, will occupy me for the duration of the journey, but meanwhile we sit on the runway with the door open. But only four of us, apart from the crew, know the reason for the delay, at least for the moment: we are waiting for someone who has gone to find her case.

If I had held up a whole plane like this, Iona would have died of embarrassment, but I suspect, have had the will to live long enough to kill me first. Whatever other havoc I may have created on this trip, at least I did not do *that* and have survived to tell this tale – or at least as much of it as I can remember. Thanks to Iona for her recollections. Without her, this tale would have been a great deal shorter. Whether that is a good or a bad thing, it's not for me to say.

And so, dear reader, we must say farewell for the present and perhaps forever as the jury is still out on whether there will be any more travels and therefore any more books. Will time heal the scars of these misadventures and will Iona give me another chance? I am hopeful but not confident. As our national bard put it in *To a Mouse:*

> *An' forward, tho' I canna see,*
> *I guess an' fear!*

About The Author

Born a long time ago in a place far, far away even from most other places in Scotland, David M. Addison grew up, at least in the physical sense, and moved away from his native North East and began travelling the globe, though he does make occasional returns to his native soil to visit old haunts and haunt the old relations who have not disowned him.

This is the fifth book recounting his travels and once again he has been drawn back to Italy for which has a particular fondness.